RACIAL CRISIS

IN PUBLIC EDUCATION

RACIAL CRISIS IN PUBLIC EDUCATION

A QUEST FOR SOCIAL ORDER

by

ARTHUR DAVIS, JR.

VANTAGE PRESS

NEW YORK   WASHINGTON   ATLANTA   HOLLYWOOD

FIRST EDITION

Copyright © 1975 by Arthur Davis, Jr.

Published by Vantage Press, Inc.
516 West 34th Street, New York, New York 10001

Manufactured in the United States of America

Standard Book No. 533-01206-6

CONTENTS

THIS book describes and examines what I consider to be the cause of the racial crisis in public education. What follows is the result of four years of observing, reading, interviewing, and teaching. I have visited about seventy-five suburban and city schools and have spoken privately and publicly with several hundred people and students of mine involved in one way or another with the education of black pupils. I have read several linear feet of books and an uncounted amount of periodical literature since my days as a graduate student at the University of Illinois. I would not say that my preparation for this endeavor is sufficient, but two full file cabinets of notes is more than enough to start with: and there comes a time when a man who teaches for a living must sit down and write his book.

The effort throughout this book has been to get at the realities of blacks' education in the American system, and to cut below the controversy to the problems of inner-city schools. Thus, this book is written for teachers, parents, school administrators, and community action agencies interested in the education of black Americans. Though I would hope that parts of this book are entertaining, I would expect also that much of it will be enlightening to people who regard the current racial crisis in public education as real and significant. Therefore, my primary purpose is to share with others what I consider to be the crisis in educating blacks and some necessary steps schools can take in alleviating this crisis. The scattered sections of description of the racial crisis in public education are presented to demonstrate the continuous existence of a problem that needs cooperative action if it is to be solved.

Much of what has been written about the education of black Americans from the past to the present would have brought this effort far closer to reality if educators responsible for their work had written in practical rather than in theoretical terms. Thus, the purpose of this book is not to provoke thought alone, but to produce action.

In writing this book, I tested my ideas and approaches with my wife Loretta. Our many debates were reflections on, and examinations of, the historical antecedents of blacks' education, which resulted in a refinement of the manuscript. The book caused her personal inconvenience and intellectual annoyance; and she had to tolerate my many bursts of fury which I employed to ward off really telling criticism of something I had written. Her linguistic abilities, her intelligence, her patience, and her stubbornness are the source of much of what quality this book may have, and she sacrificed endless hours of her time to help produce it.

In addition, I would like to thank Peggie Lagnese who worked tirelessly to help me put together the original manuscript, and Phil Feldman, who reviewed it. And finally, I would like to thank the various librarians, whose names are too numerous to mention, at the State University of New York at Brockport of which I am a faculty member, and the University of Rochester whose cooperation I greatly appreciate.

Arthur Davis, Jr.

THERE is little agreement as to the causes and dimensions of the racial crisis in public education, but there is almost universal agreement that the crisis exists. This book attempts to probe the dimensions and causes of the crisis, to analyze the crisis from a cultural perspective and a theoretical and action viewpoint.

This book is addressed to all who are interested in the improvement of education for black Americans. In recent years, more and more people have become vitally concerned about the future of the black community and its education, particularly the inner-city blacks. Unlike most books written in the vineyards of the inner-city crisis, this offering proposes a social prescription and programming for quality education for black Americans through their culture.

Individual parents and citizens and community action groups of all kinds are taking a renewed interest in the conduct of inner-city schools. Inevitably, differences of attitude and opinion have arisen; sometimes these differences have led to vigorous controversy charged with emotional overtones and rage. In a word, inner-city education has become a paramount matter of public interest that ranges in scope from the private discussions between parents and teacher in a local school, to the widely publicized debates in the legislative halls and public forums of the state and nation.

In this setting of public interest in inner-city education, as in all matters of important public policy, the hope of the democratic way of life rests upon discussion of the merits and opposing points of view. Thus, emotional appeals to prejudice and racism, reliance upon half-truths about blacks or invalid generalizations, or simply a lack of knowledge are dangerous assumptions in a democratic society upon which to form public or private judgments of black pupils, ability to achieve.

Therefore, this book is designed to provide a sound foundation upon which to base judgments about blacks' education. It is addressed not only to prospective inner-city teachers, but also to the members of the educational profession, and to the American public, who share the responsibility for the conduct of educational institutions. It assumes that all present practices and all proposals and programs for the future should rest upon some valid grounds or presuppositions about black experience and culture, as well as upon some hope or preference about school desegregation. A careful review of the educational history and culture of blacks in America is, therefore, an indispensable element in evaluating the present and in making plans for the future in the inner-city. This review, admittedly, will not solve our present problems, nor will it dictate the road to the future; but intelligent decisions about the inner-city should not be reached without it. I believe, therefore, that this review of black educational history and culture is one of the ways in which teachers and the public together should prepare themselves for making better judgments about education for blacks.

I hope this book will be especially useful in the professional preparation of inner-city teachers and administrators. It is designed specifically for use in foundation courses in education, in teachers' colleges, liberal arts colleges, and universities. It is also designed for study in connection with other professional courses that deal with the principles of education, curriculum development, and reform administration and community groups. It is the intention that it will be useful for prospective college and university teachers who are entering their professional preparation and need an orientation on the scope of the black community. It is also intended for the "on-the-job" teacher, who may need an in-service refresher course on the black community to achieve "moral" integrational perspectives after his many years of service in the inner-city schools. It is, finally, my hope that the general educational profession and the general public will find opportunity herein to enlarge their understanding of the inequities in education for black Americans.

I have sought to preserve the merit of the earlier stages of

Negro education, while avoiding their shortcomings. I have attempted to include basic factual information and criticism of the purpose and process of education for black Americans.

I have, however, tried to remedy the failures of the present approaches by attempting to take account of the newer outlooks that have come to characterize more recent writings and teaching in the field of education for blacks.

One of the characteristics of the newer approaches is the cultural approach to the development of educational progress. Recent development of black studies programs and black culture centers has stressed the importance of the concept of culture. The distinctive way of life embodied in black people's folkways and mores that developed in the traditions of the past and that lives on in the institutions, ideas, beliefs, attitudes, and customs of the black community is summed up in the term *culture*. If educators and community groups alike are to understand and to be able to deal with the problem, if they are devoted to educating blacks, they need to understand the culture in which the process of education operates and what this culture contributes to our society. Black cultural traditions are not things dead and gone; they live on in black people and can act as guides to educational thought and action.

If we are to know black people and their problems and are to design educational programs of action, we need to know their culture. If educators are genuinely to face the problems of the black community, then it stands to reason they need to study the black community as an institution among other social institutions in American society; they need to study the underlying ideas, values, beliefs, and attitudes that motivate blacks' behavior in and out of the school. Thus, if the educational profession is to analyze carefully the present problems of blacks that confront education, professional workers need to know how and why blacks act the way they do about schools.

People act as they do, at least in part, as a result of the inherited values and ideals that live in them as traditions; and the school may be incompatible with this life style. The core of many inner-city school problems may be that the curriculum does not complement the culture.

Effort should be put forth to help educators understand what blacks' educational problems are, how the problems have arisen, what the advantage and errors of the past have been, what forces from the past are still at work in the present and what we have to reckon with as we move in the future. Since I cannot bring to bear all recorded black educational history upon present-day problems, I will bring to bear upon the present that experience of the past which is pertinent and relevant to the resolution of present black educational problems. Thus, the history of black education will not be confined to the factual recital of school data of the past, but will look at education for blacks in vital relationship to the culture of its people's time. This reflection on the education of blacks will not be a simple chronological recital of happenings from year to year, or from century to century, but a recall of affirmed antecedents, educational problems, and issues of the past as an aid in deciding what should be done in the future.

In this view, the cultural approach to education for blacks becomes a reassessment of black cultural and educational traditions. This untried approach should help educators, and community groups make judgments concerning the manner in which the process and purpose of education can be integrated; what is good for the future and, thus, needs to be strengthened; and/or what needs to be changed. All of this can and must be done with no abatement or relaxation of the rigorous requirements of scholarship.

There is great value in gaining perspective on the present time by seeing how education has been related to black culture in past eras. I have tried to show how education was viewed in the South and how its methods and content have been shaped by earlier philosophical orientations. This attempt is essential to an understanding of the way these inherited outlooks and practices by both blacks and whites continues to operate at the present time. Such an understanding of the past is indispensable to a sound analysis of the conflicting points of view that exist at the present.

A characteristic of the inner-city is increased attention to the persistent problems that face educators in the black community. Therefore, the book is useful in courses that emphasize practical field experience in the inner-city community, where attention is centered upon certain critical problems or conflict areas, as related to education in culture. This phase of the book includes such topics as early school experience for prospective teachers, colleges and universities thrust toward the inner-city community, cultural programs, human relations workshops, and white teachers in black schools.

In order to preserve the value of the factual and chronological treatment of education for blacks and also incorporate the values of the cultural approach to the inner-city problem, the book is organized in the following way:

Chapter 1 deals with "The Quest for a Black Philosophy of Education"; Chapter 2 with "Impassive Dilemma in Urban Education"; Chapter 3 with "Reshaping the Process of an Inner-City Education"; Chapter 4 with "Demands on School Policy: Decision-Making in the Inner-City Schools"; Chapter 5 with "The Influence of Social and Afro-American Studies"; and Chapter 6 with "Inner-City Educational Problems: Models and Strategies."

Within each part, education is treated as a phase of the distinctive cultural development of the black experience under consideration. As philosophical orientations changed or came into conflict with one another, they produced conflicting views of the desirable role of education in their time. Many such views continue to affect black Americans in modified forms. They are the psychological, philosophical, and intellectual foundations of education from a black perspective. Much of what is discussed represents proposals for change in the inner-city that rest upon dissatisfaction with existing educational and curriculum patterns in the black ghetto schools. Here are thus described the conflicting demands made upon ghetto schools by those who hold differing educational outlooks with respect to the persistent problems of inner-city schools. These are the controversial questions with which community groups and the dominant culture grappled in trying to make up their minds with respect to the social role of education, educational control, and the educational program.

Finally, the last section describes some humanistic alternatives, practices and activities in education and the community that will bring about an interplay of social forces and experiences. As new life conditions and new perspectives press for change, they are often reflected in educational innovations, experiments, and trends. Throughout all of the chapters, I have been at pains to stress factual and scholarly information based upon the best available primary and secondary sources. In addition to the sources on black educational history, I have tried to use the results of recent scholarship. Footnoting has been kept to a minimum, except in situations dealing with various educational outlooks and conflicting proposals for black education. In situations of this kind, there is considerable quotation and frequent reference to primary source materials. Therefore, footnotes have been more liberally used as a guide to the serious reader who may wish to probe deeply into the roots of persistent inner-city or black educational issues.

The more readily available publications have been selected in order to enable the reader to widen or deepen his understanding of those phases of inner-city education that cannot be enlarged upon in a general volume of this kind.

My hope is, then, that this book will be useful in refining and enhancing the long over-looked values and culture of black Americans in education.

Throughout this book, when referring to Americans of African descent, I will use the term black or black American, the term perferred by most black people. However, the term Negro also will be used, but only when reflecting on the historical setting, which at that time seemed to be the most preferred term.

RACIAL CRISIS
IN PUBLIC EDUCATION

CHAPTER 1

THE QUEST FOR A
BLACK PHILOSOPHY OF
EDUCATION

EDUCATION has always been highly influenced by the concepts of the nature of man. The way in which man's nature was perceived determined the way in which he was perceived by such great thinkers as Socrates and Aristotle as a thinking, conceptualizing person. Man was differentiated from animals by his ability to symbolize and to think in generalities. For instance, both Socrates and Aristotle (two eminent exemplars) felt that education was the means by which the development of the mind, then referred to as the "soul," could be achieved. Aristotle is famous for his many educational ideas in this vein, including the idea that "man cannot be taught anything; that we, as teachers, can merely provide an atmosphere in which learning can take place."

The religious view of the nature of man, however, was not as liberal as the idea or ideals of the Greeks. Later the religious view was that man was inherently bad and that education would help man overcome this evil and learn to control it. Therefore, Bible reading was the main purpose of education, so that one could find the way to heaven. The naturalistic concept of the nature of man, as supported by Rousseau and others, considered man basically good, that it is society which teaches a person to be bad. In *Emile*, Rousseau advocated raising a child away from society, allowing his basic goodness not to become

1

tarnished by society. The humanistic concept of the nature of man, however, viewed man as neither good nor bad. Locke felt man was born *tabula rasa,* a blank slate, and that man learns through experience in society. He and those who advocated the humanistic concept of man felt that man could not develop into an intellectual being, a "man," as we think of it, without education in society.

From these basic concepts of the nature of man, education has changed to coincide with the concept of man. Education has been the means by which society has preserved itself. Through education, man has been able to transmit those values which society deems important and vital to the next generation. Through education, society has been able to learn from past generations and to use history as an aid in coping with present-day problems and anticipating future needs.

Education has also been viewed as an agency for change. It not only has allowed each generation to cope with change, but has enabled each generation to initiate change, for the betterment of society. A society without change is a staid and stagnant society. Education, then, has made selection in society possible; it has allowed the individuals within society to judge which things must be preserved and passed on to future generations, which things must be modified to suit the demands of present society, and which things must be changed to modify society and allow it to meet the challenge of the future.

The selection of what and in what form societal "truths" should be transmitted has been decided at times not by society but by dictators acting for their own purposes of power. The arbitrary selection of what is to be taught and the manner in which it is to be taught is one basic difference between teaching and indoctrination. Teaching may be considered an activity aimed at changing behavior, but carried on in a rational fashion, which gives reasons for all conclusions and, above all, maintains respect for the integrity and judgment of the learner. Indoctrination also has change in behavior as a goal, but there is no attempt to extend respect for the judgment of the learner. What is necessary in indoctrination is the outcome. Process, so essential in teaching, is not considered in indoctrination. This is the difference between teaching and indoctrinating. Teaching presents facts and encourages man to formulate his own ideas.

Indoctrination selects those ideas which must be learned for the preservation of one way of life. Mussolini and Hitler, for example, found indoctrination to be their means of achieving their own ends. In their regimes, the government controlled the schools, decided what would be taught, and influenced men to think as they wanted them to think. Democracy, on the other hand, could not exist without an educational system which encouraged men to think for themselves, an educational system which educates the masses and facilitates, in so far as possible, full development of the capacities and abilities of every person. The chief aim of education is to realize the fullest satisfaction of human wants. It is from this purpose of education that the American dream and ideal of equality of opportunity is derived.

Proposals For Reforms In Public Education

During the nineteenth century, the nature of educational opportunity was continually changing in the United States. Our nation was building and expanding on the concept of individualism, whereby each citizen, through his own self-help and efforts, can attain his place in society. The concept served the colonial society well, but as the nation emerged into a viable creation, there was a need for more and more extensive education.

Benjamin Franklin had already seen the need for utilitarian education as a means of maintaining the position of the middle class. Franklin's plan for a new type of school, to be known as an academy, was distinctly secular in tone and content. His proposal provided a clear channel by which the philosophy of sense, realism, and empiricism flowed into American educational thought to give support to the desires for vocational training and practical preparation for a life of usefulness in society, public service, and professional pursuits. He hoped that teachers would relate to their pupils as if they were their children, treating them with familiarity and affection. Franklin's real hope was to enlarge and make respectable an education for civil and occupational life that would not need to rest upon religious instruction nor upon the classics. The impetus of

3

Franklin's academy and its impact upon the public school was one of the basic revolutions in the American educational system for all American children.[1]

In 1779, Thomas Jefferson atempted to revise the code of laws that governed public education in the state of Virginia. He saw more keenly than anyone up to his time the need for a complete system of public education. His proposal for a system of public elementary and secondary schools was contained in his Bill for the more General Diffusion of Knowledge presented to the Virginia assembly.[2] He based his argument for public schools on the grounds that a free society devoted to achieving the natural right of its citizens can be maintained only if the people in general are well educated. He believed that all persons should have equal opportunity to receive a liberal education without regard to wealth or social status. Therefore, all children should be given an opportunity to learn at public expense. Jefferson's proposal for a short education for all, with extended education for the extremely gifted from the lower classes, was also already a part of the philosophy, but not the actuality, of education. To complete his proposals for a system of public education, Jefferson called for a reconstruction of the academic curriculum at the College of William and Mary in 1779, which was not accepted. However his proposals contained the more secular and more practical as well as less emphasis on the classical than he would have made if he had been successful. His proposals emphasized reorganizing the college so as to teach the following bodies of knowledge: law; mathematics; history; ethics and fine art; natural philosophy; medicine and anatomy; ancient languages; and modern languages. This was Jefferson's ideal of a higher education as an instrument of preparation for leadership in public service, in the professions, in science and technology.

Franklin and Jefferson took up the cause of the common man and shifted the locus of improvement from the concept of individual charity to the need for organized effort, through governmental sponsorship if necessary, to promote the general welfare of the nation. These two philosophies generated a powerful movement for social reform that included public education as its most potent weapon in the battle against poverty, ignorance, and inequality.

4

The control and continuance of education in the early 1800s was still largely a function of the home, the church, and the individual. As the frontier moved west and people saw an opportunity to attain a better economic and social position through land development and their own efforts, the eastern states began to move toward a more widely based education, seeking to keep a sufficient labor supply readily available to fulfill mercantilistic needs. Thus, in the 1830s, we see the beginning of locally supported (with some state guidance) schools. The era of Mann and Barnard as pioneers in education was emerging.

Along with their stressing the need for more education, with local support, the industrialization of the East brought other forces to bear on the educational system.

The industry drew more people from rural areas, seeking economic gains in the cities. It also brought large groups of immigrants to the country, and many centered in the urban areas for employment purposes. So the educational system was again seen as a way to remove inequities through educational opportunities for the masses and to improve their social and economic position as a means of alleviating some of their prior suffering.

Even with the immeasurable broadening of the base of education, many still did not benefit, even though public education was increasingly provided as a matter of right rather than of charity. Even though the opportunity for an education was available for this increasing flow of citizens, instead of attending schools the vast majority of the children of laborers found they could help themselves better by working. The Civil War and the resultant "emancipation" of the black people dumped another group, previously uneducated (technically speaking), upon the people of the country. Without education, they could become an unruly mob; with education, each could raise himself economically and socially.

Throughout the nineteenth century, regardless of the changes in the population's composition, institutions of learning continued to grapple with the problem of meeting the educational needs and interests of our diverse population.

The movements in our society which provided changes in educational opportunity were the emergence of technology, the mobility of people, the change from rural to urban living; the need for education became more apparent as society advanced. Public schools began to be more and more the rule rather than the exception. The right to educate passed from the hands of the parent to the hands of the state. One-room schools were consolidated to form graded schools, and emphasis was placed on expanding the curriculum and upon improving the educational preparation of teachers.

Giant steps toward equality of educational opportunity were made during the nineteenth century, and more strides were taken toward this end in the twentieth century. However, equal educational opportunity for black Americans has not yet been achieved. If equal education had been achieved in the nineteenth century, it may not have been necessary in the twentieth century to work toward integration and in an ever-increasing manner labor with all the social problems which have caused and continue to cause racial crisis in public education.

In Historical Perspectives:
The Antecedents of Blacks' Education In America

When discussing the problem of education for black Americans, most often we are concerned with the profound nature of the socio-economic structure, with family backgrounds, inadequate teachers and administrators, and a lack of financial resources. Furthermore, we tend to think that with possible modifications, the problem facing the black community, that of semi-illiteracy, will be resolved. Rarely, except by what most Americans call black radicals or militants, is black education viewed as a system which differs from that of white education in terms of philosophy and goals. Because the method of educating black Americans, as indeed the method of educating white Americans, involves the designation of certain values and roles that are essential to live in the American society, this does not mean that the philosophy is the same. For the nature of the assigned roles and the specific values in black education are the direct opposite of those in white education. For whites, the values and roles learned through formal education have been to advance a majority. For the black pupils, the majority,

6

through exercising control over the school, has attempted to impose upon blacks a scheme of education which would aid in denying them full participation in the society. Black citizens of the South posed a tremendous educational problem for that whole region of the nation.

However, being aware of the fact that segregation in the South was an important factor in shaping the philosophy of black education in the South, and the North, purported to be non-segregated, suggests that there might be some differences between the black and white systems of education.

The essential argument is that the educational system of the South, which excluded blacks as full participants, was rigged to socialize a race of people into submissive, non-violent, obedient superpatriots. The system was devised to shut off the minds and emotions of black students from all that the white race said was taboo. Although blacks knew that they lived in America, where, in theory, there existed equality of opportunity, they also knew what to aspire to and what not to aspire to; they were hampered and hedged about in what they could aspire to be and become. Their education, in many instances, taught them to believe in freedom and independence of thought and, at the same time, to limit their aspirations to thinking only. This living by contradictory viewpoints can be most frustrating and can lead to disintegration. Thus, the intent of the educational system in the South has always been to get black boys and girls to act out the roles that the whites had mapped out for them.[3]

Much of the above is supported by literature dealing with black education between the Civil War and World War II. Extensive information may be found in the *Journal of Negro Education* and *The Crisis,* the latter edited by W. E. B. DuBois. In addition, the works of Louis Harlan and Horace Mann Bond cannot receive too much praise for their value and worth in understanding blacks' education in the South. Also, black fiction gives a deep insight and understanding of black education in the Southern tradition. Good examples are Richard Wright's *Black Boy,* W. E. B. DuBois' *Souls of Black Folk,* and Ralph Ellison's *The Invisible Man.*

Before the Civil War, few black Americans were allowed the opportunity to attend public schools. Shortly after the war,

7

the federal government sought to stimulate the development of public education for black Americans in the South. The early advocates of the education of blacks were of three classes: (1) masters who desired to increase the economic efficiency of their labor supply; (2) sympathetic whites who wished to help the oppressed; and (3) zealous traveling missionaries who believed that the ex-slaves might learn the principles of the Christian religion.[4] Among these advocates, there was little or no conflict about the type and quality of black education. However, the Emancipation Proclamation and the "Negro Amendments" created a different and complex atmosphere over the question of black education. There was a real difference in opinion, both interracial and intraracial, and the opposing arguments were more than mere misunderstanding. Public education for former slaves became a very controversial issue, and the circumstances exposed the many interests concerning the kind of education necessary for the ex-slave.

The majority of black Americans in the South lived in rural areas; consequently, the black public school in the South began as a Southern rural institution. Although most educators considered it a complete failure, if the system is evaluated in terms of its objectives and its philosphy, it follows that the education offered by the black rural school has been successful in living up to its expectations. The rural black school system was designed to socialize blacks to be peaceful, orderly, and humble people. The system was carefully devised to deny to blacks a dream of plenty, to teach them to expect little, and to settle for almost nothing. William J. Edwards, telling of his twenty-five years in the Black Belt, said: "We have in the South, as everyone knows, a dual system of public schools, one for the white and one for the Negroes. This accounts in part for our poor schools for both white and colored. Such a system is expensive and, of course, the Negro gets the worst of the bargain. This is not surprising to him, he expects it in all such cases. He has been taught to expect only a half-loaf where others get a whole one, but in some cases he gets practically nothing from the state for education."[5]

Almost all advocates' quest for a philosophy of black Americans' education refers to such objectives as "training for life needs" and "training students to fit into complex and ever-changing democratic society," but in fact the educational system of the South was organized largely to prevent the black child from becoming like the rest of the participants in our democratic society. The process of education kept blacks separate and distinct. In reality, the public school was to train blacks to fit into rural life as they found it, with all its prejudices and discriminations. There was never the intention to teach blacks to strive for the reality of democracy. Democratic education would have been directed to encourage equal participation in all activities on an equal footing with all races. Instead, the purpose of the school was to give blacks a false perception of their real racial situation. The school was instrumental in developing a compartmentalized mind. In one block, one would instill the belief in democracy and the hope of someday participating fully and equally in the American society. In another block was the realization of one's obligation to submit to a prescribed role for all black people.

While the general problem of equal opportunities was pressing in the case of the Negro, the social conditions of the South posed the most important educational problem for the Negro following the Civil War: to extend and perfect the ideal of "separate but equal" educational opportunity, and to realize it more effectively in practice. Around these two concerns revolved much of the racial controversy in education during this period.

The Demand for Negro Education

While it is obvious that blacks of the South posed a tremendous educational problem for that region and for the nation as a whole, education for blacks throughout the country invoked considerable arguments and questions among whites: were blacks capable of learning at all? Many urged simply and directly that they were not. Others, more convinced of blacks' ability to learn, were faced with the question of how and what to teach them. Was the black child to attend the common school? Were blacks to receive the same education as white children or a special one? Here, too, major controversies arose. One might well begin by turning to black educators.

Booker T. Washington, an acknowledged black educator, was a notable principal of the newly established Tuskegee Institute located in Alabama. Booker T. Washington, throughout his work in behalf of education for blacks, seemed, with consistency, to advocate that education of black folk would improve their purchasing power and social responsibility.[6]

One must not get the idea that Booker T. Washington was the only black to urge universal education for blacks; other powerful black voices were heard. For example, a Northern black theologian from New York City outlined a three-point program spelling out the educational needs of blacks in the South: (1) a better system of public schools; (2) an expanded program of trade and technical training for blacks; and (3) high-grade normal schools and colleges for the training of teachers, leaders, and professional men.[7]

It goes without saying that the white people of the country found themselves bitterly divided on these questions. One of the most important problem issues involved the struggle over whether black and white would attend the same school. Many Southerners took a strong position for separate schools and vowed to give up public education entirely rather than allow their children to attend school with blacks.

Gustavus Orr, state school commissioner of Georgia, in a speech before the Florida Chautauqua in 1886, held that the two races in the South were no nearer to intermingling socially. He stated: "Vast multitudes of our best White people would keep their children out of the schools altogether and trust to giving them such home instructions as they might themselves be able to communicate, or to such private teaching as they might be able to procure, rather than place them in daily contact in the common school with children coming from such homes as have been described."[8]

The profound attitudes on education for blacks and the changes in the institutional life of black America fermenting the intellectual life of blacks, led many black educators to begin to think harder and harder about the purpose and process of education for blacks. The actual conditions under which black people lived and the changes they worked and fought for prompted them to look more critically at the kind of education they saw about them and to visualize an education that would be more appropriate to the times. New outlooks on black life and black men caused some to bring their ideas to bear upon new educational goals, content, and practice. The traditional intellectual outlooks for blacks were reflected in a reassertion of traditional conceptions of black education, whereas those who saw value in the new philosophic and scientific attitudes began to argue for a new concept of blacks' education. Carter G. Woodson, the founder of the Association for the Study of Negro Life and History, known today as the African-American Historical Association, an assiduous black scholar and a prolific writer, was a man who firmly believed that "the achievements of the Negro, properly set forth, will crown him as a factor in early human progress and a maker of modern civilization."[9]

John Daniels, at a Richmond convention on black Americans' education, said, "If we do not give them a plain schooling best adapted to their needs and useful to them, outside dreamers and fanatics will give them an education not useful to them but dangerous to the peace of Virginia."[10]

It was not the purpose of the public schools to educate black people to be intelligent laborers, trained farmers, or skilled artisans of the South. And, certainly, it was not to educate them to become businessmen or politicians. Horace Mann Bond described the role of the black Americans' rural school as an institution developed to give blacks just enough education to take advantage of their surroundings but not more schooling than is demanded by their dependent economic situation.[11] In Southern states, few blacks were encouraged to receive educational training beyond the elementary level. Those exceptional blacks what were allowed to fill certain public service positions, that whites did not prefer, like teaching, were encouraged to acquire specific training. White leaders were forbidden to teach black students. Also, the state of Arkansas Department of Education, in its annual report of educational activities in black schools, described the following objectives of the black public school: "The Negroes must be encouraged to develop leadership within their own race, therefore, the State Department of Education desires to render every possible assistance in training them for this purpose. There must be teachers, preachers, doctors, dentists, and skilled workmen and farmers who shall lead, both by example and precept, and

11

make it possible for the encouragement and assistance rendered by the State to function properly.... All Negroes, and especially Negro leaders should be trained so that they will become not only competent but willing to assume and discharge their civic obligations. They should be trained to become dependable citizens in their respective communities, and should realize with increased opportunity comes added responsibility."[12]

As has been indicated, there was considerable public response on the kind of education the Negro is best suited for by both individuals and the Arkansas Department of Education. In the case of the latter, as always, it is difficult to judge how far these pronouncements represented the views of black people or the community. Thus, the question is not only one of the extent to which institutions of learning spoke for the community, but the extent to which they spoke for the black population they purported to represent. Even with these unanswered questions in mind, it is useful and informative to survey the alignment for and against, as well as the kind of education Negroes should have in a democratic America.

The insistence on a particular kind of education as more suitable for blacks was mainly motivated by the interests of preserving the caste order. Gunnar Myrdal describes black education in the South as an "education which bothers less with bookish learning and more with life in a humble status, daily duties, and the building up of character."[13] Black economic or political power was not sanctioned by the Southern white society and was not encouraged in the black public school. Dista H. Caldwell, reflecting on some of her experiences in the South, stated: "In most southern school systems an effort is being made to keep the Negro in his place. This means keeping each generation of Negro boys and girls away from the polls and doing the same kind of work that their fathers and grandfathers did. I once heard a country superintendent say to a congregation of Negro teachers in a summer school: 'Train your Negro boys and girls to be the best Negroes possible. Train them to be what they can be. Don't train them to be senators but train them to be good niggers.' "[14]

A prevalent black-country attitude was expressed by Walter A. Watson and Paul B. Barringer, as described by Louis Harlan in *Separate and Unequal*. Watson was horrified to think that there were 2,500 black schoolhouses "turning out your voters by the thousands to meet you and to meet me at the ballot box."[15] Barringer, chairman of the faculty of the University of Virginia, said at the Richmond convention on education for blacks: "Shall we, having by a great effort gotten rid of Blacks as a political menace, deliberately proceed to equip the Black for the future as an economic menace?"[16]

Black people were also confused over the philosophy and objectives of the black public school. There were prominent black educators or "refined Negroes" who thought that blacks did not need a quality education. It is difficult to determine whether they were sincere in their opinions or whether they were expressing the will of the whites. Obviously, some blacks managed to make the system work to their advantage, and they were not willing to sacrifice their material gains for self-respect or racial pride. Moreover, they could compensate for a lack of recognition by whites by demanding excessive respect and praise from less fortunate blacks. On the other hand, there were blacks who sincerely believed that education, especially classical education, was not the primary need of black people. Joseph Winthrop Holley, president emeritus and founder of Albany State College, stated: "Literature, music, art, and philosophy are fine, but what our young men and women need first is bread and meat on the table and money in the bank."[17]

One might ask Holley how the black was to put bread on the table and money in the bank except through quality education. To this question, he would have replied: "White man and black man can live side by side, if each knows his place and his responsibility toward the whole society. It takes many kinds of people to make a world. . . . Dependent as the black man is on the white man in the south, the white gentleman needs his black brother just as much. The economy of the south is geared to the amicable functioning of the two races in the traditional manner, each realizing its strength and limitations. Formerly, this racial pattern could be stated in a 'brains-plus-brawn' equation, in which the white man furnished the managerial skill and the black man furnished the labor. . . . One is not made the less for being a black servant, so long as he is a good black servant. There is no servitude more exacting than that required of a King."[18]

13

It is almost unbelievable that a black man would sincerely express such a view. And it becomes more unbelievable when one considers that J. W. Holley had achieved everything he had through education.

The struggle between the conservative and radical group of blacks became focused on the issue of "industrial" versus "classical" education for black Americans. One school of thought took the position that black Americans' education should differ in no respect whatever from the education of white Americans. This trend of thought was epitomized by W. E. B. DuBois. DuBois thought that black boys and girls should have a classical and cultured education just as white boys and girls. He was perceptive enough to understand the evil intentions of the black public school.

"Cast down your buckets where you are. In all things that are social we can be as separate as the fingers, yet one as the hand in all things essential to mutual progress." With this statement, Booker T. Washington became the champion for the position that blacks should be taught to fit realistically into a segregated society. He was backed by the white South and the majority of Northern philanthropists. The theory expressed here is that black American education should be directed to prepare blacks for the basic jobs necessary to modern agriculture and modern industry. Any attempt to participate in the social, political, and economic life of the larger society was deemed unnecessary.

The conflict and debates among black educators are interesting but were only important in the development of blacks' ideologies. Black Americans' differences had little impact on the development of black education in the South. Southern white Americans, like Northern people, had among them all the power, and so their convergent interests molded black American education in the rural South.[19] The ideas and philosophies of black people were important only insofar as they embraced and reinforced the philosophies of the whites. In searching the attitudes that determined the course of the rural school in the South, one should concern himself mainly with the attitudes of the dominant whites. Since the attitudes of Southern whites were of greatest importance for the growth and development of black education in the South, it is important to further explore the nature of the attitudes of white Southerners toward black education in the South. The important question to which one must address himself is, Why did white Southerners support the establishment of black schools?

White Support of Black Education in the South

"Negroes would not be getting so much education as they are actually getting in the South, if the equalitarian creed were not also active." The above statement was taken from Gunnar Myrdal's *An American Dilemma*. Here, Myrdal is supporting his assertion that Americans have a deep commitment to the American creed, and as a result, they are driven to adhere to the principle of *equality* before the law. To agree with Myrdal is to imply that white Southerners supported black education because of a moral commitment to the American creed. There is the possibility that the American creed might have had a small impact on the attitudes of white Southerners toward black education.

A. McIver, State Superintendent of Public Instruction in North Carolina, stated in 1871: "As to the African race, the results of education is doubtful, but in this age of the world, the experiment must be tried in good faith. While I think no system of instruction will ever lift the African to the high spheres of educated mind, yet let the role be played fairly, and if the results should not be commensurate with the demands of Christian civilization, the error will not be ours."[20]

The possibility of the American creed having some impact upon the attitudes of whites toward black education in the South must be considered, but it is my interpretation that humanitarian reasons had little to do with the establishment and support of black education in the South.

Just as whites forbade the teaching of slaves because they felt that education was incompatible with slavery, they also became convinced that a particular type of education was necessary for the ex-slave to adjust to the role they had prescribed for him. Incredible as it may sound, there seemed to have been serious concern about blacks reverting to an animal

15

stage. A. A. Gunby, in a speech before the Southern Educational Association, in 1892, stated: "The Negroes in a colony of their own would degenerate and speedily lose the civilization they have derived from contact with whites."[21] As a result, there was a widely held belief that the South should educate blacks at public expense because it made them more useful, peaceful, orderly, and humble citizens.

Many Southerners believed blacks were influenced by Northern abolitionists and had become angry with Northern whites. Hence, they would always await the chance to avenge the wrongs done to them by the whites during slavery.

Paul Barringer of the University of Virgina, at the meeting of the Southern Educational Association in 1900, described the black as an incapable, ignorant, vengeful person, scheming to obtain political power. He envisioned education for blacks serving largely as a tool to obtain political mastery of whites. Speaking to his peers, he exhorted, "Go back to the rule of the South and be done forever with the frauds of an educational suffrage."[22]

White Southerners, somehow believing that the slaves once loved their masters, sought to counteract the suspected negative influences of the abolitionists. Thus, it became an objective of the school to reeducate blacks to love and esteem their white citizens. The history of blacks and the South was constructed by Southerners in such a way as to blind both black and white to the unpleasant and inhumane experiences of slavery. A. A. Gunby described the role and duty of Southern history at the Southern Educational Association in 1892: "I am very positive that southern history which is taught in Negro schools should be written from a southern standpoint, and the true, unvarnished facts about slavery, about the treatment of Negroes before and after the war by the southern whites as compared with the treatment of Negroes by all other people should be impressed upon their minds. They would thus grow up to love and esteem their white fellow citizens as they have done in the past."[23] It takes no imagination to envision what Southerners considered the true and unvarnished facts of slavery. The majority viewpoint was probably best represented by John Calhoun, who thought that slavery was a romantic and rewarding experience for the Africans.

16

Another reason for the support of black Americans' education in the South, which was urban rather than rural, was to increase the economic efficiency of the South's labor supply. Because of slavery, the South had lagged behind the rest of the world in the industrial revolution, and it was urgent for the South to catch up. Therefore, it became necessary for the South to train a reliable laboring class. It was obvious that the ex-slaves composed a reliable and cheap reservoir of labor.

Despite the above, many Southern whites were opposed to the support of black education. Some objected to the support of black Americans' education because the taxes were in actuality paid by white citizens who were financing the black public schools. A. A. Gunby, before the National Educational Association in 1890, expressed this discontent: "While we have cause to congratulate ourselves on what the South has done for Negro education, we cannot disguise from ourselves the fact that there is a growing dissatisfaction with the system and a tendency on the part of many to regard the money spent on Negro education as wasted or as robbery of the White children. Consequently an increasing number of people are disposed to advocate the withdrawal of support of Negro schools except to the extent of the taxes paid by Negroes, which would virtually abolish those schools."[24]

There were other reasons, though not as pronounced as the tax issue, but perhaps much more important to the white Southerner. Whites feared education for blacks because they felt it might eventually raise blacks to a level unsuitable to their environment. This was reinforced as educated blacks migrated to the North because of a lack of decent opportunities.

Obviously the necessities of educating black Americans outweighed the fears. However, the institution itself reflected both the fears and necessities of the whites, it prepared blacks well to play their expected social roles: to retreat from reality and to be afraid to disturb the status quo. The school taught blacks to believe that slavery was all in the past and not really so bad. Moreover, the student was not to investigate or be inquisitive about the facts of slavery. The school, being deliberately made separate, reflects the fear of interracial contact. The school was also made inferior in hopes that it would produce inferiors. The entire Southern educational system may

17

be seen as one designed to train white children to be masters and black children to be the servants of these masters.

Public Education of Blacks in the North

Unlike the South, blacks in the North experienced a somewhat different educational problem.

Perhaps no subject in American history has received as much attention in recent years as the development of the urban ghetto. A vivid picture of the urban ghetto is given in the writings of Jacob A. Riis, ardent exponent of urban social reform. In volumes such as *The Children of the Poor* and *The Battle with the Slum* are sketches of poverty, of squalor, of intolerable living conditions, and of a thousand degenerating influences on the youngsters inhabiting the bleak tenements of the city and poor schools. There are gauges, appealing always to the youngsters' desire to conform, to be tough and adult. There is idleness, the fertile soil for unhealthy influences to reap its harvest.

All of these prove continuing educational influences of the inner-city child. The educational problem of the urban Northern black is different in context if not in principles from that of the rural Southern black. The situation in the North is emphasized by the deep educational problem of urban life. Black immigrants from the rural South compounded the educational problem of the inner-city ghetto, for they were incompatible with influences tending to perpetuate the life and ways of European cultures of the ghetto inhabitants. The promise of the city was greater than its performance. The problem of caring for the destitute and homeless, especially among blacks, faced the North. The contemporary crisis in the urban cities impelled educators to search for the roots of the inner-city and to explore those forces which relegated black people to a separate and subordinate status in urban life.

As more blacks moved to the North, restrictions in housing and employment forced black people into separate communities, where they had little choice but to provide for themselves the facilities and services that the larger community denied them. This does not mean that blacks were merely

18

passive figures; they worked positively and actively to create a viable social and cultural life of their own. If the inner-city ghetto was the product of white discrimination, the institutional ghetto was the creation of black civic leaders and entrepreneurs determined to make the black community a decent place in which to live. Yet this development can only be understood within the context of the racial proscriptions that continually circumscribed their activities.

The educational literature on black life demonstrates clearly that the black inner-city ghetto differed in significant ways from the European immigrant enclaves because of blacks' cultural distinctiveness and because poverty prevented them from acquiring better housing elsewhere. Discrimination was only a secondary cause of the immigrants' isolation—and, indeed, once they were Americanized and reached a certain degree of affluence, they were usually able to move into the general community with little difficulty. Cultural distinctiveness, of course, played some role in the development of the black inner-city. Black migrants from the South, like European immigrants, frequently desired homes close to those of similar backgrounds and convenient to the institutions and services that catered to their needs. Moreover, poverty limited them, too, to certain sections of the city. Yet, beyond this, similarities stop.

In general, one is able to distinguish two social patterns for immigrants. First, the avenues of mobility that were open to European immigrants and their children were usually closed to black urbanites. The son of the immigrant could—and frequently did—rise to a supervisory or managerial position and moved with relative ease into the mainstream of American society. The black, on the other hand, was confined to service and domestic jobs and could rarely advance beyond his menial capacities. The rare black man who, despite the odds, did acquire a good job and make money, still found it difficult to escape the ghetto. A systematic pattern of housing discrimination confined him to the black section of the city even when he could afford property elsewhere. Breckinridge of Hull House noted that in Chicago, for instance, in the early twentieth century, the problem of the black family was "quite different from the White man and even that of the immigrant. With

19

the Negro, the housing dilemma was found to be an acute problem, not only among the poor, as in the case of the Polish, Jewish or Italian immigrants, but also among the well-to-do."

Second, the process of acculturation, which transformed the European into an American, worked differently for the black man. Coming to the Northern city with a Southern rural culture that had itself been conditioned by discrimination and prejudice, the black migrant developed a new urban subculture that became over the years more, not less, distinct from the culture of the urban white. Unlike the life-style of the European immigrants, the black subculture of the Northern city was primarily a culture of adaptation. Although increasingly rich and complex, it did not have an independent reference point outside American society and was referred to as the "culture of inherited poverty."

The need to break this cycle has brought the role of education into sharp focus. During the past two decades, many labels have been applied to the inner-city student; for instance, culturally deprived, culturally different, culturally disadvantaged, educationally, and socially different blacks were dealt with as if their learning difficulties were the results of limited mental capacity. The school's curriculum was limited in its ability to provide for ways to meet the basic needs of this special group of students. Teachers failed to understand that these pupils' limited backgrounds and impoverished experiences inhibited their learning responses. Educators tended to define basic needs in terms of what would make teaching easier or what would keep the school's curriculum stable. Basic needs were defined more as school curriculum expectations, and as educational needs. It is purported in educational literature, that a culturally disadvantaged student is as he is because he is reared according to the standards of one culture, but when he enters school, he is expected to function according to the standards of a different culture. He is, therefore, when compared with the majority of the students attending American public schools, culturally at a disadvantage. Because of his different preschool experiences, the student is likely to be at a disadvantage from the very start of his formal schooling. His language, behavior, and value systems frequently are entirely incompatible with what the school, as an agent of the dominant society,

20

assumes or actively advocates for its students. In brief, the student's education is handicapped or disadvantaged by his cultural background. Thus, because of a student's cultural difference, he is disadvantaged in obtaining preparation for the society which dominates his education.[25]

A Sense of Reality

During recent years, there have been a number of studies describing the effectiveness, the structure and functioning of inner-city school systems, scholarly and polemical, friendly and hostile. A number of these have sought to portray the impact of inner-city schools on students and teachers and to examine the unintended, as well as the intended, consequences of forms of school organization. The questions raised are not new; the intensity of the debate, however, is unprecedented.

Perhaps no other period in human history has witnessed such extensive growth of inner cities and such widespread diversity of ideas and beliefs. The dialectical process of urbanism, changing ideological beliefs, and advances in technology have altered the thinking of the community, pupil composition in inner-city schools, the school curriculum, and ways of meeting responsible social and educational needs. So pervasive are the effects of the inner-city that no one can escape its ungovernable penetrating impact.

However, in a persistent manner, the involvement of educators in the special problems of the urban community, and particularly the inner-city, has been sustained and intense. For many years, the flood of ideas, programs, funds for research, and experimental projects has been so rapid that it was difficult to sort them out or to come to many well-based generalizations. In reflecting on the rapidity of change in the modern world, at this point, a major outline of the field of inner-city education is not sufficiently clear to permit an organized approach to an understanding of the basic structure of the programs and an assessment of proposed solutions.

Because of the major uncertainties, instead of presenting a consistent set of propositions and generalizations, as is often possible in a settled area of knowledge with a long history of

21

development, let us emphasize the controversies that enliven our particular field of interest, and the aspects of inner-city education. Hopefully, such consideration will deepen and extend our knowledge of inner-city schools.

Many of the educational problems of inner-city children need to be understood in terms of the underlying social conditions which afflict them. Harry Miller and Marjorie Smiley put it this way: "In a normal classroom in a suburban school, when one child is unruly, or another is not working up to his capacity, or a third is failing to read on grade level, we look to individual circumstances, to special problems of adjustment, in order to fashion a solution. But when children in the big-city schools are, *on the average,* reading one or two grades below the norm, when half or more of them drop out of high school before graduating, we must look to fundamental structural problems in the school as an institution and in the society at large."[26] Understanding these "fundamental structural problems" is the first step in evaluating the policy alternatives available today in the education of the disadvantaged. To choose wisely among these alternatives, however, will also require an examination of the process and purpose of American education, the roles of professionals, and the value of commitments of segments of American society; here will enter ideology as expressed in institutions, attitudes, and behavior.

Many have considered the problems faced by both the culturally disadvantaged student and the public school in the educational process. For instance, Virgil A. Clift, in "Factors Relating to the Education of Culturally Deprived Negro Youth," and Edmund W. Gordon, in "Characteristics of Socially Disadvantaged Children," write in the ecological vein about the inner-city diadvantaged.[27] Clift offers some "premises and facts" about contemporary education and American society. He begins by stating that neither the public nor the schools are convinced that the disadvantaged students can be educated to perform on a high level, because faults and weaknesses seem always to be attributed to the individual or his group.

Clift says that rarely is there criticism of the "conditions in the system that affect the individual's total development."[28] He declares that the problems of poverty cannot be solved without understanding the social pathology of various subcultures and

22

the psychopathology of the people who live in poverty. Specifically, he advocates programs that will "help youth to overcome psychological degradation and injury to self-esteem which result from the negative valuation society has placed on individuals because of caste, social class, race and economic standing." Recalling that fifty years ago the schools were expected to educate the disadvantaged (i.e., the immigrants) in "about three generations," Clift notes that today the same result is supposed to be accomplished in one generation or less. Therefore, Clift declares that the school is obligated to develop both academic competence and the highest order of occupational, citizenship, and social skills in its students.

Clift also maintains: "Schools must deal with the problems of racial segregation because it is directly related to inequality of opportunity and poverty." He holds that the human mind is "our fundamental resource" and that education "must remain the keystone in the arch of freedom and progress if we are to keep our system secure and our society stable."[29]

John Niemeyer, in "Some Guidelines to Desirable Elementary School Reorganization," describes research done at Bank Street College in New York City, on the question of how the problems of such schools cannot be solved merely through the incorporation of "more services" or by "changing family backgrounds." Instead, the schools themselves must undergo "a functional, and probably structural, reorganization."[30]

Bernard A. Kaplan, in "Issues in Educating the Culturally Disadvantaged," discusses the education of culturally disadvantaged students in its total social context. He proposes that "the problem of the disadvantaged" can be solved only if the society as a whole gives evidence of "its undifferentiated respect for all persons." Kaplan quotes the Educational Policies Commission of the National Education Association as follows: "The problem of the disadvantaged arises because their cultures are not compatible with modern life. One of the greatest challenges facing the United States today is that of giving all Americans a basis for living independently in the modern age. The requirement is not for conformity but for compatibility. To make all persons uniform would be as impractical as it would be inconsistent with American ideals. To give all people a fair chance to meet the challenge of life is both practicable and American."[31]

Samuel Tenenbaum advocates that "we will have to adopt fundamental reforms, radical and crucial in nature, so that the school as an institution will be more nearly in conformity with the cultural and behavioral patterns of this class. . . . What has long been a national fetish, almost religious in fervor, is the effort to shape all children, regardless of their state or condition, in the middle class mold. . . . In our sanctimonious way, we have assumed that this, our middle-class culture, represents the best of all possible worlds. We have never examined lower-class culture with the view of asking: Is there perhaps something in another way of life to alleviate our own sickness? (i.e., the often unbearable demands made on the middle-class child by his parents and his sub-culture). Like my house neighbors we have regarded every deviation with moral condemnation."[32]

Harry S. Broudy, a philosopher and historian of education, traces previous attempts to overcome poverty and its consequences, and he notes that in one important respect they have differed from the problem that the United States is now working on. The difference, he points out, is that the ranks of the socially disadvantaged Americans include disproportionately large numbers of people who have been subjected to color discrimination. He asserts that, as far as educational and economic opportunities are concerned, it is unrealistic to pretend that the problems of the disadvantaged white are the same as those of the disadvantaged Negroes.

He says that all who work in educational situations designed for culturally disadvantaged students should be professionally prepared for that particular work. Such preparation leads to routinization and intellectualization of the activities involved and makes it possible to perform even unpleasant duties. He warns that the ultimate educational goals for these students should be as high as for the "culturally replete" students and that remedial, compensatory measures must be viewed as temporary only. Therefore, he advocates, for the disadvantaged students, a basic program of general education in the sciences and the humanities, rather than merely a "literary repair job preparation type of schooling."[33] Broudy argues that improving earning capacities does not necessarily change the way of life, the values, or the aspirations of anyone; these changes come about only when a person is also able to improve some of his

24

other capacities. For Broudy, economic repleteness and cultural repleteness are not identical, nor even synonymous. Affluence, in the form of a "good job," does not produce the peculiarly human qualities of life; it simply lessens the economic pressures that tend to militate against the intellectual, moral, aesthetic, and religious qualities in man. Broudy also considers the question of what the culturally deprived segments of the total society may have to contribute to the middle-class segments. He suggests that the schools might learn from the slum child how to make the culturally replete child more self-reliant, less dependent, and less demanding of his parents for the newest and the fanciest in things and recreational activities, as well as in other areas of life. Conversely, Broudy is highly dubious that all of the middle-class traits are good ones to foist upon the culturally deprived students. He says: "Now while the middle class is still the backbone of the nation, it is also the stuffed shirt of the nation."[34]

The better model on which the culturally deprived and the culturally replete should both consider patterning themselves, he suggests, is a classless model, combining traits from the traditional wisdoms of both the West and the East. Broudy writes: "In this model, I dare say, the solid virtues of thrift, cleanliness, honesty, industry, and dependability will be written large; but I am equally sure that the quickness of mind and hand, the independent spirit of the gamin, the willingness to take life in its immediacy with all of its fresh flavor, the readiness to laugh, to love, and to enjoy the vividness of experience will not be missing. In equalizing educational opportunity, let it be opportunity for the best."[35]

Betty Levy writes about her experiences as an elementary school teacher in Central Harlem. She declares that, for most teachers who grew up in and are trained to work in a middle-class environment, working in a black slum school is much "like going to a foreign country." She deplores the fact that the school usually attempts to transplant itself unchanged into the different environment. Consequently she observes that the barriers to understanding are great on both sides.

Levy emphasizes the special need to prepare teachers to deal with and attempt to overcome their own "cultural shock" and cultural bias. She advocates that teachers must have an understanding and appreciation of the slum community if they are to understand and appreciate their students; and, as a result, be able to reach them and teach them. She pleads that an entirely new approach and that new curriculum ideas oriented specifically to the values, interests, experiences, and the entire culture of the lower-class Negro students are demanded. Levy writes that there is a need for basic changes and radically new solutions to the problems that she encountered.[36]

Betty Levy issues a challenge to school administrators whether they are directly concerned with the education of culturally divergent students or not. She maintains that efforts which seek to solve the problems of culturally disadvantaged students do not necessitate the lowering of the standards which are held by the school. Part of showing respect for a person is letting him know that he is expected to perform up to his ability and to meet standard rules of conduct. She further declares that a student need not be made to choose between the values of his home and the school.

The development of empirically based generalizations about the black child has shown a curious mixture of rational viewpoints. Their prevalent tone of thought has been ardently rationalistic about the educational deficiencies and needs of black pupils. Three general points of view were given considerable emphasis. One view has urged a reform of the curriculum, notably through including programs that help "disadvantaged" youth "to overcome psychological degradation and injury to self-esteem." A second view, promoted almost exclusively by John Niemeyer, urged that more attention should be given to "functional, and probably structural reorganization of the schools." A third position, promoted largely by Broudy and Levy, argues that teaching culturally divergent children is clearly a job for a well-chosen, well-trained teacher, and that the school should promote objective studies of the black experience and its role in American culture.

Such characteristics of the black pupil's educational deficiences and needs, taken as they are without elaboration or refinement, do not indicate and project universalistic social norms for all and a forced conformity to traditional ideas and practice for black pupils. In many instances, the scholars' analyses represent a movement away from the blind conformity

26

of the past, and face up to the problem of the blacks and their schools as we turn away from the past toward the emerging future. Furthermore, the scholars' observations in and of themselves give social guidance for the work to be done in predominately black schools.

It would seem that if a teacher is engaged in teaching black students, he is obliged to help them by relating to them through their culture. Moreover, if teachers are intimately concerned with the "natural development" of black children, they should study the nature and culture of black people to properly guide their development and to adjust instruction to their needs. When viewed in cultural perspectives, what is needed is an educational program that brings a variety of humane concerns, understanding, and methods of teaching and inquiry to bear upon the developed black culture to achieve more adequate guidance for work to be done in the inner-city schools. Part of the problem in dealing with black students as they relate to their environment is that of understanding the relationship between inner-city environment and the blacks' culture.

We have, I believe, wholly overlooked a vital moral principle in black Americans' education. This oversight is largely responsible for the limited success of the black community, and the great problem of national education of blacks will never be solved until we take it into account. The principle is: that education has long been viewed as playing a decisive role in the historical continuity of culture.

Culture, as an intellectual concept, has been developed by anthropologists and sociologists in dealing with human behavior. It developed out of a need for a basic theory or concept to deal with the variety of ways of believing, feeling, and behaving, characteristic of different societies and different social groups, which increasingly came to be known and studied. From one point of view, we might define black culture as the total patterned way of life of black people in which human personality and human experience are shaped; or, as a kind of additional environment which our American society has created for itself. From this perspective, black culture is the process by which the dominant group attributes meaning to, or projects it upon, blacks who are not willing to or cannot comform to the traditional model envisioned by the majority.

27

This general approach to the idea of black culture is to be distinguished from the late Oscar Lewis' concept of the culture of poverty. As used here, black culture refers basically to the higher, refined aspects of the black experience—art, music, literature, philosophy, the inner and outer reinforcement of black people, the appropriation of which presumably produces the "cultured" individual. Nor is black culture used here to refer to the culturally disadvantaged aspects of the black experience exhausted in literature in the late 1950s and early 1960s which viewed black pupils as a kind of veneer of deviant customs and manners.

Some Basis for Change

The dominant early genre in the history of blacks' education in this country is a version of comparing and contrasting the education of black Americans with that of white Americans, as if there were only one educational means to an end. Like their predecessors, contemporary white educators often think of evolving school racial compositions and increasing ideological consensus from the perspective of the professional scholastic, especially school administrators. Their thinking is linear, evolutionary, and often perceives the community as a geographically homogeneous unit with a single curriculum and philosophy of education.

As stated earlier, in the 1960s it was common to read about the disadvantaged. When others recorded the educational experience of black pupils, they normally reported the facts administrators chose to divulge, such as statistics of attendance and dropouts, and learning difficulties. In short, it was a promotional account of underachievement and problems that could be handled only within compensatory educational programs. This was an insider's view of education for blacks seen from the top down.

In the 1970s, there have been some changes in this establishment view of black American education. Educators and community laymen have paid increasing attention to ideological debates about which educational model should dominate the inner-city schools. These studies have illuminated

28

a number of ideological choices as well as the various rationales underlying curricula and teaching strategies, but none has raised questions about the basic purposes and process of black education. Educational philosophy and culture are closely linked and center on ideas about education rather than on empirical investigation of the actual impact of schooling. Indeed, many of the ideologically minded have assumed that commitments to different theories automatically resulted in differences of the product produced by the school. As a result of this tradition, one which has produced useless analyses of ideas, we know very little, if anything at all, about the impact of these ideas on blacks and the black community.

In many respects, the traditional educational philosophy has served its time and purpose well. However, it has not perpetuated and institutionalized the Freedman's Bureau vision of a common school which could transform blacks. The Bureau, inaugurated after the Civil War for the relief, guardianship, and education of Negroes, undertook to provide "unity and a systematic approach" to the many uncoordinated efforts of schooling for Negroes. In my opinion, this dream of the Freedman's Bureau for Negro schools was a great social invention. It gave a miscellaneous procession of educators a goal of becoming a united profession. Moreover, it provided a simple linear model for institutional research, thus enlarging the body of empirical knowledge; and it helped to explain and justify the education of blacks during the period of their most rapid growth by expressing a consensus on certain values of an education. Nevertheless, in spite of the Bureau's efforts, there was often little understanding of local conditions, values, feelings, and a failure on the part of the philanthropies to take community sentiments into account.

The present turmoil in black education suggests that it is perilous to take familiar educational models and ideologies for granted. Today it is clear that the black community and patrons have lost confidence in teachers and administrators, for the clients are rebelling against the educational means to a democratic end. Furthermore, today there is increasing evidence that the inner-city schools are not—and were not—serving the culture that justified them. Familiar facts need to be turned into puzzles; today many want to ask, Should education meet the needs of the culture? Should the process or purpose of education change to meet the culture of the inner-city public schools?

Increasingly, blacks have channeled the investigation of Afro-American education into the historical mainstream. Scholars have sought insight into the wrenching policy issues of the present by asking new questions of the past. Naturally, such revisions have produced conflict between advocates of old and new interpretations. Much of this conflict has really been a form of academic status politics, a quarrel between school officials and the black community. I do not intend to go into details about these polemics beyond expressing the opinion that both sides have often obscured and stereotyped the issues rather than clarified them. Both groups have pointed out that new approaches are needed to give guidance in educational policy questions today. School officials lack in educational imagination, and the black community leaders, being highly sensitive and defensive about the inner-city schools, have exerted a monopoly over educational policy-making.

The Problem in Perspective

Before projecting into "A Concept of Education for the Ghetto Blacks," I would like to deal briefly with four influential essays: the pamphlet, *The Role of Education in American History;* Bernard Bailyn's *Education in the Forming of American Society;* Lawrence Cremin's *The Wonderful World of Ellwood Patterson Cubberly;* and Stanley Ballinger's *Education And Culture.* In varying ways, these studies made two central points: (1) that education is far broader than schooling (indeed, that "in a profound sense, it *is* the life of the young as they move toward maturity"); and (2) that schoolmen should analyze the impact of education upon the society, not simply "the character that education has acquired as a creation of society." The Committee on the Role of Education in American History put the latter conviction in this manner: "The historian may . . . and we trust he will . . . approach education saying: here is a constellation of institutions . . . what difference have they made in the life of the society around them?" The committee urged scholars to investigate the influence of education upon such matters as the assimilation of immigrants, economic development, equality of opportunity, the development of political values and institutions, and "the growth of a distinctive American culture over a vast continental area."

In his provocative narrative, Bernard Bailyn suggested a hypothetical history of education in the colonial and revolutionary periods which would take into account changes in the family, religious life, race relations, and economic development as crucial determinants of the transmission of culture from generation to generation. Rather than tracing in linear fashion the institutions of the present from seeds in the distant past, Bailyn urged historians to regain a sense of surprise, a sense of discontinuity. The transformation of education in America, he wrote, "becomes evident . . . when one assumes that the past was not incidentally but essentially different from the present; when one seeks as the points of greatest relevance those critical passages of history where elements of our familiar present, still parts of an unfamiliar past, begin to disentangle themselves, begin to emerge amid confusion and uncertainty. For these soft, ambiguous moments where the words we use and the institutions we know are notably present but are still enmeshed in older meanings and different purposes . . . these are the moments of true origination."[37]

Lawrence Cremin continued the monologue in his essay on Cubberly published in 1965. In this study, he traced the historical tradition as it flowed into and from Cubberly's influential *Public Education in the United States.* Acknowledging Cubberly's astounding industry, his clear organization, and his service in giving professionals an "unflagging commitment to universal education," Cremin nonetheless concluded that Cubberly's analysis had obscured the full character of education in America and "had helped to produce a generation of schoolmen unable to comprehend . . . much less contend with . . . the great educational controversies following World War II."[38] He urged historians to examine educational agencies other than the school, to bring revisionist interpretations in general history to bear on educational questions, and to place American educational history in comparative perspective.

Stanley Ballinger's essay projects that "education reflect the culture; that education should adjust itself to the changing culture; and that education should address itself to the needs of the culture, and a difference in degree of culture entails a difference in the quality of education."

These four essays constitute excellent points of departure for educators desiring to investigate the role of education in Afro-American life. Each sketches topics which could absorb a lifetime of research. The essays by Bailyn and Cremin include valuable bibliographical aids. Since the publication of the first pamphlet of the Committee on the Role of Education in American History, many insightful studies have appeared.

This body of writing has demonstrated that an analysis of education can be intellectually respectable. Perhaps in the 1950s this was a point that needed reinforcement. Today, however, I suspect that a large group of educators will be moved by concerns not so prominent before the mid-1960s. I am thinking especially of the crisis in race relations and urban education and the signs of strain and conflict apparent in all educational institutions. We have developed a double system of public education, one central-city-suburban and predominantly white and middle class; the other inner-city, predominantly ghetto blacks and poor. On the surface, the schools in central city and inner-city are similar, both loomed over by the same schoolmen, curriculum, and philosophy of education. Often their lists of courses, their organization, and even at times, their rhetoric are identical, but they are not the same. One group leads from better homes, through well-financed schools to higher education; then on to the lucrative life in similar communities. The other takes ghetto blacks through dark and aging buildings, then back to the ghetto welfare rolls or compensatory educational programs. The inner-city process of education adds little cultural value, prevents the accumulation of social and economic resources, and leaves the next generation of ghetto blacks with no more than the last.

In the past, most critics of public education have come from the right side of the political spectrum. Today, critics on the left have been pointing out that the facts of inner-city schooling belie the ideology of the common school, which originally sought to give each child equal opportunity, to mix all social groups under one roof, and to place schools under meaningful public control. Writers like W. E. B. DuBois,

Nathan Wright, Jr., Preston Wilcox, Leslie Campbell, Benjamin E. Mays, and C. Eric Lincoln have been trying to tell the story of ghetto education from the bottom up; titles like *Death at an Early Age*[39] and *Our Children Are Dying*[40] indicate that the prospect is not a cheerful one. Studies like *Racial Isolation in the Schools*[41] and *Village School Downtown*[42] show that schools have become more and more segregated along class and racial lines, creating in effect two public school systems, one for the white middle- and upper-class central-city-suburbanites, and the other for the poor. James Coleman has revealed how far we are today from genuine equality of educational opportunity for ghetto blacks; surveys in ghettos like Harlem reveal that children there fall further and further behind in educational credentials that have become essential for occupational mobility in our society. And research by Kenneth B. Clark indicates that the public has only the remotest control over day-by-day school policies in the large urban bureaucracies.

Movements for community control in black ghettos daily remind us of the seriousness of the current crises in education. We read of new proposals which would fundamentally alter traditional educational ideology and structure; people ask why free education has to be a public monopoly and suggest tuition vouchers for the children of the poor; blacks demand decentralization of control; students and teachers reach for power over matters formerly dominated by their superiors; scholars investigate what the mass media and the educational industries may do to our customary notions of education in the classroom; new definitions emerge of what genuine equality of opportunity in education would cost in resources and effort. While it has been traditional in America to see education as the answer to social problems, today many disenfranchised blacks regard the schools as part of the social problem. This crisis, and this new social research, make it even more imperative to recast the philosophy of education, for the inner-city to analyze those critical turning points which may have led to the present situation.

A Quest for Quality Education

There are many reasons for working to strengthen the black

33

communities, but in the last analysis the most incontrovertible of these reasons is that millions of citizens—including many who have no special commitment to living in an all-black neighborhood—are living there now and will continue to do so for the foreseeable future.

Secondly, the development of institutions in the black community affords an opportunity for many whites and blacks to solve the educational dilemma of black youth.

Black youth are confused, not simply about what is going on around them, but about the intellectual equipment they have at their disposal. Other educational models and educational ideas do not apply; indeed, they never applied.

It seems to be perfectly plain that most black youth's rage and individual uncertainties are rooted in social and educational disorders; and if they do not know what to believe, or what to believe in, the reason is not the turmoil within, but the fog outside. To see their way through this fog, they need social ideas, and an educational philosophy, not compensatory programs.

But if black Americans do not know how to diagnose their social ailments or how to proceed to deal with them, if they do not know where to turn to get a grip on black affairs or what dimly humane outcome might possibly be seen in them, it is partly because of the ideas they have inherited for guidance.

Thus, the time has come for blacks to place in perspective some of this confusion. This is an offering to get greater order, clarity, and consistency about the ideas we can use for interpreting the plight of black Americans, and for turning them from a fatality in an affluent society in which we must live into an opportunity for the generations of blacks to come. In the process of considering these ideas, it is quite possible that certain persons will find some greater serenity of spirit. This will be a fortunate by-product of my inquiry, for I am interested in developing ideas, not as a means of personal salvation, but as instruments of social planning and action.

Most blacks grew up in a climate in which the prevailing winds blew favorably for an infinite number of beliefs, attitudes, and values. We thought, for example, that the existence of a variety of social, educational, and philosophical interests and values would result in desirable outcomes. Fixed distinctions

34

of class or status were looked upon as gratuitous. Where there were conflicts of social, educational, and philosophical interest, or disagreement between black social classes, something like a rational compromise was considered out of order; and add to this the existence of a kind of general solvent of selfishness which led further to disintegration. Common beliefs about ends have never universally been shared by blacks as a race of people. It has been this diversity which has set the tone and standard of public discussions, added bitterness to the civil rights debate, and destroyed the hopes of most blacks who permitted themselves to have any hopes. The black leaders who are celebrated in our public ceremonies and implicit in their public manners, in many instances attempted to provide clear-cut answers to all problems, be they political, economic, or social. Behind this was a set of half-articulated attitudes and expectations about the "real problem" plaguing black Americans, about the factors of himself and his environment on which he might depend, and on the ideals it was reasonable and most important for him to pursue in his effort to control his destiny. This outlook is seen as being the main cause of the present unhappy situation. It is responsible for compensatory programs' most disastrous failures, it is said, and even for the contemporary efforts of model cities programs. In many ways all the present uncertainties come to a focus in the decline of rational ideas and of the wisdom which stood behind them; and the general validity of these ideas and this wisdom, its relevance to the present problem, its usefulness and its prospects, are the first things with which Negroes must come to terms in any assessment of the substantive utility of black Americans and their aspirations, which they must contend with.

On its intellectual side, the crisis in public education of our time is a crisis in our interpretation of the Negroes' educational needs and problems; in particular, it is a crisis in the attitude they ought to take as blacks toward the type of educated black human product they envision, and would like for schools to produce as the next generation.

It is this writer's opinion that the future of Negroes lies along a radically different path from the one that they have been following. I am convinced that a misrepresentation of the facts is itself a major reason for our present educational troubles;

and when we put their criticism together, they constitute a rejection of black culture almost in its entirety. In examining the sources, we are entitled to a full-dress reappraisal.

I believe that these ideas, notwithstanding all the criticism that may be made of them, are essentially correct—correct in their logic, right in their estimate of what is possible, and right in their estimate of what is desirable. At the present moment, with its emphasis upon ideological correctness, it is probably necessary to say, however, that I do not regard the view I have reflected on in this chapter as waves of reform in public education for blacks. I am trying to lay down an exclusive definition of what is necessary to eliminate the plight of blacks. How successful I am only the reader can conclude. My effort is based on logic and is, I hope, useful. It is an attempt to formulate an outlook which, I believe, expresses the working principles of producing a valid product, which I hope will help those teachers with inclination to help blacks achieve, to see further, to move with fewer lost efforts, and to help them take command of their problems in a systematic way. I do not insist or assume that every black share my point of view, and I am willing to acknowledge that more than one means can lead to the same end, if the end is agreed upon. But the means I describe, I cannot help but believe, lead there more quickly and more efficiently.

To be explicit, I am talking about developing a black philosophy of education. What I envision is a theory of education that the school administrators and community leaders, working together, can develop and institute in trying to deal with the present educational problems of black children.

No doubt, a black philosophy of education has an arrogant sound about it. However, in looking for enduring values, a black philosophy of education offers a larger context for the measurement of current problems and temporary solutions. It gives us a chance deliberately to erect safeguards so that basic values will not be lost in dealing with emergencies, so that we will not needlessly complicate other problems in our preoccupation with just one problem, urgent as it may be. A black philosophy of education offers a long view and a hard view. It gives us a chance to keep first things first and lifts political action above the level of expediency and opportunism. For the

36

attempt to develop a philosophy of education has been the way in which other men have tried to make a sober and circumspect appraisal of the cultural resources available to them, remove limits upon their power, and heighten the alternatives open to them. It is an attempt to deal with problems, not in isolation from one another, but in some systematic way, to take account of long-range considerations, to safeguard primary ideals, to pick out the most important variables in the social process. A black philosophy of education can be a way, at once, of making the social and educational imagination more responsible by pinning it down to what is immovable, and making it freer and more flexible by giving it a larger vision of human possibilities. It is a theory of how to get things done, and of what blacks can make of their experience. As such, it is an explicit strategy of social and educational action, and it can be a sober prelude to the development of a coherent educational program for the inner-city public schools.

Such a black philosophy of education results from the ideas that once sustained us. For example, an impressive variety of leaders was urgently seeking a new black cohesion. In one sense, the answer to this question constitutes the rationales of compensatory educational programs and model cities programs. By and large, these reformers believed that they spoke for the black population, rather than to it. They assumed that community leaders everywhere shared the same ethical system, the same dedication to public service, and the same aspirations to unity. Their task, in other words, was not to convince people, but simply to arouse them, and like-minded legions across the land, community by community, would translate their dream into practice. It is this misunderstanding and misinterpretation of what would later be called compensatory education that specified the type of education for blacks. It was within this framework, which had no single canonical statement, which was sometimes fuzzy around the edges, and ambiguous about some of its most fundamental conceptions, which disintegrated and disenchanted blacks.

The climax—the solution to black problems—lies, of course, in education serving the black community, harnessing the energy of the masses, showing them the truth, and as the late W. E. B. DuBois grandly predicted, all the resistless forces of nature become our auxiliaries and hasten the process of development on to certain prosperity and triumphs.

It is an optimistic message, one in which both teacher and learners knew they could walk the edge of damnation in the early part of the ritual with full assurance that ultimately the path would lead them on to success.

Some Tentative Guidelines

I should like to discuss a possible approach to building a black philosophy of education, which, it seems to me, would be central to a reinterpretation of our educational policy, the purpose and process of education in the inner-city, the education of black Americans.

Two questions are relevant: (1) How would you build a black philosophy of education? (2) What problems would you endeavor to solve? These are questions of perspectives.

The present crisis in black education is prompting educators to look with new perspectives at institutions we have long taken for granted and to ask new questions about familiar subjects. This is not so much another form of present-mindedness, a defeat which has produced much anachronistic writing on the education of black Americans in the 1950s and 1960s, but an insistent educational revolution which is slowly penetrating the black community that is forcing educators and schoolmen to understand blacks' existence in new terms.

In the face of the present racial crisis in public education, the task of developing a black philosophy of education can be a complex and controversial undertaking. Therefore, the responsibility for developing a philosophical scheme should not be that of the school administrators alone, nor should it be assigned to the community leaders, but it should involve both. School administrators and community leaders, with the aid of scholars in higher education, should study realistically philosophies that complement black children's interests and needs.

All of us have some philosophy, though it may not be carefully thought out and placed in an organized form. However, before school administrators and community leaders develop a black philosophy of education in all of its various details (aims, content, procedures for teaching, and other factors), they should have a creed or belief in the things that they wish to accomplish. They should be imbued with the spirit and belief that what they plan to undertake is valid, worthwhile, necessary, and that it has inherent in it rather unique contributions to the educative process which they can and will promote and defend.

In developing a black philosophy of education several conditions must be kept in mind by the developers if the philosophical scheme is to be relevant:

1. It should be based upon an analysis of black people, their needs, interests, physical and mental capacities, aptitudes, abilities, and short-comings;

2. To be sound, it should be arrived at through the techniques of the scientific method of research, particularly as applied to reasoning;

3. It should reflect the recognition of our acceptance of the concept of individual rights to creative, artistic, economic, and occupational development;

4. It should embrace any and all relevant factors, such as: aims, subject matter, teachers, school and classroom organization, methods, time, psychology, resources, standards, grading, tests, and other factors;

5. It should provide for present intelligent social living as well as preparation for adult economic living;

6. It should reflect the fact that some phases of the learning experience will focus on the cognitive essentials, and other aspects are personal, "special-interest" learning, and that there are certain well-defined relationships between these two divisions;

7. Finally, it should recognize its somewhat unique educational contributions to white children and adults, but simultaneously accept and cooperate and coordinate its educational activities with general cultural education and other special interest areas.

Any concerned group of school administrators and community leaders must have well in mind the problems they wish to resolve. In short, they need a pattern of problems of the black community which they must apply to the works of each philosopher studied. Such a pattern of problems affords several advantages: (1) it serves to direct the study and research; (2) it provides a means of localizing the main issues; (3) it should motivate inquiry; (4) it should help in organizing thoughts; (5) it provides a consistent means of comparison and contrasting of the various philosophies; and (6) it should give a pattern for working out a black philosophy of education.

Such a procedure may be very eclectic in nature. It may result in glaring inconsistencies within one's personal philosophy. However, in building a black philosophy of education the eclectic stage of development is necessary as a step toward the later synthetic stage of harmonious thought on integration. Hence, we should plunge into the difficult task of abstracting and integrating the valid elements from various sources of philosophical and educational thought toward our own unified philosophic outlook of black Americans.

Thus, as DuBois has stated, and I embrace his approach, an inquiry into the problem plaguing the black community should not be a conventional type of "social science adventure," an instantaneous photograph of a sample group; but should be planned to approach the status of a complete situation, continuously photographed, and rephotographed, measured and remeasured; so that our knowledge of the problems of the vast and momentous social-educational understanding of the black community would attain a completeness with order, clarity, and consistency that would be unquestionable.

In terms of the problems we must determine the facts, meaning, and evaluate each philosopher studied. This kind of critical thinking is absolutely necessary to black scholars if we are to experience a real learning and have any degree of success in building a black philosophy of education.

Finally, this idea is nothing new. The attempt to develop a philosophy of education has been the way in which other men have tried to make a sober and circumspect appraisal of the cultural resources available to them, remove limits upon their power, and heighten the alternatives open to them. It has been an attempt to deal with problems, not in isolation from one another but in some systematic way, to take account of long-range considerations, to safeguard primary ideas, to pick out the most important variables in the social process. A black philosophy of education can be a way, at once, of making the social and educational imagination more responsible by pinning it down to what is immovable, and of making it freer and more flexible by giving it a larger vision of human possibilities. It is a theory of how to get things done, and what blacks can make of their experience. As such, it is an implicit strategy of social and educational action, and it can be a sober prelude to the development of a coherent educational program for the inner-city public schools.

CHAPTER 2

IMPASSIVE DILEMMA
IN URBAN EDUCATION:
REVENUE SHARING AND EDUCATION

THE growth of large urban populations and metropolitan areas in the United States has been one of the challenging and fascinating phenomena of the modern era. As towns merge with towns, and cities with cities, overlapping state boundary lines to form continuing giant urban complexes, a whole new set of forces arise to affect the political, economic, and social life in America.

This shift in the human landscape is visible almost from day to day. In contemporary America, the movement toward metropolitanism has become the unit upon which the local government, business, and educational leaders are now planning. Within this frame of social affairs, the rapid shift from suburban influence to an overwhelmingly metropolitan economy is the emerging new form of urban society. What lies behind the rapid and accelerating growth of metropolitan development is a change in pattern of social life.

As social products of this historical process, we have witnessed the concentration of the population in large cities, as well as increase in the size and quantity of metropolitan areas. We have witnessed a change in the scale and mode of social activity; a change in the quality of social and individual life. Today, urbanization represents a change in the structure of social organization. It refers to the process of crystallizing society at a certain point in time and is conceived of as a characteristic of the total society.

The trend toward increasing metropolitanization and the determinants of shifts among metropolitan areas in the form of widely diverse growth experiences is one phase of our problem. But equally striking shifts have been taking place within cities—changes in community and school pupil composition which, particularly in the case of the larger cities, pose at least as many social problems as do the broader shifts and are closely related to them; namely, the educational and sociological problems attendant upon a society which has shifted from urban to suburban, and now metropolitan, and the problems of the black communities affected by this sociological shift.

Sociologists, more than any other group, have studied the process and have developed the subject of urban education with a large literature which educators have neglected to their cost. But few of these people, even the sociologists, saw more than isolated facts, and none used urbanization as the basis for a new synthesis.

The old sociological models describing the conditions of the black community have been strained to the breaking point. We are no longer dealing with the sort of phenomena we knew even one generation ago. To be accurate, we are no longer talking about the "dark ghetto," but an open ghetto that has become a giant of elephantine proportions. Thus, our emerging city population can be viewed on a number of levels: the city schools and their role in meeting the needs of minorities; the problems and challenges of the black community itself; and the difficulties faced by the school in meeting the needs of the minorities.

Regardless of the level of analysis, easy solutions to the problems of the black community and the public school are difficult. Most of us have a few pet theories to offer as answers to these vexing problems. Even the layman at the community level is sure that, given the authority, he could have the difficulty eliminated in short order. A solid step toward a solution will be taken when we persist in isolating the difficulty and seeing its relationship to the rest of community life in terms of its culture. To summarize the challenge, two fundamental needs are highlighted. First, the city school must deepen

43

its awareness of its functional role and service to minorities. Second, schoolmen must rediscover a sense of cultural diversity that is present in urbanized America.

"As the term society expresses the organizational characteristics of a group of people living together, so the term culture represents the shaped and agreed-upon values, attitudes, and behavior norms which control the selection of appropriate behavior."[1] For example, the white teacher, suddenly thrust into the midst of black pupils, finds that the "traditional wisdom" which he or she brings from his culture and education collapses under the new pressures, his established value of an education, his way of viewing life, his dealing with people, and rearing a family prove him to be inadequate as an agent of change.

The teacher is suddenly confronted with the need for new knowledge, new teaching techniques, and new social modes. That which is true for the teacher gradually has become true of all social agents. We are experiencing in the inner-city a period that knows a collapse of deep-rooted traditions. The public school at all levels is having great difficulty in serving as it did in the past. New problems and new knowledge must be integrated with the accumulated wisdom as new demands are made by the inner-city community.

Even more frightening is the fact that the social unrest and racial strife of the community have been transferred to the schools. The frustrated community way of life has become an integral part of city schools. All of this serves as commentary on the basic fact that a vast transformation in urban education is taking place. These factors combine to produce a certain type of attitude that is evolving in the school. Within the past two decades, the social transformation has been tremendous, and the need for systematic study of the trends and conditions in urbanized areas has become increasingly important.

The Miller and Woock book, *Social Foundation of Urban Education,* brings together a collection of studies on the urban setting. The documentary sources flavoring this book authenticate the emerging urban movement taking place in America.[2] This movement has always existed. Arthur M. Schlesinger, in "The Rise of the City," greatly illuminates the increasingly dominant role played by urban development in late nineteenth-century America.[3] In this, he tried to use the urban movement

44

to synthesize the events of American history from 1878 to 1898, when the United States was trembling between two conditions of life, one rural and agricultural, the other urban and becoming industrial. Currently, the urban way of life is the rule, not the exception. Researchers, on an ever-increasing basis, are attempting to place in perspective the pieces of the emerging social arrangements.

Internally, we move from one neighborhood to another, one community to another, all within the city area; externally, from one town or village to another, in search of better opportunities, a place in the economy, and status in the social order. This search has always followed certain integrating patterns until recently. For example, minorities, as they arrived, tended to settle first in the older and less desirable sections of the city, where once the now-declining white population lived. Because of this polarizing trend within the metropolis, a salient feature of the emerging urban society is a dominant minority group attending public city schools.

For example, Washington, D.C., our nation's capital, as an extreme case in point, epitomizes the type of pupils our city school must educate.[4] This comes to the heart of the question of responsibility. In the culture that is developing, should the school be associated so exclusively with this community? Should it deliberately seek to associate itself with the sphere that has become the arena of minorities? This residential area, like most others, is characterized by family life, peopled during the workday by women and preschool children.

The complexity of public education in the city is great, and the magnitude of the educational problems plaguing the black community, related or isolated, inevitably will become the new American dilemma. Unless we as educators are able to gain some newer perspectives of community conditions and problems, and offer some meaningful changes, the renaissance in public education that we are experiencing in the city schools will hamper instead of enhance the education of non-whites. Schools in the black community will not be as they are now, polarized along racial lines only, but will become schools that are based on the Hindu caste system. The organization of the American public school system along social and economic lines can be consistently associated with the ancient doctrine of caste, and

45

is advocating, under the authority of schoolmen, precisely the same philosophy of life as governs the Hindu caste system under which, by alleged divine or natural law, the people are organized in groups according to the occupation for which they are supposed to be fitted, the domestic in the domestic caste, the executive in the executive caste. As Karl Marx would state it, the ruling class and the working class.

From almost any perspective, particularly socioeconomical and educational, because of racial differences, city schools are shaped and dominated by the culture and life-style of minorities. The current status of city schools, marked by a growing population of minorities demanding equal educational opportunity and institutional inclusion, constitutes new social forces and change. To illustrate this point, in public schools, new demands are being placed upon schoolmen and teachers to alter the curriculum to the needs of their new clients. This demand has reverberated through the entire nation.

Inner-City Profile

The inner-city is an integral part of the metropolitan community; in fact, it is the heart of the metropolis. Within the last decade, a growing number of articulate black leaders have joyfully entered the urban scene, along with the federal government, to take part in the task of creating an urban society scaled to the full life of all of its members. This task is to move minorities into the mainstream of the emerging urban way of life in the metropolis.

Without a doubt, there is literally nothing in the other segments of the metropolitan community directly comparable to the inner-city of ghetto blacks or even the enforced community of isolated small-town America.[5] Consequently, the residential neighborhoods of the city, as important as they are to their inhabitants, seldom provide more than a minimal sort of "community." Homogeneous and graded by their social rank, the various local areas still support and control only a limited amount of the vital energy of their inhabitants. Quite similar to the loosely defined structure of the inner-city, within the metropolitan complex is the black community. Here, again,

46

a line is drawn on the map, affording a certain identification and orientation, separating the residents. The black community, however, neither has the resources for real autonomy in educational matters within the metropolitan complex, nor can it establish a meaningful relationship with other communities in the same metropolis. As a concomitant, they are unable to integrate their unit in any effective way with other units outside their boundaries.

The black community is not a mere agglomeration, it is not a self-contained neighborhood, but a group organized along special lines. The behavior of its members is subject to structured patterns of interaction regulated by norms and values which give the group continuity and order and are intrinsic to the community. This suggests a reevaluation of the mode of life in the modern urban community and emphasizes the significance of taking the perceptual, as well as the behavioral, context into account in educational matters.

The existence of subcultures in our society has been recognized by social scientists and educators and has helped to explain some of our educational problems and to suggest solutions for them. The description of the black community's paradox has highlighted the contrast between our ideals and our practices and has shown the conflicts between our real learning and the learning goals formulated by the schools. Inevitably, the problems outlined above become political problems, but our present political structure is ill-suited to deal with such issues.

The large-scale bureaucratic centralized system which controls the non-whites' work, rewards, rights, and, in large part, thoughts, are neither territorially nor socially inclusive. There is, in consequence, considerable overt and covert conflict between the effects of the system on the black community. Such conflicts are evident, for example, between equal opportunity and the ethos of democracy, between representation and the municipal government, between producers of commodities and consumers. An obviously dramatic example is the racial strife in schools and race relations on and off the job. Less obvious, but probably as important, is the struggle in the intellectual market between the schools and the mass media for control of the socialization process; assimilation and diffusion of the culture, with blacks sometimes neutral bystanders and sometimes third parties.

If the black community is to have a substantial role in the metropolitan community, a major step in the right direction lies in an inevitable decrease of bureaucratic centralization, not only in civic and governmental community, but also in education. The total function of education in the city should be broken down into component parts, enabling a large array of community members to become involved in the achievement of their children. This suggests some form of community control for social order. The term *community control* connotes a form of rational organization that is in opposition to the centralized concept which we now have. The urban schools of today themselves form a useful illustration. Public education in the inner-city has experienced the growth of a widespread bureaucracy in the last two decades. Professional schoolmen have increasingly occupied administrative positions, and dominated policy- and decision-making in place of citizen participation. The black community is systematically excluded. Because of this exclusion, the seeds of controversy and rage are ready to germinate and blossom into overt action at any time.

The goal of education in any society should be to empower persons to act in the interest of self and society. The school gives to all citizens the skills, experiences, and understandings vital to maintenance and survival in contemporary society.

It has been recognized that today's emerging, complex, metropolitan society can actually restrict rather than expand personal living. Uselessness, centralized control, depersonalization, prejudice, racism, monotony, and anomie are seemingly by-products in the black community. In the context of social relevance, the many problems of the inner-city schools must be given high priority status among the overall complexities of metropolitan society in the mid-seventies for social order.

In acknowledging the complexity of educating minorities, a Mayor's Advisory Panel on Decentralization of the New York City Schools, better known as the Bundy Panel, was created in response to a request of the New York State Legislature "to prepare a comprehensive study and report and formulate a plan for the creation and redevelopment of educational policy

48

and administrative units within the City School District of the City of New York, with adequate authority to foster greater community initiative and participation in the development of educational policy for the public schools . . . and to achieve greater flexibility in the administration of such schools."[6]

The primary purpose of this plan was "to increase community awareness and participation in the development of educational policy closely related to the diverse needs and aspirations of the city population."[7] The basic recommendations of the Advisory Panel can be summarized as follows:

1. The New York City public schools should be reorganized into a Community School System, consisting of a federation of largely autonomous school districts and a central education agency.

2. From 30 to no more than 60 Community School Districts should be created, ranging in size from about 12,000 to 40,000 pupils, each large enough to offer a full range of educational services, yet small enough to maintain proximity to community needs and to promote diversity and administrative flexibility.

3. The Community School Districts should have authority for all regular elementary and secondary education within their boundaries and responsibility for adhering to state education standards.

4. A central education agency, together with a superintendent of schools and his staff, should have operating responsibility for special educational functions and citywide educational policies. It should also provide certain centralized services to the Community School Districts and others on the Districts' request.

5. The state commissioner of education and the city's central educational agency should retain their responsibilities for the maintenance of educational standards in all public schools in the city.

6. The Community School Districts should be governed by the boards of education selected in part by parents and in part by the mayor from lists of candidates maintained by the central education agency. Member-

ship on these boards should be open to both parents and non-parent residents of a District.

7. The central educational agency should consist of one or the other of the following bodies: (a) a commission of three full-time members appointed by the mayor, or (b) a Board of Education that includes a majority of members nominated by the Community School Districts. The mayor should select these members from a list submitted by an assembly of chairmen of Community School Boards. The others should be chosen by the mayor from nominations made by a screening panel.

8. Community School Districts should have broad personnel powers, including the right to hire a community superintendent on a contract basis.

9. Community School Districts should receive an annual allocation of operating funds, determined by an objective and equitable formula, which they should be permitted to use with the widest possible discretion within set educational standards and union contract obligations.

10. All existing tenure rights of teachers and supervisory personnel should be preserved as the reorganized system goes into effect. Thereafter, tenure of new personnel employed in a particular District should be awarded by the District.

11. The process of qualification for appointment and promotion in the system should be so revised that Community School Districts will be free to hire teachers and other professional staff from the widest possible sources, so long as hiring is competitive and applicants meet state qualifications.

12. Community School Boards should establish procedures and channels for the closest possible consultation with parents, community residents, teachers, and supervisory personnel at the individual school level.

13. The central education agency should have authority and responsibility for advancing racial integration by all practicable means. The state commissioner of education should have authority himself, or through

delegation to the central education agency, to overrule measures that support segregation or other practices inimical to an open society.

14. The Community School System should go into effect for the school year beginning September, 1969, assuming passage of the necessary legislation in the 1968 Legislature.

15. The main responsibility for supervising the transition from the existing system to the Community School System should rest with the state commissioner of education. The principal planning and operational functions should be assigned to a Temporary Commission on Transition, which should work closely with the current Board of Education, the superintendent of schools, and his staff.

16. The transition period should include extensive programs of discussion and orientation on operations and responsibilities under the Community School System and on educational goals. School board members should be afforded opportunities for training and be provided with technical assistance on budgeting, curriculum, and other school functions.[8]

These recommendations deal with four main problems: the nature of community control of educational policy, the composition and selection of community boards of education, relations between community boards and higher authorities, and the reform of the personnel system. It may be helpful to examine the issues confronting the panel in each of these areas and to understand the reasoning that led to its final recommendations.

Decentralization as proposed by the Advisory Panel is seen as a means to a fundamental change: the full entry of the black community into public education. These recommendations for decentralization of the New York City school system ignited passions far beyond the borders of the state. The results have reached national proportions that are inducing change in public education.

Needless to say, the decentralized school district was not without problems. Initially, it was thought the problem was one of antiquated school organization. But the problem was deeper than structure or policy. New programs for the disadvantaged and new curricular materials made teachers uneasy; when they failed to effect the desired change, despair deepened. It became apparent to schoolmen and parents that they were dealing with a problem of deeper dimensions than they had realized.[9] Despite this setback, the decentralization idea is spreading rapidly across the country. The New Jersey State Commission on the 1967 racial riots called for decentralization of the Newark public schools into small locally governed subdistricts. In Washington, D.C., plans are actually under way for a decentralization project. Decentralization efforts are also being planned in Detroit and Philadelphia. Even in smaller districts that do not suffer from bureaucratic sprawl, the ideal of meaningful parental participation has caught hold. To be effective in the type of society we now live in, it is necessary to plan many endeavors in cooperation with other communities and schools. The decision to decentralize must be rethought in the light of needs elsewhere. This demands cooperative planning.

The Black Community and School

The black community, prompted by a desire to set itself apart in order to preserve some cultural values, is a defensive response to external forces which threaten its creative existence. C. Eric Lincoln has asserted that "it is a unity born of the wish not to conserve, but to escape a set of conditions."[10]

The black community has fluctuated in its relationship to the rest of the nation. In the period when the nation seemed extremely polarized, the black community adopted the monastic reaction of withdrawal. To bridge this canal, black educators sought active contact with the community in thought and culture by attempting to present a philosophy of education in as favorable a light as possible to the thoughtful skeptics. They were conscious of the pitfalls that lay on each side. But, they also were convinced that a paralyzed refusal to act by the community is not the answer.

Pride, stubbornness, and a burning desire to labor alone have made it difficult to evaluate the motivations of the children and community that prefers to "work alone." Social scientists who have looked objectively at the crisis situation in the inner-city, for example, have bluntly said that excessive decentralization will continue to handicap the children. In their judgment, only schools with integrated student bodies will be able to weather the storm of the inner-city.

I am not advocating a return to the status quo. My plea, however, is that we move beyond our present inability to meet problems where necessary on a higher level of authority because of a view that restricts the operation of the school to the local community. Some communities are striving to meet this need through strengthened parent participation. Some schools are reorganizing so that the school boards are representative. We need minority representation that refuses to permit necessary services to go undone because of deep-rooted, unrelated, cultural traditions in the local school.

The culture of the inner-city is a complete reverse of the suburban culture. The basic folkways and the specific mores that so ably served the suburban community failed to make contact with urbanites.

With vision and trepidation, often with more commitment than knowledge, the public schools in the city are confronted with a new role—the role of adjusting themselves to the "now" culture; such a change evidences the work of the community school. This is the initial hurdle in trying to provide quality education for a changing school district and community.

Public education in the city must be reevaluated. We have clung to traditions more than we will allow ourselves to believe. We have depended on our traditions more than we have attempted to innovate. Loudly we have proclaimed our arduous work for a quality education for the poor, but in the witching hour we wonder whether we were exerting ourselves for our own personal ends. The life conditions that plague city schools at many points have become little more than a weak echo of the basic beliefs and attitudes of this nation. True, the terminology is more pious, but too often the school and local community reflect the affective mode of the nation. We attempted to reform the city schools, but we stopped short. The face of complacency is seemingly intensified by the way liberals beat their breasts and, at the same time, continue to function along traditional lines.

53

In a thorough reevaluation of the school, we should examine the antecedents and purpose of education and the sources of our problems. We should cease pretending that a new program of compensatory gimmicks will change the basic conditions of the community. The 1960s probably will go down in the annals of urban education as the decade of "the project." Mass educational training programs of every variety were promulgated by the agency bureaucracies. Each promised to be the panacea to revitalize the school and the local community. These action programs continue to grind away in the 1970s— though with noticeably more skepticism and less enthusiasm than a decade before. The basic need of the black community is relevant education. We must move back into the community to see its conditions. The present inner-city schools need a face lift—an extremely difficult relationship for us in modern America to grasp.

The black community, with its peculiar pathological conditions, has commanded both public and professional interest. Subsequent compensatory program developments in the field of education fall short of what their advocates envisioned. The Coleman Survey reported that most of the conventional measures of school resources, for example, prestudent instructional expenditure, accounted for very little of the variance in achievement scores of students.[11] When one reflects on the fact that black children possess a wide range of inherited abilities, and are products of different preschool environments and other social influences, this finding is not as surprising as it might appear at first glance. Analytically, a comparison and contrasting analysis of the measured prepupil expenditure does not reflect the differences among students in the amount of instructional resources devoted to their education. What is suggested, however, is that the variation in expenditures among schools within a district is likely to follow a systematic pattern. This overstatement on the expenditures of schools attended by students from the lower class by averaging the expenditures over an entire school district suggests a restricted educational program and indicates an inequality of opportunity for inner-city children at many strategic points.

There are many ways of developing educational standards, but the four criteria most often appearing are: (1) the length of the school term; (2) the estimated value of property per pupil enrolled; (3) the average yearly salary of the teacher; (4) the cost per pupil in daily attendance. The Coleman Report threw light upon some of these points. By all standards of measurement, the inner-city school, in comparison with suburban schools, ranked low.

National Effort to Solve the Problems of the Black Community School

Various sociological and educational efforts have been promulgated and advanced to relieve the inner-city schools at their most distressing points. These were in part: (a) educational surveys and campaigns which led in many instances to the passage of laws which brought about school desegregation; (b) compensatory educational programs; (c) definite standards set up to the ensure equal educational opportunities; (d) voluntary transfer plans for racial balance in schools; (e) more community-parent participation; (f) more equitable distribution of funds and special aid; (g) requirements of special training for inner-city teachers. Some imaginative educators devised the idea of matching pupils (the Princeton Plan) —an inner-city school having specific needs with a suburban school that needs to avoid the smug isolation which can close in so quickly. Many of these programs are not successful because the deep needs of the black community were not met; because the outsider came with preconceived goals and plans. The needs of the two communities differ greatly. Where a false type of paternalism can be avoided, these programs have been helpful to both the giving and the receiving schools.

In spite of the impressive attempts to solve this problem, one of the significant features of this effort has been the persistence of the ghetto school. While the desegregation of black schools will no doubt, and properly, continue, the indications are now that the movement will be slow and that the black community school will persist. I take the position that according to the present social trends, I not only predict such persistence, but believe it is inevitable. It is my opinion that, because of the high population density of the ghettos and topography, it will be impossible to dispense with schools as long as people live in the areas these schools will serve.

Whether or not this prediction will come true, it is impossible to escape the pressure of present facts. The fact that the vast majority of black Americans live in instituted communities in the United States creates special educational problems which challenge the attention of education.

In order for blacks to have a quality education, the educational experience should be intimately related to their personal needs. Blacks, as one major class of human beings, have distinguishing needs. This does not mean to imply that all their needs are either distinguishing or alike. Nor does it mean that the present situation, so far as distinguishing needs are concerned, is assumed to be permanent.

The recognition of students' needs as a basis for educational planning implies the judgment that people learn best what they feel they really need. Studies conducted have pointed out several life needs with which blacks feel the school should be concerned. Though in some instances blacks have been studied repeatedly, no attempt has hitherto been made to discover the degree of importance blacks give to these areas of life needs or whether they feel that public schools are the agencies that should meet these needs. Studies have not shown whether there are additional needs that rise from the cultural fact of being black, nor has any attempt been made to discover whether there is a discrepancy between what they wanted for schooling and what schools actually gave them. Studies have not revealed whether suburban schools and city schools meet the same needs or whether additional needs arise because of the different natures of these schools. Studies have focused, however, on the common human needs of education that are shared by all—black and white, male and female—in their revelation of what is desired in public or private education.

We are at a historic crossroads in public education, much more momentous than that of a decade ago. We have witnessed enormous progress for minorities, especially blacks, in the 1960s. One might argue that the situation we face is not new to history, for the story of America is the story of people reshaping their community. However, for decades this change was slow and gradual. The set of traditional ways in the urban community was directed to the preservation of the status quo. Change in the school curriculum was seen as a danger; innovation was viewed as a threat and federal support as control. The problem of urbanization is greater than a mere series of isolated difficulties. For even if the urban problem of educating minorities and racial conflict were solved, a fundamental urban problem would still exist. We are confronting a change in the black "cultural mentality"; a black society questing for identity and participation. Schoolmen are tinkering with solutions which seemingly change given pieces of behavior. They can institute massive compensatory programs and even include minorities in decision-making; but the basic concerns of culture which confront the black community remain.

The rate of change in public education has now become so great in the urban community, with the sum result so massive, that our accelerating trend toward the education of minorities poses one of the greatest problems with which we must wrestle as a nation. The demand for equal opportunity is so great it suggests that the school must change to complement the diverse culture and ethos. The inclusion of blacks' culture in the curriculum is inevitable. The external signs of this massive shift was charged by the Kerner Commission Report.[12] The urban community is polarized. The gulf between the white community and that of the black has increased to the breaking point. We have passed the tipping point of integration into resegregation. How can we overcome this? First, we must learn more about the community culture by entering into its life. We must face the community as it is, not as we would ideally reconstruct it. This step is more than a translation of suburban concepts into inner-city equivalents.

Second, the organization of the curriculum materials in the inner-city schools should be different from that in the traditional school. It should be different in ways that it can build upon the nature and needs of the children. The integration of subject matter should be effected through large units of work developed around genuine life interest and experience of blacks. The pupils should not be classified in closely homogeneous groups on a basis of achievements in skills or factual knowledge, but work together, as people do in life outside the school, on enterprises of common interest in which each participates according to his ability. This is schooling and opportunity. Many of these children are creative.

The way black children learn should be of much concern to schoolmen. The process of learning need not be an agreeable process, and under the same conditions and the same guidance as white pupils. This is no new idea in education. What is new is the ability to try it. Rousseau was equally concerned with the learning process of children.[13] His concern was more sentimental and less scientific than that of the contemporary school, but he studied the child for his technique of teaching and made his way by the light which he had, dim as it was. From this study, Rousseau put forth the following principle: children learn through a series of satisfying experiences.

This approach should be used in the inner-city school, but not to the exclusion of all other techniques. The teachers of ghetto schools should provide opportunities for the necessary "experiencing" of their children. They should promote individualized and group planning.

At the heart of the school should be a sincere regard for the individuality of children; this, too, belongs to an older ideology, Rousseau first, then Pestalozzi. The intellectual and cultural development of children should be the foundation of their education, and from it the whole movement of self-development should arise. In the school, therefore, the personality of the child should be respected, his work should be significant, his leisure should be important, and the integration of the two a pleasure. The school should be a place to which children go with willing feet because they find there work that is challenging, leisure which is satisfying, and a social group which gives them a feeling of adequacy and security.

In order to bring the ideals of the school to fruition, certain characteristics of the inner-city school to be served are necessary. These are: (1) groups of children small enough for the teacher to know each child intimately; (2) the opportunity for checking the tool subjects and individual instruction in them, if necessary; (3) rich community organization which provides opportunities for democratic living; (4) community programs that supplement the school program; (5) an adequate supply of learning materials; (6) teachers who think in terms of children as well as subject matter.

The average inner-city community provides a "million dollar" laboratory for nature and social study, to which children can be scientifically introduced. Within this homogeneous grouping, the teacher should see an opportunity for education as a vehicle for upward mobility, cultivating an aspiration to overcome and rectify these conditions, remotivation and refinement of their cognitive skills and affective mode. The inner-city schools, considered for many years as a liability, in the hands of a skillful teacher become an asset. In this way, the child is taking account of the tortuous trials and pathways of experimentation and the many failures encountered in the attempt to relate empirical fact to scientific models and theories. But he is also beginning to mention certain *traits* of the scientist; the need for care, for much patience and perseverance, the ability to withhold judgments and to coordinate complex means-end systems of action over extended periods of time.

Revenue Sharing and Education
Realities of the Present

The need for studied and realistic thinking about the inner-city public school, and particularly about its effectiveness in overcoming the educational deficiencies of a large population of minorities, is clear. The realization of equal education for inner-city pupils is an arduous task complicated by inadequate financial support. Empathetic schoolmen who are aware of these deficiencies and the increased financial needs of minority groups' schools are few in number and are frustrated by the numbness of this problem. These policy-makers seem divided in apathy between those who are vaguely satisfied with what they have in terms of revenue and those who grossly misunderstand the method of providing for anything better.

Why the failure of city school districts to have a first-rate, or even an adequate, school system? In answering this question, I would say that the lag in quality education is caused by the perpetual financial crisis in public education. The financial crisis in public education may be frighteningly apparent to a special group of informed citizens, but it seems to have escaped the vast majority. Perhaps this is because the crisis has been acute for so long that it seems a state of normalcy.

The alarming statistics about illiteracy, drop-outs, delinquency, undertrained teachers for inner-city schools, urban blight—none of the concepts are new. But, recognition has failed to arouse indignation. No consensus has been formed in or outside the community. The schoolmen and the surrounding communities collectively have not expressed their wishes for something better. Consequently, the controversial disputes: white vis-a-vis black, the internal division of the city school district into inner-city and outer-city subdistricts has broken the city school battle into skirmishes. Because of this detachment, some way must be found to alert citizens to the fact that meaningful reform is necessary in order that city schools can provide the type of education for low-income minorities living in the inner-cities plagued by our shifting and relocating society.

This residential isolation breeds school segregation, which can penetrate to the roots of American democratic values. Foreseen as one of the major challenges of our society, we have not yet learned how to coordinate two different subschool systems within the same district in the city proper. Add this to the controversy to achieve integrated schools and this matter of dualism has resulted in an impassive dilemma. Until the school districts find a way to synthesize this dualism, or bring it into useful coexistence, we cannot expect to have a strong metropolitan community.

The Perils of Stringlessness

The operation of the cities' public schools is a heavy financial burden for most American urban communities, and the expenses have increased greatly in the last ten years. Within larger cities—for example, New York City, Chicago, and Los Angeles—the educational costs often amount to a large proportion of the cities' expenditures. Moreover, this increasing cost of education is compounded by innovations in the traditional order, such as busing enacted to achieve a measure of integration, and compensatory educational programs for children from low-income families that include special programs of guidance, mathematics, and remedial reading. These programs alone present serious problems in city school financing.

More than ever before American communities are distinct

in characteristics both in their financial resources and in the proportions of children in their population. For instance, in most states the financing of public schools is dependent on funds generated from local property taxes. Taxable real property, assessed on a per-pupil basis, varies widely from one school district to another; and receipts from local property taxes per pupil vary widely in adversity as well—even though many of these states provide aid to school districts pursuant to a formula that purports to equalize interdistrict disparities.

Congressman Henry S. Reuss, while concurring with the way state aid to education is distributed, simplified the extreme inequality in educational opportunities that exists both among the states and within the states: "Overpayment to some localities results in underpayments to others. State Aid, instead of being distributed on a basis of need, is frequently distributed on a per-capita basis, which means that wealthy suburbs get as much per child for running their affluent schools as the central city gets for running its poverty schools."[14]

In what many minorities would regard as a most important decision, the California Supreme Court, on August 30, 1971, in the case *Serrano* v. *Priest,* tentatively concluded that the state's system of public school financing denies children the equal protection guaranteed under the Fourteenth Amendment, because it produces substantial disparities among the school districts in the amount of revenue available for education. Also, in December, 1971, in *Rodriguez* v. *San Antonio Independent School District,* the United States District Court, the Western District of Texas, ruled that the method of financing schools in the state of Texas likewise violated the Fourteenth Amendment. These cases in point are enlightening, however, only in the context of the facts of the law. The contention that this finding was sudden belies the antecedents of school financing in America. The real and inescapable fact is that children from low-income families are heralded by this distinguished unmistakable process of funding. Thus, extreme inequality in educational opportunities exists among the school districts.[15]

Today, the greatest single means of adequately financing city public schools is the folk practice of depending heavily upon federal aid to education through the Elementary and Secondary Education Act (ESEA) of 1965.

The ESEA, signed into law, was not only the largest commitment, $1.3 billion, by the federal government, but also represented the most comprehensive federal effort toward alleviating the vicious educational neglect that has attended poverty. However, through an extensive use of Elementary and Secondary Education Act of 1965 (ESEA), city schools have increasingly come to recognize that equalizing the school facilities within their borders is no easy task. Presently, city schools, for example, are utilizing ESEA funds from the federal government to underwrite a minimum of compensatory educational programs for public schools in most large cities.

The consensus among schoolmen and politicians at this time is that the situation in city schools has steadily deteriorated in the years following the initial inception of the ESEA. Few are inclined to disagree with this sentiment. The moderate position among some schoolmen holds that racial integration is steadily being achieved but that the command of the government through ESEA's guidelines for reasonably prompt integrated schools is destroying the base of healthy, amicable race relations on which the ESEA was purported to rest.

Needless to say, the principle of federal aid through the ESEA for the education of the disadvantaged has declined unrealistically in the economic circumstances of American life. The dwindling, ill-managed fortune of federal grant programs has been highlighted by complaints relative to confusion, duplication, fragmentation, and lack of coordination, and has resulted in pending special revenue sharing and reformed guidelines.

Caught between an inadequate and shrinking tax base and the phase-in of unstipulated revenue sharing, city schools are facing greater uncertainties. Thus, the critical question is whether revenue-sharing funds to education will substantially supplant the ESEA. In the light of many minorities who are already beginning to formulate their composite verdict, it is superficial to believe that a distribution of revenue-sharing funds for equal education opportunities for the disadvantaged will be an integral part of the plans to continue the attack on unequal education.

General Revenue Sharing in Restrospect

The advent of revenue sharing is an obvious change in financial aid to education. In fact, it is a domestic Marshall Plan. "In a mood of invention, the Marshall Plan was created to place $5 billion a year at the disposal of the European countries. The big condition, right at the start, was that the European countries themselves prepare programs of self-help and modernization in order to qualify."[16]

Instituted in 1972, the domestic General Revenue Sharing Program involves returning to each state a portion of the federal income tax collected within the state. An impediment inherent in revenue sharing is the creation of a distribution formula satisfactory to large and small communities within counties and states. More than 38,000 units of government—states, cities, villages—have received $8.2 billion in revenue-sharing checks since December, 1972. Furthermore, within the next five years, a total of $30.2 billion will be distributed. This is substantially less than the cost for elementary and secondary public schools in the United States for the school year 1969-70, which was about $38 billion.[17]

In Phase I, revenue sharing was discussed as a donation in addition to existing "categorical grants," that is, federal funding of specific programs. Then came Phase II, which became the substitute for categorical grants, placing federal subsidies to social service programs under the control of the local government. Even if social programs are sufficiently supported through this arrangement, without specific guidelines clandestine decisions can be made on the use of revenue-sharing funds: ". . . it is undoubtedly true that some funds would flow into the educational budget. However, there is no assurance that the funds would go to those schools where the educational quality is lowest, and where the funds are most needed to provide equal opportunity."[18] Therefore, the financing of education in the cities from revenue sharing exclusively, if not carefully planned, can inflict an injustice upon the residents of the heavily populated inner-city areas, for citizens and school districts in these areas have long relied on financing education through federally supported projects and programs.

It is not clear how an educational burden, which is virtually impossible to bear locally, becomes much easier when the more flexible resources of the federal government can be made available, and still easier when it is regarded as a federally supported program with no guidelines that categorically include minorities' interests and needs.

For the past twenty years, the quality of public education in predominantly large cities has tended to reside in federally funded programs, and these have been almost entirely in the inner-city communities, whereby controlling guidelines have accompanied the grants of aid. Consequently, an extension of federal aid through tax sharing must then bring into consideration the question of whether federal control should also be extended. The logic of revenue sharing, as I see it, should point directly to the need for a large-scale program of federal aid for public education to help equalize conditions among the diverse communities, as well as states.

The principle of local autonomy in public education is a longstanding and firmly established administrative practice. Within each state, both tradition and legislation have delegated the actual administration of the school to local boards of education. While it has been usual for the states to have retained some degree of regulation and supervision over the schools within their boundaries, the latter have been operated primarily as local school systems. Accordingly, to successfully meet specific interests and needs, revenue-sharing funds for education should be placed directly under the control of the local school boards to decide their use, enabling school districts to make further equalizations in education within their districts.

But, even under the control of the local school board, the distribution of revenue-sharing funds for education, and what they are to accomplish, should be sufficiently detailed to permit translation into observable and measurable indices or criteria. Furthermore, there should be a satisfactory and valid basis for developing such concrete indices by which the distribution of revenue funds will be distributed, and, consequently, the effectiveness of these funds as a response to the educational needs of low-income families. To deliver this type of human service requires no special effort. Enough is known and documented in the historical record of public education financing and human needs to ensure that adequate distribution of funds by the school district can be planned and administered.

The Need for Guidelines

First, the need to earmark tax-sharing funds as an aid to public education for the inner-city must be noted. The problem of adequate funds for education in the city arises because a limited amount of public funds must be used to finance a large number of municipal services. For example, within the major cities across the nation, non-school total per capita expenditures for services related to high-population density and large welfare populations are much higher than those of suburban school districts. In addition to these costly services for the direct aid to low-income minorities, the city must provide the normal range of urban services in the areas of criminal justice, fire, sanitation, and transportation. Although these services are provided for throughout the metropolitan area, the need for them is often greatest in the section of the metropolitan community marked by high levels of minorities who are poverty-stricken. Furthermore, research studies have reported in complete detail the financial inabilities and the educational needs of inner-city pupils. The inability of low-income families—urban-complex taxpayers—to generate, through tax resources such as personal income tax, sales tax, and property tax, adequate funds for the education of the disadvantaged is authentic.

Secondly, the real difficulty in enacting federal legislation for revenue-sharing of a more specific nature is not a question of citizenry needs or ability to pay, but the crucial issue is whether to use revenue-sharing funds for the support of private schools.

A substantial number of state school districts are segregated, and revenue-sharing funds, if not clearly earmarked, can be used to foster segregation of schools. One of the strongest arguments that can be made for sharing of revenue to remove inequalities among school districts is, essentially, humanism. All children deserve equal opportunities to learn, even under the provision of tax sharing. The financing of the public schools with revenue-sharing funds at any given time must be established by the effectiveness of a formula in meeting the needs for public education in our democracy. Persistent efforts have been made through federally funded programs to equalize educational opportunities within inner cities, and much progress has resulted from those efforts. Nevertheless, despite the unprecedented success, the population has not benefitted uniformly. In comparison, only little has been done to ameliorate inequalities that exist between city and suburban schools. The educational inequalities that exist between city and suburban schools, or individual city schools within the same school district, is a fact of life and is no longer denied.

Perhaps the most appropriate solution to alleviation of educational inequalities of the cities' schools is revenue-sharing. A substantial program of revenue-sharing to education with the "right" formula would accelerate the progress of equalization of educational opportunities.

A revenue-sharing formula for school districts in the urban complex is needed, one that distributes resources in a manner that will overcome educational disparities. Such a program that fairly draws and effectively distributes funds for schools in the metropolitan community will require federal, state, and community participation. This concept will make possible a shift from the earmarking principle as applied to property taxes, to a composite approach to a comprehensive tax-sharing program for school districts with the greatest identified needs.

William Anderson, a leading scholar in the field of intergovernmental relations, in a letter to Senator Harold H. Baker, Jr., stated: "In a nation with a highly mobile population, and one imbued with the high purpose of advancing the level of its civilizaton, it is necessary that all children and young adults be educated up to at least a minimum standard. In the national interest, the functions of public education cannot be left solely to the many states, with their different levels of ability to provide that education and diverse ideals in the field."[19] This, in itself, should bring schoolmen and decision-makers to a closer scrutiny of the basic elements of educational equality and a consideration of the ways in which revenue-sharing funds ought to be distributed for educational purposes to ensure such equality.

In urbanized America, segregation is not only rising but shows signs of approaching complete separation into totally distinct residential and school districts. The three principal reasons quite frequently given to explain the nearly universal prevalence of segregation are poverty, high crime, and poor city schools. Thus, because of these social problems, there is no basis for anticipating significant changes in the segregated school unless this attitude toward city schools is attended to. Such alteration is possible through revenue-sharing as an opening wedge for integration.

There is a possibility for serious deliberation, for a conscientious way for new arrangements and adjustments to meet the needs of minorities that will enhance the efficiency and effectiveness of the local and county government while guarding against the danger of unresponsiveness or exclusion of minorities' needs in distributing revenue-sharing funds. To illustrate this, the suburbanization of the last several decades has been an almost exclusively homogeneous white phenomenon. This can be depicted through the popular ecological theory of Ernest W.

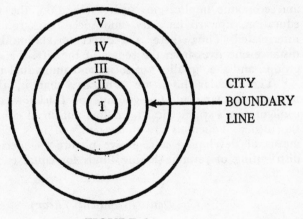

FIGURE 1

Burgess and R. E. Park, better known as the concentric zone theory. According to Burgess, a city can be divided into a series of five concentric circles or valences around a core, usually named, in turn, the central business district, the zone in transition, the suburban zone and the commuters' zone.[20] See Figure 1.

In Burgess' theory, Zones I and II in modern times are observed as being the focus of commercial and civic life blended in with residential deterioration that is saturated with a predominant group of minorities who are, according to modern standards, poor and uneducated. Zone III, the new central city, an integral part of the city proper, is occupied by professional people and businessmen. Because of municipal laws, many city decision-makers reside here; for example, the school superintendent, the city manager, the mayor, school board members, and councilmen. Zone IV is a ring of suburbs. Zone V is the metropolitan community.

Because of the similarities in life styles and exhibited characteristics, the legal boundary line that separates the city from the suburbs is the only visible way one can differentiate the inhabitants of Zones III and IV. (See Figure 1.) Quite often, this is made visible to citizens by signs that read, for example, Rochester City Limits, Welcome to the Town of Brighton, or the Village of Spencerport. Zones III and IV, thus, have social and economic implications such as location, the value of an education, upward mobility, and social background that are interrelated. Thus, there is a direct correlation between the distance one lives from the center of the city, the status of the groups, and the "quality" of social and individual life.

The circular lines are arbitrary, that is, they neglect natural and man-made topography, and I acknowledge that the configuration's symmetrical form does not fit all cities. However, the theory's adherents are numerous, and it is suggested as a means of developing a cognitive picture for decision-makers' distributing of revenue-sharing funds for equal education.

The Density-Gradient Theory

In addition, another systematic way to distribute revenue-sharing funds in terms of educational need is possible through

Colin Clark's Density-Gradient Theory.[21] In a rather theoretical manner in describing the distribution of the population, Clark generalizes that the density of the population declines with distance from the city. He expresses the density pattern by the exponential formula $Y = Ae^{-bx}$, in which:

$Y =$ the population density at any given point.
$A =$ the density in the center.
$e =$ the Naperian logarithmic base 2.718.
$b =$ the rate at which the density declines.
$x =$ the distance from the city center.

(See Figure 2.)

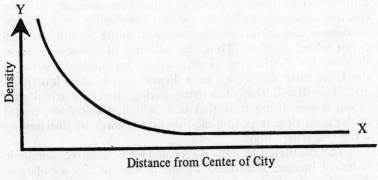

Distance from Center of City

FIGURE 2

The quantities x and Y are variables, e is a constant, and A and b are parameters fixed for each city at any given time. A high value of b indicates a compact city; a low value betokens a sprawling cluster for example, New York City. Assigning a constant value of b throughout a given city is necessary to keep the formula from becoming unwieldy, providing a single Formula for Funds Distribution.

While the Concentric Zone Theory and the Density-Gradiant Theory display graphically the density in zone areas, they are, nevertheless, of some value, if only to indicate the density of various school districts in various parts of the metropolitan area. Both of these theories are feasible and applicable to the problem at hand. Their explicit directness, as well as the assumptions on which they are based, point up the need for utilizing in conjunction with such approaches a direct measurement of some concrete, economic indicators for revenue-sharing for education to remove disparities in educational funding within and between school districts. Thus, the plotting of density-regression lines for the distribution of revenue-sharing funds, in terms of the Concentric Zones, can be a logical means to a functional end. The distribution of revenue-sharing funds for equal education is seen being consistent with school districts' needs and at the same time impeding metropolitan growth by distributing revenue-sharing funds.

The calculated formula I recommend is based on economic index of income, multiplied by the density of the population, divided by the distance from the center of the city. The formula:

$$\frac{Economic\ Index\ X\ Density\ of\ the\ Population}{Distance\ from\ the\ Center\ of\ the\ City}$$

In summary, the formula:

    1. Provides for comprehensive problem diagnoses and educational planning.

    2. Brings local elected officials more directly into the delivery of educational services.

    3. Transfers the burden of responsibility for getting appropriate educational assistance from the people to the system.

70

4. Encourages and enhances the creation of local, integrated, educational plans through a project-planning authority.

5. Promotes the development of unified delivery system, one that gives people a clear point of access, treats their problems as a whole, and tracks their progress.

6. Permits the transfer of funds among school districts to achieve maximum effectiveness.

This should bring schoolmen and revenue-sharing decision-makers to a closer scrutiny of the basic elements of educational equality and a consideration of the ways in which revenue-sharing funds ought to be distributed for educational purposes to ensure such equality.

CHAPTER 3

RESHAPING THE
PROCESS OF AN
INNER-CITY EDUCATION

THEORETICALLY, the role of American public education has been to socialize individuals into society; to prepare them to live in the social environment through the teaching of socially useful skills, and the normative structure of the democratic systems. This has not been the case in the twentieth century for the urban inner-city dispossessed. Only recently has attention been put forth to refine the process of education to include the inner-city poor, other than to describe the situation. Until recently, research and scholarly studies have provided an adequate description and diagnosis of the problem of inner-city children in our mass society, but fall short in attempting to provide an adequate social philosophy and plan for solution of the problem.

In most inner-city schools, black children are expected to perform as well as whites, when the schools' historical role has been to provide for the dominant culture, where middle-class values have been taught. How can inner-city students relate to a middle-class-oriented course of study if they come to school with a different background? Black children are expected to perform as well as whites in schools whose curriculum and administration reflect middle-class society and background due to different cultural, economic, and social backgrounds. Poor people, usually those with the greatest educational need, are forced to "adjust" to programs of little relevancy and of little functional value to them. Students who don't adjust to such circumstances are often left with the street as their only alternative.

The educational factor in the inner-city has been widely, if not well, understood among urban educators in the North since the 1954 *Brown* decision of the Supreme Court. For nearly the entire decade from 1955 to 1965, the causes of this cumulative failure were for the most part attributed to two sources: (1) family conditioning, and (2) deficiencies in the facilities and programs in the inner-city schools. Those inside the educational establishment emphasized family deficiencies. Those from the community pressing for reform from the outside emphasized the failure to teach effectively.

Within the confines of the inner-city ghetto, there were other reasons yet to be explored for the intensification of public interest in inner-city education during this decade. An absolute doubling of the youth population and an automating economy combined to stimulate public demands for effective educational performance on all fronts. Some of these demands—for example, the hopes of inner-city youths to get into higher education, should have been met quickly to the satisfaction of all. In a democratic society where full competition should prevail, education is essentially the avenue to overcoming social differences and to success. The role of education has been to socialize individuals into society and at the same time, to allow the individuals to expand their constructive creative abilities. Yet, the inner-city contains too few effective schools in a sea of administrative confusion and inept construction to effectively carry out the socializing and educational process. The entire concept of inner-city public education is inefficient, ineffective, and out of date.

Several monumental federally sponsored research studies describe the situation. For example, The Civil Rights Commission Report (Racial Isolation in the Public Schools), the Coleman-Campbell Report (Equality of Educational Opportunity), and Project Talent, reinforce each other profoundly in identifying the prime sources of inner-city school success and failure. Each demonstrates that student achievement is influenced mainly by family conditioning, personal motivation, and the social climate of the school. The major documents of

73

academic success or failure are *inextricably* connected with race or ethnicity. In the inner-city black ghetto of the North, social and economic differences in family conditioning amount to differences between blacks and whites, with more than half of black families subsisting at or below the poverty level. Likewise, the social climate of inner-city public schools is also heavily affected by racial and cultural isolation. Coleman and Campbell describe the situation vividly, stating, "of all the characteristics of school which distinguished the education being provided the average White and Negro students, it is the environment provided by the fellow students where the differences are most dramatic." Social climate thus depends upon who goes to school with whom and where. But, in racially changing communities, the social climate is becoming predominantly that of one culture and race.

As for personal motivation, this factor blends aspects of individual personality with environmental conditions and the social and cultural influence of the school, as these are perceived by the students. For these reasons, the most urgent inner-city educational challenge of our time, along with curriculum and instructional reform, is educational progress that reflects the culture of the people. This is an alternative, a challenge of changing the attitude and aspirations of inner-city youth, and a means of remotivation for an education.

If inner-city teachers are failing, they are failing at the point where the newly emergent culture of the inner-city society itself is not being challenged; for instruction in the three R's, in itself alone, is not the total process of being educated, but is a means to an educational end. When the cultural orientation of the inner-city school changes, the teacher, if she is to continue to be an effective agent, should adjust to the culture in order to foster the growth and development of the inner-city child.

Education in the inner-city should have a unique special function; what is needed is not merely equality of resources, but equality of results. For example, the primary purpose of education in the inner-city should be to develop the potential of blacks by relating to black culture and experience through black culture in our society. The schools as they now exist should be reformed to be functional to the black community. The curriculum should start with black people as a specially and uniquely cultural people. Therefore, if the ultimate objective of education is to socialize students and make them productive members of society, the processing must include the norm and culture of the community being served.

Education should place a high premium on reaching a higher level of survival than previously known. Every effort should be put forth to make blacks aware of the fact that education perpetuates a given society and has a larger societal purpose by passing on collective wisdom through black culture. Education should play a substantive role in training blacks to think. It should be a system of intellectual legitimacy which defines the activities and experiences of blacks as a universal yardstick of human existence.

Black studies programs today pay particularly close attention to the place of blacks in the social structure, examining their functional and substantive roles in the existing institutions. Because of the nature and structure of our society, the role of the institution (i.e., educational system) depends upon the totality of relationships, processes, and facilities which people develop to meet a specific social interest or need. However, the consideration of needs of minorities, whether racial or economic, have not been properly considered. One has only to reflect on the rituals of the institution, particularly public education, its functional usefulness within society to minorities. Blacks across the nation are echoing a fear for the security of life, the safety of their community, and the preservation of their liberties and institutions. This is the apex of the racial crisis in a time of extraordinary promises and commitments that are logically inconsistent and traversed with the ideas and feeling that our institutions are showing signs of openness to minority values and culture. This profound period of incorporating minorities is a new phase of the racial confrontation in the inner-city that warrants reforms in terms of blacks' and whites' basic education. For example, inner-city public education for the black community should be reformed into a concept that places emphasis on universal values, the black community particularities, and culture so as to allow the inner-city pupils positive-creative relationships between themselves and their community. Thus, the program should provide individuals with identity, purpose, and direction. Until recently, this potential

75

for the development of a quality education for blacks was possible in Southern schools where the black experience could have flourished. Today, in public schools in both North and South, even though the black experience is being taught, it is treated in most cases as a unit of instruction, but never becomes an integral part of the curriculum.

The ultimate focus of inner-city public education should be to meet the needs of all cultures and the school should be eager to provide this service, serving all citizens, harnessing the energy of the masses, showing them the truth and the way to certain prosperity and triumph. It should be an optimistic process where pupils can move from the edge of damnation with full assurance that ultimately the path will lead them to success.

A changing public school purpose, process, and curriculum have, depending on the needs of the community served, for some time been characteristic of American public school education. The tempo with which this change has occurred in public institutions has not remained constant. The tremendous increase in knowledge available to be taught, the expanding knowledge concerning learning and the learner (be he "disadvantaged" or "affluent"), and the variety of societal factors influencing the public schools have contributed to an ever-increasing need for program and curriculum change specifically designed for the inner-city schools.

One very prominent factor noticeable during this century is the increasing tendency for people to change their place of residence. For example, ways of meeting our needs differ substantially from an era when the majority of families lived on farms—a technological age has forced rural people to find non-agrarian employment in urbanized communities. A large portion of these mobile families include school-age children.

This trend has been accentuated since the beginning of World War II. Minority group members, frequently from cultural levels where unstable employment was already a problem, have migrated to industrial centers in the seemingly never-ending search for new jobs. Millions of these persons are now centered in urban areas, frequently creating serious social, economic, and educational problems. These are the disadvantaged,[1] termed by Conant as "social dynamite."[2]

The urban cities suffering badly from a serious unfavorable influx of people who drain off their resources have entered a state of disintegration. Today, the cities are attracting both commuters and immigrants, the former paying little for the privilege of crossing their borders five days a week; the latter is an important drain on meager resources.

Providing resources and programs to meet the needs of these millions in large urban cities is a genuine challenge, both to the city school systems and to the entire nation. Perhaps in no area is there greater need for an education than in locations containing a high concentration of diverse people. The failure of urban communities to meet the demands of a changing technological society and a changing diverse population results from an inability to readily adjust institutions and educational policy. Living in an age of technology, no one is ever completely educated—at most, one can only be a student of the daily incidents as they occur. Consequently, despite extensive written and oral exploration of continuous expansions and alterations of the purpose and progress of education, very little, if any change at all, takes place in inner-city schools without turmoil. Change is the basic factor necessitating continuous education of all people and particularly of the inner-city child. Without continuing study, inner-city pupils' knowledge and performance soon become obsolete and continue to lag behind the masses.

The crisis in the inner-city can be attributed to the expansion and growth pattern of the cities, dividing the city's inhabitants into ethnic ghettos and various subcultures. This nature of the community setting, the accuracy with which it can be understood, and its import on the purpose of education to a great extent determines the outcome of the educational process. The process is one of the many activities carried on in the social setting in which it takes place.

Ethnic ghetto and community subcultures are basically social institutions. Their primary function is to preserve and perpetuate to future generations the best of the knowledge, ideas, and customs of their culture. As a social institution, the inner-cities are necessarily affected by the educational policy decisions made in surrounding ethnic ghettos.

The American culture is a multiplicity of many subcultures which are both unique and interrelated. There are many races and ethnic groups. Often, but not always, the distinctions between cultural groups may be readily apparent. According to Harold M. Hodges, the composition of the cultures quite often today falls into three categories. They are: rural, urban, and suburban. Hodges has developed a frame of reference in which one can examine society as being on a continuum. The list below shows Hodges' culture continuum.

A. Folk Culture

I. Tradition oriented; strong resistance to change and novel ideas; pattern of life static, unvarying, community centered; "behavior is traditionally spontaneous, uncritical, and personal"; rigidly unified culture.

II. Social controls vested in mores, folkways rather than codified laws; controls enforced by informal community pressures, threat of gossip, or ostracism; behavior regulated by firm, inflexible custom; little allowance for individual choice; no tolerance for deviates, dissenters.

III. Social relationships long-lasting, intimate, personal; dependence upon others for approval, affection; slight privacy and anonymity; dominance of primary and quasi-primary groups (family, neighborhood).

IV. Little division of labor except between men and women; "range of alternative patterns of behavior open to individuals is held to minimum"; emphasis on ascribed (hereditary) rather than achieved (competitive) statuses; people know what to expect of others; sex and age roles rigidly prescribed, starkly different.

V. Component parts of society are closely articulated, fitting together with a minimum of friction or conflict; little or no social disorganization (divorce, delinquency, suicide, etc.); although life strict and narrow, level of adjustment was relatively high.

VI. Pattern of life dictated by custom: "tradition.direction" prevails; little urge to challenge status quo, innovate, or flaunt tradition.

VII. Particularistic social system (with emphasis upon inherited, feudal-like status); rigid social-class structure; intense conservatism pervades all segments of life; people tend to accept their own assigned statuses as inevitable; governments (like family, community) often autocratic, aristocratic.

VIII. Ethnocentrism and correlative suspicion of "outsiders"; intolerance toward deviates from prescribed norms; little or no acquaintance with other communities, other values and ways of life.

IX. Community is economically self-sufficient; a simple technology in which virtually everyone is a primary producer; minimal division of labor; agrarian and handicraft economy with minimal competition (mutual aid is frequent).

X. Simple, "folk" type entertainment (folk songs, carnivals, fairs); emphasis more on participants than spectators; simple leisure tastes involving community-wide or family-wide participation.

XI. Patriarchal, male-dominant family systems; marriages based on tradition, utility; marital unions stable, life-long; life familistic (family centered) in orientation; extended families frequent; family occupies central place in social structure, performs major obligations (educational, religious, economic).

XII. Scanty, informal education except for clergy, aristocrats; slight value attached to formal schooling (emphasis more upon practical knowledge); illiteracy widespread.

B. Urban Culture

I. Future oriented: undergoing rapid change and consequent breakdown of traditional values, practices; social structure loosely articulated; "composed of welter of conflicting, competing groups and ideologies."

II. Mores have been weakened and folkways redefined; legal norms and laws have supplanted unwritten codes; few universally accepted beliefs, values, standards of behavior; mass movement of heterogeneous peoples to the city broke control exerted by family, neighbors; complex formal agencies of control, such as police.

III. Relations with others more transitory, impersonal, superficial, anonymous (people expose only segments of their total selves in everyday interaction); indifference toward strangers replaces rural hospitality (or hostility).

IV. Proliferation of social roles and intricate division of

labor; few fixed, ascribed positions (individuals must seek out and compete for positions) ; "individuals must fit into a complex social structure in which they occupy statuses and play many different and unrelated roles"; tendency for sex and age roles to converge, becoming more alike (and more confusing).

V. Communal dissensus replaces consensus; social organization increasingly atomistic and ill-defined; value orientations of various subcultures automatically clash; soaring rates of social disorganization; uncertainties beget anomie, marginality, mental illness.

VI. Philosophy of "rugged" individualism, experimentation; "progress" becomes goal; emergence of "inner-directed" character; deviates, mavericks, "characters" become more common.

VII. Universalistic social system (emphasis upon individual achievement, same norms for all) ; more open, permeable social-class system (and consequent emergence of class consciousness, status striving, conspicuous consumption) ; emergence of rags-to-riches theme; emergence of labor as political force, resurgence of political liberalism, democratic government.

VIII. Growing contacts and familiarity with people from diverse cultural backgrounds encourages tolerance, "people rub elbows with and become indifferent to extremes of all kinds," but early phases of growth promote ethnic and racial conflict.

IX. Increasingly complex economic system with elaborate division of labor; quick transfer of goods and services; gradual demise of individual enterpriser and increasing potency of big business; but specialization, competition continue to prevail.

X. More "sophisticated" (and synthetic, manufactured) entertainment fare; growth of "spectatoritis," mushrooming of competitive spectator sports; increasing potency and pervasiveness of mass media; variegated tastes and publics; work and leisure sharply distinguished.

XI. Children, wives break free of father domination; children leave families as they gain economic independence; marriages increasingly based on "love-at-first-sight" romances (with spouse often from totally different backgrounds) ; life decreasingly familistic, increasingly individualistic; family loses central role, divorce rates soar, families become smaller.

XII. Emergence of mass education, progressive ideology;

education increasingly democratic, available to all; burgeoning of school population; professionalization of teaching; illiteracy disappearing, "diploma" goal for all.

C. Suburban Culture

I.   Comfort-oriented; security and freedom from want becoming ideals; social structure increasingly cohesive, well integrated; quest for certainty; cult of adjustment supplants cult of individualism; reemergence of community, nationwide norms, consensus.

II.   Social controls reinvested in neighborhood, family; increase of informal primary-type contacts strengthens role of peer group; rural and quasi-rural values take root.

III.   Relations with others less superficial, transitory; growing dependence upon others for approval, affection; friendships, cliques increasingly based on mutual interests and values; social distance between strangers less marked.

IV.   Increasingly communal consensus; gradual dissipation of religious, ethnic, racial subcultures (with consequent attenuation of value clashes) ; indications of various indices of social disorganization (divorce, delinquency, etc.) leveling off, occasionally decreasing.

V.   Lesser encouragement, toleration of deviates, mavericks; emergence of "other-directed" character type; emphasis upon "teamwork," group harmony, "togetherness."

VI.   Trend toward "mass society" with correlative mass middle-class-dominated culture; lesser proportion in upper and lower classes; class lines increasingly vague, boundaries more and more fluid, class-linked value and life-style differences less marked; masses more liberal politically but left-wing radicalism blunted; labor, business, and other power units countervail, balance.

VII.   Diminution of ethnic and racial conflict and increase of libertarianism (popular belief in civil liberties) ; increasing cosmopolitanism, breakdown of regional and national barriers (in face of rear-guard, diehard ultranationalists, hyperconservatives) .

VIII.   Postindustrial economy of "plenty," service economy dominant; increasing dominance of corporation (and demise of "Main Street" businessman) ; automation of industry increases; series of "common markets" supplant national competition, trade barriers.

IX. Mass media of communication increasingly geared to demands and taste of "lowest common denominator"; new spectator sports supplant old (but increase in participant sports); "upper bohemian" market for sophisticated entertainment challenges mass market; proliferation of specialized hobby groups.

X. Families increasingly democratic, companionship in nature; marriages increasingly stable; marriages more homogamous "likes marry likes"); families become larger; resurgence of single-family dwellings, family-centered activities; long-time trend toward earlier marriages reversed.

XI. Increasing proportion of population attends school, mean years of schooling continue to rise; popular reaction against excesses of "progressive education" movement; greater demand for college preparation; college degree becomes prerequisite for "upper-middle-class status."

Like many other sources, an examination of Hodges' continuum reveals that his characteristics of the urban culture are synonymous to inner-city culture and excludes suburban culture. This is a contradiction. The 1950 census' definition specifies a community as an urban population consisting of all persons living in the following types of settlements:

(a) Places of 2,500 inhabitants or more incorporated as cities, boroughs, and villages;

(b) Incorporated towns of 2,500 inhabitants or more, except in New England, New York, and Wisconsin, where "towns" are simply minor civil divisions of counties;

(c) The densely settled urban fringe, including both incorporated and unincorporated areas around cities of 50,000 or more; and

(d) Unincorporated places of 2,500 inhabitants or more outside any urban fringe.[3]

Obviously, Hodges' divisions are based on ideal types which do not exist; however, the characteristics of the divisions provide a valuable point of departure for analyzing contemporary society.

The web of social relationships and subculture, taken all together, constitutes an urban society and is never completely

82

homogeneous. However, homogeneity may be good for milk, but it does not work well with people; perhaps urban communities may be defined as an emulsion, not really blending, but mixed together, while at the same time allowing each person or group to retain an individual identity. People in the same urban community differ in interest, in taste, in occupation, and in status and power. These characteristics are purported to be responsible for the urban way of life.

A number of urban ecologist models have attempted to describe the growth and expansion of American cities. However, two descriptive models of cities' growth are the "Concentric Zone Theory" by E. W. Burgess,[4] which has been previously cited in Chapter 2, and the "Sector Theory" of Homer Hoyt.[5] These two theories illustrate the pattern that many cities seem to follow.

Briefly, these theories describe the outer-most valance bands as the high-rent residential suburbs' and commuters' zone. The inner-zone comprises the inner-city, the central business districts and the slums and is heavily populated by the lower-income classes. In between these two sections is the out-city. The outer-city is a residential section on the fringe of the suburbs where most municipal employees who work in the city live (for example, city judges, the school superintendent and the board of education members, the police and fire chiefs, the city manager, the mayor, etc.) Civil service rules require all employees to reside within the city limits.

More than 10 million persons are gainfully employed in government service, most of them residents of cities and working in organizations whose functions are mainly carried out in urban and the inner-city community. The expansion of various services, some of them hitherto considered the exclusive function of public education, has resulted in the multiplication of educational agencies, departments, and administrative divisions operated by personnel occupying different positions and making educational policy for inner-city schools. A vast amount of wealth is spent in developing and maintaining an inner-city educational system whose function is both the transmission and collation of knowledge. In a folk or rural society, it is possible for an individual to learn from his kinsmen most of the essential features of his culture. But so complex is the inner-city com-

83

munity, so much is there to be learned, that the transmission of the cultural heritage can be adequately carried out only through facilities established exclusively for this purpose. The demands of the inner-city are such as to attach particular importance to public institutions of learning.

The relationship between the inner-city and education is still further evidenced by the ever-increasing demands for education.

The growth of the inner-city and the spread of urban values has awakened the inner-city people to the fact that simple folk knowledge is not sufficient.

Under the conditions of inner-city life in a mass society, the educational process cannot be carried out on a mass basis. There must be organization, and small-scale organization at that, at the grass-roots level. To provide educational services appropriate for such a community, an organizational system capable of meeting the needs of the inner-city community must be developed. The decentralized system should be a part of the government apparatus, although much of the process of education is carried on under the auspices of community organizations that may also be bureaucratic in character.

Every American community—including suburban communities—has a bureaucratic educational organization that provides not only the traditional educational service to all the people, but, in addition, reflects the cultural heritage.[6] From kindergarten to college and beyond, the suburban culture is reflected in its educational values. James B. Conant, in describing the college-oriented suburbs, stated: "When one finds a high school from which eighty percent or more of the graduates regularly enroll in some four-year college or university, one can be certain that a relatively homogeneous residential community is at hand. In such a suburb the vast majority of the inhabitants belong to the managerial or professional class; the average level of income is high; the real estate values are correspondingly elevated. In these wealthy communities, one is likely to find effective school boards, great parental interest in the public schools, high expenditure per pupil. Since the citizens are interested in good schools and ample resources are available, the public schools are as good as the professionals know how to make them."

Unlike the suburbs, the inner-city schools are staffed mostly by teachers living in the suburbs, the board of education members and administrator living in outer cities, leaning toward the suburban culture, but making policy decisions that affect inner-city schools. An important paradox is white teachers teaching in predominantly all-white suburban schools seem to be successful in preparing suburban youth for college. "Suburban schools today are challenged to 'get' boys and girls into top-flight colleges and, consequently, to maintain high standards in the academic courses. These schools are also faced with a dilemma. The problem comes in cases where the parental ambitions outrun the offspring's ability; that is, where the boy or girl has difficulty mastering academics in a school with high standards and yet is expected by his parents to attend a prestige college, the parents are likely to blame the public school. . . ."[7] But in inner-city schools staffed mainly with white teachers in a predominantly black setting, the dropout rate is high, and the blame is usually attributed to the environment and the home.

If education is to reflect the culture, an organized community-controlled school is necessary for the inner-city to provide service. Major policy-making functions should be performed by a community board whose members are elected to office by popular vote of the community served. Immediate responsibility for carrying out these processes of education and administrative functions should be centered in a professional administrator appointed by the community, who is accorded the necessary authoritative power to keep the system functioning. This includes a community superintendent, principals, and various specialized supervisors of teaching personnel, directors of special curricula, and managers concerned with maintaining the physical facilities. The production worker, being the teacher, should be selected by the community and the school administrators.

A Conflict of Values

The inner-city school's future orientation is clearly in conflict with the school board of education, producing some conflict in inner-city students, who are now demanding a meaningful realistic education. One difficulty with inner-city schools, and one reason why there is a great deal of argument among those responsible for them, is that various groups having to do with inner-city schools are spread out between the so-called traditional educational and the more recent community educational values. The school board, having gotten where it is through succeeding in the system *as it is,* feels a heavy commitment to the status quo (traditional educational values), while the inner-city groups who have no roots in the traditional educational system and may not admit and enjoy indeterminacy, may be closer to the relativistic, less individualistic, community-controlled schools.

Community interest groups have always been interested in the community schools. For example, private and parochial schools and even today suburban ethnic ghettos control their schools.

This is only one tenuous example of something which must be watched carefully. Many groups in the community at large would like to get into the schools or the school program in order to sell things to pupils. Many community and interest groups support the use of certain text materials, and texts, which somehow manage to project the organization's culture or point of view to the pupils. In similar fashion, publishers of textbooks, who determine a considerable portion of the public school curriculum, are not always immune to an organized interest group's values and culture. They must produce a version which will sell both in the rural and suburban communities which have a central adoption or purchasing committee.

There are seldom any inner-city parents serving on textbook adoption or purchasing committees for their community. Thus, many texts used in inner-city schools, particularly in the area of history and social studies, represent a rather ineffectual compromise. This compromise is easily seen in treatments of black history or black studies.

Again, it should be made clear that various interest groups are interested in selling ideas, values, and culture to pupils. The black community groups want to make sure that their points of view are treated academically in the schools, while other interest groups wish to protect pupils from influences and knowledge which they term "un-American." For example, one only has to scan or examine textbooks on social science or

86

literature to discover that the total black experience is encompassed in one paragraph or excluded. This type of exclusion cuts off black institutionalized avenues leading to success. This inhibits learning, accurate perception, and attitude formation. The "unlearned," the "unmotivated," the inner-city pupils whose perception, because it is academically exclusive, does not permit an orientation past the here and now; the black pupils whose attitudes are frequently classed by the whites as "immoral," and those blacks whose socialized behavior does not meet the standards of the majority group, are no justification for excluding their culture.

One of the best ways to sell things is to eliminate competition by setting up barriers to keep out a person or class of persons from what is open and accessible to others. Thus, if you have a point of view to "sell," it is often a very successful move simply to remove from public access other points of view which conflict with or threaten yours. This happens often in inner-city public schools. Robert K. Merton, in describing American values, had this to say about the excluded:

> Americans, generally, whether they represent the excluded or not, hold in high regard a relatively common set of values. The realization of these values is outside the experience of most excluded persons.

> An important part of American values is achievement and success. Culturally excluded individuals seldom taste success or achievement. Achievement comes in many forms, i.e., education, financial success, occupational advancement, family status, etc. The political, economic, educational and religious systems have inadvertently and purposefully blocked the avenues of achievement and success for most excluded persons.

> Another set of values is activity and work. To be occupied at all times is necessary, expected and demanded. "Idle hands are the devil's plaything"; if one is not working then he is loafing. Unskilled and unschooled minorities are more frequently unemployed than employed. Seldom are the culturally excluded in the unemployed position by choice, but by necessity.

> Efficiency and practicality are beliefs held by most

87

Americans. The best way to do things is the practical way. Persons who do not succeed economically, or who hide themselves in "ivory towers" aren't "down to earth," don't have "their feet on the ground," and are not "practical." Members of the lower class desire, as much as anyone else, to be practical and efficient. Although practicality and efficiency may be lacking in terms of middle-class Americans functioning, the culturally excluded are practical in terms of their necessities for living.

Progress, freedom and equality are other aspects of the American value system seldom experienced by the culturally excluded. Access to the sales pitch for material comforts, without gaining them, frequently stimulates inactivity, lethargy and retards motivation.

Institutional contacts reinforce these values. Excessive failure and constant frustration while trying to obtain access to these values does not necessarily decrease the value's importance, but it significantly stifles motivation.[8]

The inner-city schools of a truly pluralistic society should be either open to all perspectives and cultures or else closed to all, with the former perferred over the latter. At the present time, certain perspectives and culture have greater dissemination through the black community's schools than others. These perspectives are not necessarily superior in terms of their logical structure, but they are often held to be self-evident truths, and not areas of debate. This perspective represents the community-at-large's educational values for more than the inner-city black community's educational values.

The greatest service the city schools and school boards can perform in our society, with its increasingly bureaucratic and single tendencies, is to implement a model of pluralism. The way to fight certain perspectives or tendencies is not dogmatically to denounce them, but to provide, through the curriculum, a confrontation of all perspectives, not just those which are passively accepted as the truth at the community level. In periods of educational history, in some communities, local educational programs were geared to local values, for most of the pupils lived in the local community, and a case was made for helping the young to "fit in." Today, however, in America, we have a double school system in the city—not mentioning the suburbs, but the city. The responsibility of the board of education is divided between the outer-city and the inner-city.

The educational problems of the inner-cities' school are everybody's problems that cannot be solved with a suburban school model. Its problem is everybody's problem because it is the unsolved dilemma of the twentieth century. Educationally, this dilemma has resulted in two school systems of education. There are similarities in their organization, structure, curriculum, but, of course, in many cases, their rhetoric is not identical, and productively they are not the same. Collectively, this system of education adds little, if anything at all, of cultural value; it stiffens the opportunity to accumulate social and economic resources, it impedes cultural and social enrichment and intellectual growth, and it leaves the next generation of children with no more than the last. The sooner the city school board perceives this reality, the sooner it may begin to collaborate with the community to solve this problem.

An Appropriate Time for Change

This section moves beyond specific empirical studies of the inner-city "culture of poverty" and black education, and beyond generalized accounts of them to directly and explicitly raised questions about the black community, "where we are going," with respect to ethical considerations. The ethical considerations are two: the quality of the black community and individual life; and the quality of education and social life, which, in turn, heightens or stultifies the quality of community and individual life. The argument is that education is, as typically we find it historically to be, reflective of more fundamental cultural institutions and processes. When the more fundamental cultural institutions and processes lose integrity or harmonious relationship, then education follows suit and becomes in its own way just as confused and inchoate as they.

Beyond a narrow statement of the process and purpose of education and a few principles at a very high level of general-

89

ity, little, if anything, at all can be said applicable to the new situation society is confronted with in the inner-city schools and the black community. The new situation in the black community is trivialized by attempts to assimilate it into a timeworn and depreciated purpose and process of education. The image envoked by these words suggests a reconstruction of the process and philosophy of education in the inner-city. If one accepts the argument that education reflects the culture; that education is to adjust itself to the changing culture; and that education addresses itself to the needs of the culture, then a different inner-city culture entails a different approach to quality education; and it becomes obvious that educators and others in positions of responsibility are in need of a philosophy of education of inner-city schools which will enable them to describe, predict, and hopefully control the process of education in order to achieve quality education and produce a "quality product." The position is this: many of the inner-city educational problems—the "patchwork" curriculum, student personality problems, etc.—can be traced to cultural exclusion in our democratic society, to which the inner-city schools have not made a creative adjustment. To develop a meaningful educational model involves the development of a model which is built on the assumption of multiple causation in explaining social affairs.

A model of this kind requires the school to give an account of the fragmented, confused nature of our society, and to trace this fragmentation and confusion to a similarly existing situation in the general culture. This situation in the general culture should be examined; the cause underlying changes in the general culture should be described; and evidence of cultural conflicts should likewise be described.

When most of us think of the purpose and process of education we are apt to think of it primarily from the standpoint of our particular cultural heritage. For many purposes this approach is legitimate and necessary. But it is something more than the sum total of any single cultural heritage; all of us share, in some degree, responsibility for the educational enterprise as a whole.

In the last analysis, the process of education should be mediation between the young and the culture; that is to say, it is the process by which the child acquires the habits, beliefs, knowledges, attitudes, and skills required to make him an effective and acceptable member of the society into which he is born and in which he must live. It is within this general framework that the black communities must find their place.

Whatever else this may mean, it means that the work of schools can be intelligently conducted only as it is related to the nature, the needs, and the problems of society, as well as to the nature, the needs, and the problems of children. To put it another way, the study of education must be as firmly grounded in the understanding of the culture as it is in the understanding of the learning process.

The main arguments to this point have been to the effect that there is little racial harmony in inner-city schools and that there is a marked absence of argument upon fundamental intellectual and moral postulates.

Thus, the question arises of how racial harmony or integration can be attained, its basis seemingly being absent. The answer is that there are latent values and beliefs which have in fact sustained us, but which are progressively losing their force. The task is to make these implicit and covert postulates explicit and overt, a task to which education is assigned a primary role.

The postulates are those of the democratic tradition or, the "American Creed."

The fact that the postulates are latent and still somewhat operative does not necessarily mean that they can easily be made overt and fully operative. *Social direction is not easily changed deliberately in crisis periods.* Moreover, the democratic philosophy is challenged by alternative ideologies, and it has historically been fraught with interpretative conflicts and by practical, internal difficulties. Some democratic reasons to justify altering the process of education and the context for schooling in the inner-city are:

1. The dual system of public education.
2. Ethnic ghettos.
3. The consequentially different social structure.
4. Inadequate representation.
5. Disaffection of authority and responsibility.
6. Needed curriculum reforms.

7. The redefinition and relocation of power in educational policy.
8. The emergence of a different self-consciousness of black Americans, together with a desire to control their community.

The obvious facts should not delude educators about a fundamental reality. The black community is of a new mind with respect to its education. They want schools with the essential quality of providing schooling that enhances the identity of blacks. Many are convinced that the inner-city schools project the culture, value, and life-style of the dominant group.

The black community wants to achieve power, to control its own institutions, and to make good schools for its own. It must be stated that separatism is not necessarily in conflict with a vision of an integrated society. The black community points with accuracy to history and the course taken by other ethnic groups to give themselves self-confidence and a control of their affairs. Through devices of separation, other ethnic groups achieved for themselves status from which they were accorded the esteem on the basis of which they were more fully integrated into the institutional framework.

What we now have is a situation in which the inner-city, ghetto schools and the appropriately perceived problems are radically being transformed. The assigned task of education for the inner-city child has been to hack away at the child until he fits into at least one of the predetermined shapes or slots, while attending to his needs, both the natural needs, and presumably the needs growing out of the routine surgery being performed on him by the provisions of counseling, congeniatory programs, gripe sessions, a simulated air of personal interest and warmth, and other compensatory gimmicks. What was appropriate education in the inner-city in the 1960s with reference either to content or method for the ghetto schools today is no longer appropriate. In fact, it may well be counter-educative today.

What I advocate is that in inner-city schools, particularly in the black community, the curriculum and methods must be updated because the logistical growth of knowledge in the ghetto has added a great deal, and much of the literature of the 1960s is shown to be in error. In addition, I argue that each successive wave of inner-city pupils, like students in other communities, is radically different. I attribute this to life conditions and the crucial problem in the inner-city educational process and the inappropriateness of the educational modes, which do not complement the culture of the community. The inappropriate image once was, and still is now, characteristically described in literature on the inner-city, and it should not be. The image of the inner-city child should rest on a preponderant sense of cultural respect, running both ways, so that the teacher can be comprehensible to the pupil.

But what is now more nearly the situation on both sides of the desk in the classroom is more nearly caught by the image of the visiting anthropologist. The inner-city pupil and teacher find the other very hard to understand; each is effectively insulated against and resentful of being changed; each has an origin, fate, and future quite different from the other; each is naturally hostile to the other and capable of making the hostility felt and effective; neither can understand the other except by a sophisticated, sustained, and delicate effort to enter empathetically into the culture of the other.

Community Unity

There is no need to take the inner-city bustling, energetic, black community's word for it. A visit to any inner-city confirms as "something we've not uncovered elsewhere" their escalating influence in community betterment. The inner-city black community's organized strength is affecting local politics. The black community, standing alone geographically, has not been recognized until recently as a powerful voice.

When anyone alludes to inner-city black community strength, he has to be talking in part about the ramparts at the grass-roots level. To name a few, the black community groups and coalitions rally around a common force—the black community. Across the nation, there is at least one in every city. For the major urban cities, add scores of others springing up in the ghetto soils of discontent. Make no mistake about it, many of these communities devote their efforts to an improve-or-perish level. Stokely Carmichael and Charles Hamilton, authors of

Black Power, state, "We are aware that it has become common-place to pinpoint and describe the ills of our urban ghetto. The social, political and economic problems are so acute that even a casual observer cannot fail to see that something is wrong. While description is plentiful, however, there remains a blatant timidity about what to do to solve the problem."[9]

All the black community battlers aim at such common foes as political power, deterioration of properties, harmful zoning variances, ill-advised urban renewal projects, inferior city service, education, and encroachment of various kinds. The main thrust of this effort is to preserve and protect the character and identity of their community and to be acknowledged as a people of dignity who have a contribution to make to the "open society," which they can make only in their way and not through assimilation.

In a way, history repeats itself in the flowering of community organizations. In early American history, the settlers banded together in groups for mutual protection against hostile forces. Today, their black descendants are doing pretty much the same thing.

We are dealing with an inner-city society and this suggests that the schools' leaders must learn the art of collaboration and negotiation, rather than the tricks of administration and methods of governing. The task of a formal education proper to the environment and the future should be to encourage the co-emergence and enhancement of mind, self, society, history, and culture. Present problems in the inner-city schools require that the privileges guiding schooling operating at a high level of abstraction define an essentially different operation. Since the inner-city is a different culture, teachers and administrators must learn the ways into that culture, not write it off as inferior.

If the schools confront minds, culture, and values, in the deepest sense differently made up from the dominant group, the teachers in inner-city schools must learn and help them learn the difficult and delicate art by which alien minds see into each other in ways that are enlarging and enhancing of both. And since the black pupils' history, his ontogeny, as well as the history he has experienced, the historic moment at which he stands, and the historic task of black people's education, are different, the school must recognize that education for the

94

dispossessed must be at the center of all schooling in the inner-city.

As the bearers of two cultures confront each other, the mandate upon each should be to explore the other in a tender, respectful, collaborative, and perhaps mutually elaborative and enriching relation. The exploration in mutuality should be by people who are different ethnic groups, with a view of learning from each other. Whatever may be empirically discovered should be of value to both, with a view single to the benefit of both. Thus, "integration," then, will have a new importance and a new meaning.

The air of inclusion should prevail. This type of integration characterizes a good conservation; a valued social relation in which distinctness, not separation, is preserved, something that is common and valuable to all. Moreover, the prerequisite for a truly integrated school is an atmosphere of acceptance and mutual respect. In the absence of such support, desegregation may lose a good part of its favorable impact.

An Educational Philosophy

Inner-city life and education is not, nor can it be, removed from social life and relationships. It expresses some social philosophy and rests upon some moral conception. It also is a positive and creative force capable of attacking the problems generated by the movement of ideas and interest in society. It serves inner-city people by providing the service necessary for a full life and the welfare to make explicit the social philosophy which underlies the curriculum. An educational philosophy implies a commitment, and I would like to reflect what I think the commitment of the coalition of decision makers on educational policy should be. They should be committed to:

—Making education more meaningful to the inner-city child.
—An emphasis upon the cognitive and affective mode development.
—The development of an individual who can astutely observe and analyze his society and meaningfully interact with his total environment.
—A demand for realism in teaching.

Since the inner-city school is the real confrontation point, it might be useful first to examine these points in terms of the black ghetto. We can, quite easily, discuss the input factors that bring about change and improvement in the inner-city school. Such things as more and better materials, multimedia usage, new ways of deploying students, and varied teaching strategies would all be an admirable place to begin.

However, even though they are essential, this is not the crucial input factor at this time. Certainly, teachers would like more relevant materials in their inner-city school and more modern media available for their use. The above elements of and by themselves will not help very much. The important factor in the improvement of inner-city education relative to the treatment of black pupils is obviously the primary factor. We all know that we teach for knowledge, skill, attitude, and value attainment, but these different goals suggest different means for inner-city blacks, and attention to means becomes crucial if we are to bring all inner-city black pupils a more relevant education. The Kerner Report makes one point explicitly clear: "Without major changes in educational practices, great expenditures on existing elementary schools serving disadvantaged neighborhoods will not significantly improve the quality of education." The statement is obviously applicable to the inner-city, as well as to the black community. Unless immediate priority is given to this area of the inner-city, pessimism will continue to loom on the educational horizon and continue to produce blacks who are passive onlookers to society.

Just as important as the concept of education in the black community, and intrinsically tied to it, is the concern for developing the child's self-concept and showing him his relationship to society in a positive way.

The problems of equal education for the black community can be viewed as a curriculum task, and it is susceptible to the same kinds of problems and amenable to the same kinds of solutions that lend themselves to curriculum questions. Therefore, if the conditions of inequality are to be righted, we need commitments of action from all teachers, administrators, and the school board; from the colleges and university community. Some possible commitments that might suggest action are:

Board members, school administrators, and teachers can commit themselves to:

(a) Human relations;
(b) Develop a realistic, meaningful curriculum.

When one supports the position that education is a process of indoctrination, and that black teachers certified by the same state certification board have the same capabilities as white teachers who are in suburban predominantly white schools to indoctrinate white pupils to be patriotic citizens, how can white teachers in inner-city predominantly black schools indoctrinating blacks to be patriotic be posing a threat to society through their indoctrination of black pupils? How can one rationally explain being in opposition to community control where black teachers in inner-city schools indoctrinate black pupils to be patriotic Americans? This is a contradiction of things in our society that must be hammered out.

Harold Benjamin, in *The Cultivation of Idiosyncrasy,* retorted: "How much uniformity does this society need for safety?" In answering his own question, he stated: "It needs only that uniformity which the achievements of its greatest goals require. It demands security of life and health for its people. It demands wide opportunities for its people in work and play, in song and prayer. It must provide each individual with maximum aids to the development of his powers to contribute in every way possible to the great goal of his people." Posing a series of leading questions that required reflection, he asked and replied, "Are there necessary restrictions on the individual's development? Of course there are. Should there be guidance, direction, in the building of his abilities?" Of course there should be.

The child with an idiosyncrasy of aggression cannot be permitted to develop it into an idiosyncrasy for brutality, mayhem, or murder. He must instead be helped to develop it into an idiosyncrasy for fighting disease through the practice of medicine, battling hunger by farming, breaking down isolation by blasting highways through mountains, or doing some other aggressive job commensurate with his pattern of abilities.

Benjamin further projects and replies: "How much deviation does this society require for progress?

97

"It requires just as much deviation, just as many uniquely developed peaks of ability, just as much idiosyncrasy as the attainment of its goals will allow and need. All societies are wasteful of the capacities of their people. That society which comes closest to developing every socially useful idiosyncrasy in every one of its members will make the greatest progress toward its goals."[10]

Chances are, if given the opportunity, the concept of community control enhances the development of useful idiosyncrasy in inner-city blacks toward society's goals.

Some Major Criticism—Inner-City Schools

An explanatory analysis of the literature on urban educational problems and possibilities reveals that the following criticisms of inner-city schools are being made by community parents and teachers, by organized groups, and by educators:

1. Inner-city schools are not effectively teaching dispossessed pupils the fundamental skills.

2. Inner-city schools in many ways fail to stimulate competition among and within dispossessed pupils and to reveal to parents the comparative standing of their children.

3. Inner-city schools are having difficulties in developing obedience, respect for authority, a sense of responsibility, or a sense of the importance of learning.

4. Inner-city schools are trying to educate many dispossessed pupils who cannot profit sufficiently from such education.

5. Inner-city schools have not been effective in interpreting their programs to the black and Puerto Rican community.

6. Inner-city school personnel are incompetent to deal with the complex problems the ghetto schools face.

This critical analysis may be valid for certain inner-city schools and under certain varying conditions, while in other situations it may be unjust. Certainly some ghetto schools may neglect the so-called fundamentals to deal with the complexities of the ghetto community, and for this neglect they are criticized.

The above postulates represent, in a sense, values and opinions rather than facts. If all the ghettos of the nation could be placed on a scale made up of these postulates, undoubtedly the range in variation would be great. Some would exemplify these statements to a very large extent; others not at all.

Ghetto schools should provide a rich and varied program designed to meet the needs of the pupils in the community served.

1. Only two decades ago, inner-city schools enrolled a large percentage of black and Puerto Rican boys and girls who were not expected to go to college and enter one of the professions. The drop-out rate was high and was quite diversified and avocational. Now the inner-city schools enroll more than seven out of ten dispossessed pupils, and the percentage is gradually increasing. Less than half of the graduates will try to find jobs immediately after leaving school. The majority are being encouraged to attend college.

All this means that inner-city schools must extend their program to include courses that help dispossessed boys and girls solve practical problems and be successful students academically. Thus, ghetto schools are faced with two major problems: (a) to provide the best way to develop academic programs for the ghetto child, and (b) to provide adequately for specialized interests and needs. Ghetto schools generally have not adjusted their programs to these new demands, but many are attempting to move in this direction.

2. The ghetto school administrators should recognize the different abilities, interests, and needs of their pupils and organize their programs in terms of their differences, at the same time recognizing that people must live together.

The school should cherish differences in pupils and try to protect them. It should study each student as a person and help him to meet his personal problems, extend his interests, and help him work out for himself a satisfying pattern of living, always remembering that he is a member of a group and has an obligation to improve the quality of living of all members of the group.

The Education of Inner-City Youth

While many worthwhile efforts have been made and successes achieved, the problem of providing a viable education to inner-city minority members in public schools is still a long way from solution. Only a new approach can equalize educational opportunity for the inner-city minority.

Hostility, aggression, hatred, racism, bigotry, violence, anger, these are all strong words—they connote sharp feelings and desperate passions. Moreover, these harbingers of grief, dismay, frustration, and despair are commonplace in contemporary American urban life. They have come to symbolize much of our society in general and are an everyday part of our inner-city schools in particular. Inner-city schools are under siege—a siege brought on primarily by the schools themselves swept into public view through the mass media.

Despite the information blitz afforded us by modern systems of communications, inner-city public schools have been taken for granted by educators, teachers, pupils, and parents for so long a time that the central question has not been asked for generations. That question is simply—What is the purpose of education? What is the purpose of education in an urbanized society? What should be the purpose of education in the inner-city? In 1632 John Amos Comenius, the didactic, wrote: "The education I propose includes all that is proper for a man, and is one in which all men who are born into this world should share. . . . Our first wish is that all men should be educated fully to full humanity; not only one individual, nor a few, nor even many, but all men together and single, young and old, rich and poor, of high and lowly birth, men and women—in a word, all whose fate it is to be born human beings; so that at last the whole of the human race may become educated, men of all ages, all conditions, both sexes and all nations."

Unfortunately, in the urban American experience, we have not only eschewed the way of Comenius, we have refused even to question the aims and goals of education for our time. Our reluctance to probe this issue, both intellectually and humanistically, is painfully clear when such a distinguished scholar of education as James B. Conant disdainfully declares that he feels a sense of distasteful weariness overtaking him whenever he encounters anyone discussing educational goals or philosophy. Conant further postulates that the appropriate definition of education is what goes on in schools and colleges. Equally disturbing are Martin Mayer's comments in his book, *The School,* where he states that: "We know very little about the process of education; and the reason for our lack of knowledge is probably the complexity of the process. We were not put here as we are. We have evolved from eons of animal life and we carry within us both the remnants of an unknown past and the seeds of an unknowable future. Much that occurs in the education of the child is and always will be incomprehensible to the fully formed adult. If ever all is known that can be known about the schools, there will remain a large element of mystery."[11]

The attitudes of Conant and Mayer are similar to those held by most teachers, educationists, and administrators in urban inner-city schools. Such blind refusals to question the purpose and process of urban education were made abundantly clear in Charles Silberman's book, *Crisis in the Classroom,* which is the result of a three-and-one-half-year study on the education of educators sponsored by the Carnegie Corporation.[12] Silberman and his study colleagues have described this attitudinal vacuum as "mindlessness"—the refusal to question the validity of what goes on in classrooms, or, to put it another way—Is what goes on in American classrooms what should be going on in them? The answer to this question is a resounding no, at least from the inner-city minorities. Education should deal with the development of the whole person—his cognitive abilities and his affective perceptions. Perhaps no other country in the world in modern times has placed so much emphasis on cognitive skills development at the expense of affective growth. For example, our technology is unsurpassed as compared with the rest of the world, and our ability as a nation to make things mechanical and scientific is considered the pinnacle of the industrial revolution. Yet, our society is morally on the verge of bankruptcy— we are a violent, racist, bellicose people.

American schools, elementary and secondary, have traditionally viewed the imparting of skills as being possible only through a strict authoritarian hierarchy, one in which the teachers talk, the pupils listen, and where silence is mandatory. Silence and discipline are considered prerequisites for classroom functioning. Thus, it is easy to see why most American inner-city schools are joyless, dull, tedious places where the spontaneity of children is mutilated and destroyed; where the rules are petty and oppressive; where the atmosphere is intellectually sterile and aesthetically barren; where there is an appalling lack of civility toward the children by the teachers and administrators; where this lack of civility unconsciously manifests itself as contempt for the students; where a premium is put upon "being good," rather than on asking questions; where, in short, teaching is considered all-important and where learning is barely ever considered. It is assumed that since there is a teacher in a classroom, whatever the teacher does constitutes teaching, and for far too many that is sufficient for the requirements of teaching in the inner-city.

In order to understand the implication of these truths for the education of inner-city children, we must briefly recall the history of education for disadvantaged youth and their special place in contemporary society.

As a group, the inner-city dispossessed have in the past been virtually excluded from formal education. For example, before the Civil War, schooling for blacks was generally prohibited by law in the South; and in the North, educational opportunities were severely limited. By 1890, most states had established a system of free public education which, until the 1930s, meant six to eight years of education for most Americans. For blacks, almost without exception, this meant attending inferior segregated schools de jure in the South and de facto in the North.

Pleas by blacks went unheeded for one hundred years before this country decided to deal with black demands for equal educational opportunities. In 1954, the U.S. Supreme Court recognized the obvious, at least to blacks, that state-enforced segregation in schools had invariably resulted in inferior schooling for the segregated group. Nevertheless, the Court permitted local school districts and states to continue this practice for an undetermined period of time. Blacks recognize this as nine men in black thinking white, for, by this act, the Supreme Court showed its willingness to tolerate unconstitutional inequality rather than to disturb the white community too suddenly. Blacks also knew that, as a result, another generation of their children would be doomed to an inferior education.

Shortly after the Court's ruling, the establishment began with renewed vigor the process of isolating blacks into ghettos. The nation's capital, Newark, and several other municipalities rapidly became predominantly black cities as whites, liberal and conservative alike, fled from integration as if it were a plague. White-controlled state legislatures approved school-aid formulas that favored white neighborhoods. School district lines were used to void administrative efforts at integration. Suddenly, the neighborhood school became a cherished concept. But blacks recognized such agonizing, twisting, and turning for what it was—racism pure and simple. Some recent court decisions have recognized this truth as well.

In September, 1971, a federal court judge found that Detroit's public school systems are not creations of chance, but are deliberate; that racial patterns are not happenstance, but grow out of state action or inaction. Actions at all levels—federal, state, and local—have combined with those of private organizations such as banks, real estate associations, and brokerage firms to cause segregated housing patterns. "For many years," the judge said, "the Federal Housing Administration (FHA) and the Veterans Administration (VA) openly advised and advocated maintenance of 'harmonious' neighborhoods, racially and economically harmonious. The segregated housing patterns thus state-created and enforced are the most direct cause of contemporary educational segregation."

Only recently, however, have the courts been willing to deal with educational disparities between neighborhoods. Two specific cases come to mind. A District of Columbia court recently ruled that the Washington, D.C., public schools may not deviate in the allocation of school funds from the district's average by more than 5 percent. Perhaps the most significant court action to date, however, has been a ruling by the California State Supreme Court that the state may no longer allow gross disparities in educational opportunities between neighborhoods. The decision in *Serrano* v. *Priest* questioned whether the state can first make education mandatory, by law, and then finance its school system so that some students get a poorer education than others. The court further stated that:

—Education is essential for a "free . . . democracy."

—Education is necessary for preserving an individual's opportunity to compete successfully in the economic marketplace, despite a disadvantaged background.

—Education is universally relevant. During his lifetime, an individual may never have to call for the police or fire department, or go on welfare, but everyone requires education.

—Public education shapes a child's personal development in a manner not chosen by the child or his parents, but by the state.

—The state considers education so important that it makes it compulsory and forces children to attend particular schools and districts. Although a child of wealthy parents has the opportunity to attend private schools, such choice is usually not available to the poor.

This is a landmark decision for, in the public service sector, education is certainly unique. Getting a good education is almost always a once-in-a-lifetime opportunity. If you have not received your share of basic education before your 18th birthday, there is a good chance that you never will.

American racism has imposed the task of educating the black child upon our inner-city school systems. The 1970 census shows that 50 percent of the black population resides in 50 cities and three-fourths of the remaining 50 percent resides in other urban areas. It is now clear that efforts put forth by inner-city schools to provide the black child with a good basic education, have been a tragic failure. Scores on academic achievement tests consistently show black students two or more grade levels behind whites. There are many here and elsewhere in and out of the educational establishment who place the blame for this failure on the child and/or on his family. Like Pontius Pilate, this is a sorry effort on the part of a guilt-ridden majority to absolve itself and its school system from any responsibility. To most blacks, this is a confirmation of white racism; create the inequity at every level of the economic, social and political arena; freeze the black adult and child alike in a second-class or no-class status; then blame him for the failure—not the system.

Racism in our school systems takes many forms. In addition

to the gross disparities in the allocation of educational resources for schools attended by blacks, many school officials and teachers feel that black students simply cannot achieve a high level of academic competence. Professor Robert Merton of Columbia University calls "the self-fulfilling prophesy" one where teachers expect minority children to be noisy, disruptive, or unwilling to learn. Understanding how this works is critical to an understanding of why so many black children experience failure in the public schools. Merton's theory of the "self-fulfilling prophesy," stated simply, is that in many if not most situations, people tend to do what is expected of them. A teacher's expectation can and does affect the performance of the students. Too many teachers in ghetto schools assume that their students will not be able to learn and will be disruptive, and sure enough, that is usually exactly what happens. Is it, then, so difficult to understand why these children spend so much time trying to devise retaliatory schemes, such as fighting, swearing, or destroying school property? Indeed it is a self-fulfilling prophesy.

As to the claim that blacks have lower native intelligence than whites, many liberals maintain that blacks are not inferior intellectually, but simply are retarded educationally because of their deprived backgrounds. Such liberals view the schools' job as providing massive *compensatory* education. They consistently fail to recognize that their attitude is condescending, patronizing, and offensive. They teach the black child to look upon his parents and home with pity and contempt. In my judgment, most compensatory programs are a "cop-out hiding the inadequately staffed and poorly housed schools in the ghetto."[13] They invariably have been too little and too late—artificially induced, sporadically financed and usually do more to salve white consciences and finance the establishment than to educate the black child. Thus, in general, neither liberals nor conservatives expect black students to achieve much in school.

The Carnegie study team was not surprised to discover that teachers in ghetto areas overwhelmingly considered discipline the most important aspect of their classroom activities, whereas suburban teachers considered the most important thing for their students was the ability to get along with each other and to have acceptable standards of behavior. Although the outlook of the suburban teachers is indeed preferable to that of ghetto teachers, neither approach really considers the importance of what the students learn or how much of what they absorb will be relevant for the moral and social issues and problems they will have to face as adults.

Despite the magnitude of the problems in nearly every public school, the problems in the lower-income, predominantly black schools are so staggering that the gap widens markedly and continuously between the white middle class and the black poor. Kenneth Clark, in his book, *Dark Ghetto,* succinctly insists that black children do not learn simply because "they are not being taught; and not taught, they fail. They have a sense of personal humiliation and unworthiness."[14]

The research report released by the Council for Basic Education charged that "the failure in beginning reading typical of inner-city schools is the fault not of the children or their backgrounds but of the schools!"

In yet another study undertaken for the New York State Commission on the Quality, Cost and Financing of Elementary and Secondary Education, the truth of this allegation is made eminently clear. Its most important finding was that the patterns of increased academic retardation which tend to accompany increased minority-group enrollment in a school are not constant. The study states, "Indeed the pattern changes drastically, casting in serious doubt the prevalent conceptions held not only by the uninformed but by distinguished scholars in the field of education and by the practicing professionals throughout the school system."

After detailing the patterns of reading achievement from 1958 to 1971, in the New York City schools, and plotting the trends in direct relation to ethnic composition changes, the researcher-scholar states:

"Above all, we must conclude that the children themselves have very little to do with these changing patterns. Remedy would have to be sought not by changing the failing children (or their families) but by changing the attitudes of the schools that have failed them."

The report's conclusion states in part: "Primary in determining how well children will achieve are changes in community and school system attitudes toward minority groups, rather than changes in the absolute members of minority group children in the school population and its influence on school policy. Hence, remedy must be sought in combatting racism and in entrusting school policy, to those least influenced by racism—i.e., the parents and communities from which the children come."

These findings point up some pressing and difficult questions about education that must be answered by the black community.

While American public schools have historically conveyed middle-class values and attitudes, it is an oversimplification to attribute the failure of slum schools to the students' inability to accept or understand such values. Rather, the failures come from the middle-class attitudes which teachers and administrators hold toward poor people and their role in society. The school conveys a middle-class image of how low-income and welfare children are and how they should be—an image which emphasizes obedience and respect rather than ability, responsibility, and initiative, and which expects unruliness with regard to behavior and apathy with regard to cognition.

Compensatory Education

The hodgepodge of programs that emerged was compensatory education united only in the loosest sense but not a common rationale. It was in thousands of separate communities rather than in the lecture halls or the legislatures that public education took root, and it was always there that the schools acquired their peculiar form. The rapid, persistent growth of cities encouraged other modifications. Until whites came to determine public education for the freed black, the industrial sections of the city had represented the sole exception to the community-controlled schools. As Barnard told the Rhode Island legislature in 1845, civilized men had to decide for the urban poor how best to raise them from barbarism.

Those decisions from above increased in importance and variety as the slums multiplied. The word *ethnic*, which had long played an especially prominent role in slum education, now more often took the form of so-called practical training in factory skills, and spokesmen for the dispossessed fought these experiments in caste schooling just as the workingmen's group of the 1930s had. Slum dwellers by and large received an indifferent version of the standard fare. Meanwhile, as long as the cities remained a collection of semi-autonomous subdivisions, substantial citizens moved to those areas where they could usually control their own schools as they chose. In sum, the patchwork of urban education reflected the general disruption around it.

In order to meet that changing relationship, compensatory education was relocated as the subsidiary part of a larger scheme. Is the concept of compensatory education a fourteenth year in high school or a fifth year in college? If so, are black people aiding and abetting that concept by accepting special school aid for black schools? Inherent in this notion is the assumption that blacks cannot be taught the 3 R's using regular school resources; special efforts are needed to achieve such ends. The Elementary and Secondary Education Act, ESEA, of 1965, the major source of compensatory funds, has yet to really benefit black students. Many ESEA programs were only "paper" ones; they were ill-administered, inadequate, or not educationally sound. Yet, Arthur Jensen, two years later, used these compensatory efforts as proof that even with special help, black students cannot achieve academic success. In New York City, city and state compensatory funds are tied to low reading test scores. All you need to do to get extra money for your school or district is to insure that students continue to score low on reading tests. Is this what blacks have been fighting for? If not, then what?

Another question: *Can blacks trust the education of their children to others?* Are the Chinese in San Francisco, who are refusing to send their children to integrated schools, trying to tell us something? Did the high academic achievement of Jews in New York City result from Jews' gaining control of the public school system? Why do so many black students from Southern black schools with all-black teachers and administrators do better, educationally, than so many of their Northern brothers and sisters under white teachers and administrators?

Let us assume that all of a sudden the black child is given his share of so-called good teachers, instructional supplies, and so forth. Wouldn't there still be cause for concern? In the public sector, merely receiving service from qualified personnel does not guarantee quality service. Blacks have never received good service from well-qualified personnel in the public sector such as city hospitals, police departments, and welfare departments. So far, blacks have been fighting for their share of qualified teachers; but what guarantee do we have that qualified teachers will give qualified service to black students? Can this problem be resolved with more black teachers and administrators, community control of neighborhood schools, or a combination of both?

What Should Be the Educational Goals for Blacks?

During the 1930s and 1940s, the NAACP mounted a national campaign encouraging blacks to finish high school. At that time, a high school education was considered a necessary prerequisite for getting a good job. Today, however, a college education is the requirement for really getting ahead. Regardless of the verbiage, the public school system currently is not providing opportunities for a fair number of blacks to enroll for and complete a college education. According to John Kenneth Galbraith, 96 percent of all jobs paying $15,000 or more are occupied by white males; the remaining 4 percent are split between women and blacks. It seems safe to conclude that slightly less than 2 percent of these positions are held by blacks and that, in the main, only college-educated blacks will enter this category. It's not just money that's at issue here, for these are the policy-making positions.

Thus, the so-called power structure remains 98 percent white. Today, 50 percent of the college-age population is enrolled in institutions of higher education. The black college-age population is 18 percent of the total college-age group, yet they constitute only 5.8 percent of all students now enrolled.

Therefore, the challenge is to define what is a "good education." It is not realistic to believe that large groups of Americans who fall outside the norm of the so-called white middle-class can go on indefinitely accepting the handouts of this middle-class group. To continue to deny blacks real voices in educational policy adds to and increases the polarization in

109

this society, heightens the degree of racial hatred and unrest and encourages deplorable conditions in inner-city schools and in the communities. In short, to keep the power as unevenly distributed as it is at the present time is to deal with the symptoms of problems and not with the causes. The form and substance of the changes will emerge more clearly as answers to the basic questions begin to take shape.

One thing is certain. We must solve the crisis in public education in the United States for inner-city children. We must make society accommodate all peoples of this land, or we shall surely lose our ability to solve problems, let alone ameliorate them. Jean-François Revel, in his book *Without Marx or Jesus*, gives us a controversial and unexpected view of the United States when he says that the social problems of the modern world, i.e., education, racism, human rights, ecological pollution, and so on, must be solved first here, in America, and if they are not, they will not be solved anywhere else in the world.

In a manner vaguely reminiscent of the college preparatory schools of the early twentieth century, the compensatory educational program now acts as a conduit into channels of education for minorities. However, increasingly compensatory education is seen as a frill, as an alternative means of acculturation through segregation, a commercialized concept of the culture of poverty, which renews an earlier sense of education for blacks before an impersonal society. An ongoing revolution cultural, social, and skills education have won ground very unevenly. Compensatory programs' major victory has been the establishment of new standards, altering the framework of educational institutions, even where they have not changed content. What substantive changes they have brought have widened the class differential in the public schools. The new scheme selects a minority already motivated and generally well-to-do for favored treatment often in separate classes—and by the very nature of its objectives then helps to extend the distance between those who remain in the traditional classroom and those who do not.

Questions of equity and balance have traditionally fallen beyond the scope of public education. From its origins the public school had relied upon the leading members of a locality to define its role according to their sense of society's best interests.

110

The indoctrination in the island communities and the devotion to skills in our time have all been functional precisely in these terms. What leeway the schools have enjoyed since 1900 has covered the manner of achieving goals, not the goals themselves. The legal setting for the schools, the emotional defenses of local autonomy, and the self-concept of educational administrators merely underline the historical record of education as an aura reflecting the primary place of compensatory education in American social ideology rather than as a comprehension of its place in American social structure. Beginning with slavery and running to the present, a strong rhetorical liberal tradition has continually raised expectations that quality education for blacks, more or less as autonomous agents, could promote a basic national reconstruction of public education, even if school officials grew wise and courageous. The burden of this thesis is, quite simply, that dominant groups in American society have bound public education far too tightly to their cause for rhetoric alone to move them. However, public education, especially that in the inner-city, has come to be seen by people of all ethnic backgrounds as virtually synonymous with compensatory education when a school has any significant proportion of black students enrolled.

Reconstruction of Inner-City Education

Reconstruction is a comprehensive, systematic process of change that involves the participation of the total inner-city community in the redefinition of its children's needs. As a change strategy, reconstruction of the inner-city schools should not be concerned only with defining goals and designing programs to facilitate those goals, but concerned with the developing of an administrative strategy for operationalizing the program to produce pupils graduating from inner-city public schools.

While inner-city community involvement in achieving more effective and efficient education is a key element in the reconstruction process, community leaders also can play a significant role. The role is perceived as being one of facilitation, guidance, encouragement, stimulation, and motivation.

111

A bit of educational jargon which has become trite is reference to "meeting the needs of the children." The phrase has lost its meaning largely because of its use in an ambiguous context; however, the goal it represents is the ultimate aim of education. Schools should be designed to meet the needs of the child and his culture; the responsibility of education should not be confined to the physical structure of the school.

Cultural heritage is one of the necessities of life. Black culture as a necessity seems as vital to black humanity as freedom itself. Black culture should be an integral part of the public school system. Like any culture, it is of interest to note that there exists no record of people, past or present, no matter how primitive, without some understanding of their cultural heritage.

Black culture, like all cultures, constitutes the learned behavior of people by means of which, in a particular manner, they endeavor to embrace the world; to take what they can of it; and to give it what they are able of themselves. The position is this: the inner-city teacher's understanding and knowledge of black culture, and to a greater extent, its appreciation can significantly improve teacher, pupil, and parent relations; and help the pupil to a more efficient development of his potentialities and meeting his needs. Black studies should become an indispensable part of the educational process in public schools and higher education.

I place great emphasis upon the need for black culture and studies in inner-city schools. Black children are born without the kind of hostile aggressiveness which has so long been attributed to them, because once we drop the notion that black children are born hostile little brats, we are likely to give them a good deal more of the understanding attention they need, and so much less of the "bringing up" that they don't need. The way to produce warped, conflictful, warring, hostile human beings is to frustrate them as children. The way to produce warm, friendly, peaceful human beings is by being warm, friendly, and peaceful to them as children, to satisfy their need to grow in all these qualities as in others.

Since inner-city pupils' educations have been one of the areas of white blindness to the seriousness of the black community's educational problem, it may be unlikely that improved education at the community level is the answer. Some of the past attempts to educate blacks have actually been attempts to rob them of their culture. In addition, the treatment of blacks in the traditional American school curriculum and textbooks blots out any serious consideration of their dissent from, or contributions to, the emerging American society. The basic problem which has existed between blacks and whites has not only been one of race but of culture. The black community has been stirred, ambition fired, and community groups created, which have not readily found constructive substitutes for the traditions that have been corroded.

Therefore, it becomes the black community's obligation to exercise the cultural influence of its members in a helpful way and not be content to allow the doctrines of the past tradition to provide nothing more than the inspiration for uncontrolled development and education. This is essentially a black cultural task, requiring a clear conception of our own values and of the way in which we want to share them with others.

What William O. Stanley, in *Education and Social Integration,* calls the "culture core,"[16] has become an inextricable part of black lives. It is not merely in the more obvious realms of politics and economics that this is so, but in the minds of black people. The diffusion of cultures and the interpenetration of the ambitions and frustrations of people from other communities means that a meaningful exchange of ideas, of learning and of information, are a major reason to suggest that the concept of the black community must be clarified from within.

Cultural Activities—A Part of the Educational Process

An understanding of the cultural and social environment of the community in which the community has to carry out its educational policies is indispensable to the effectiveness of those policies. In a very real sense, therefore, the cultural core does not consist of expendable frills, but should be an essential ingredient of community affairs. So far, the words acknowledging this have not always been followed by deeds, and an adequate concern with the black community for the cultural ingredient in educational policy has yet to be translated into an effective demonstration that its importance is in fact recognized.

The majority of community leaders and substantial community-action programs for community betterment have, all too often, suffered from an inadequate appreciation of their cultural environment in which they operate and a failure to weigh the cultural and social—not to say the educational—consequences of these activities. As a result, they have often lacked effectiveness or have had results different from what was planned or anticipated. The black community-action programs with their far-flung influence and activities throughout the inner-city are under a special obligation to understand the environment in which they are working and the effect their actions have on the cultural traditions and social attitudes of the community.

Moreover, cultural activities themselves have often suffered from the disdain of being regarded as nice but inconsequential, or from the unreasonable expectation that they are capable of solving immediate problems. Activities which should have their sole justification in their own aesthetic, educational, or humanistic qualities are too often expected to achieve results that are unrealistic or blamed for not achieving results, the responsibility for which lies elsewhere. This results from the frequent failure to distinguish between the different purposes that cultural activities in the community are intended to serve, or capable of serving. An incorrect analysis of situations is the result and, all too often, leads either to naive prescriptions for complicated matters or to recriminations because of the inability of cultural activities to solve problems or prevent unfavorable situations which are, in fact, due to other causes. Conversely, because of the substantial universality of many forms of scientific, artistic, and intellectual pursuits, cultural activities may be under suspicion for fear of their undermining rigidly held social attitudes.

Contemporary Thoughts on the
Education of Black America

The period 1965-70 witnessed sufficient explosions within American cities to lend credence to the contention that the

114

United States did, indeed, consist of two armed camps engaged in preparations for a second civil war. The communications media daily dispensed enormous dosages of revolutionary rhetoric. Today, several years after Watts and Washington, D.C., riots, this rhetoric still abounds, although no longer punctuated by frequent violent eruptions. Nevertheless, there is, indeed, a revolution in black America, a revolution which transcends political exigencies and is by nature fundamentally cultural. Assuming the truth of this contention, it becomes obvious that Americans recognize the important implications and serious challenges such a cultural revolution presents to the educational structure. For it is this institution perhaps more than all others to which the responsibility of cultural indoctrination and perpetuation is entrusted. The extent of black disaffection with American education—"schools are insidious instruments of this society . . . savagely ripping all dignity from Black children"[17]—compounded the problem of an already disintegrated institution. What black educators demand from the system is no less than the liberation of the mind and spirit of the black student from years of cultural subjugation. What the American educational institution has offered instead is a culturally homogeneous system which abhors the parochial and attempts to unify and democratize society by providing "equality of opportunity" through public education. Today, this drive is represented by the government's attempt to "blend statistically into our school system a uniform formula of racial elements—black, brown, yellow and white."[18] Blacks suggest that such attempts at desegregation mask more fundamental educational programs designed to maintain the status quo and discourage the introduction of knowledge which would upset the basic institutional values of white European supremacy, male supremacy, and the supremacy of people with money.[19] Critics further contend that urban schools require schizophrenia as a means to success by forcing the inner-city youth to live by two standards, that of the so-called normal society, and that of the street society. School dropouts attest to the fact that it is easier to live by only one set of rules. By emphasizing the function of unifier and democratizer, the school, in both its instruction and its procedures, attempts to persuade youth that all groups share a common language, common political and economic institu-

115

tions, and common standards of right and wrong behavior. The failure of the schools to recognize the importance and legitimacy of cultural diversity is apparent. The rationale for the adherence to cultural homogeneity is, according to Seymour W. Itzkoff, a product of mass society, itself: "The great national educational machine can be managed, manipulated and controlled only by utilizing the impressive powers of all our social institutions towards the quest of standardization."[20] Briefly stated, it is Itzkoff's contention that mass technology precipitated a major social problem by transforming the traditional relationships between men. Such transformations have altered both the content and form of our educational institutions by necessitating an increase in management and control to stem the tide of chaos. Thus, in the name of order and clarity we accept homogeneity and bureaucracy. Public education perpetuates the myth of national unity by supposing that equality is contingent upon conformity and similarity. Itzkoff's goal would be a condition in which men could be equal yet different; a condition in which diversity could be maintained without the loss of social status or power.

Black educators echo this concept of cultural pluralism in their contention that the only legitimate education for black children is one which recognizes and includes their culture in the school curriculum. "Faced with an onrush of white imagery from every corner of their learning environment—books, teachers, bulletin boards, mannerisms, values, etc.—they withdraw and begin to fulfill the prophecy of the educational system."[21] Assuming, then, that the educational system designed to preserve the status quo cannot provide a legitimate educational experience for the black student, and further assuming that an inclusion of black culture is imperative to the success of such an effort, educators are faced with the dilemma of defining "black culture." It has been suggested that the basic question confronting the black intellectual is just that: "What is black culture?" One answer which has been advanced is that "most of us do not know what 'Black Culture' really is; mainly because Blacks have been denied the luxury of defining their own culture, as well as having to always depend upon the whimsical discretion of White people to tell us what we are and what we can do."[22] Whites have traditionally imposed a unity upon

116

blacks, stereotyping them and discriminating equally against them, giving no recognition to the heterogeneity of the black population. Although a high level of heterogeneity exists in the urban black classroom, the educational program fails to reflect this.[23] Public education, by adhering to the white middle-class norm of behavior, facilitates a mass, stereotyped classification of black urban children. So engrossed in the concept of cultural unity is the school that it fails to consider the premise that the supposed cultural deficiencies of the lower-class black child may be merely cultural differences—critical differences which represent the child's realistic and intelligent response to his environment and his survival therein. "Education, whenever and wherever it is carried on, must assume that every individual with whom it works has reflected upon his experience; that he already has some implicit or explicit view of the meaning of life; that he lives by that meaning and interprets new experiences, including his educational experiences in the light of that meaning. Every educational activity has its most basic significance in terms of its effect upon the meaning of life being developed by the subject."[24] The success of urban education depends upon the realization that no child is deprived of a "culture." The public school must discard as the measure of culture, that white middle-class behavior it views as "normal" and recognize that the black urban child has assimilated a very real, authentic, pragmatic culture through which his formal education can proceed.

Nevertheless, it would be foolhardy (some would contend suicidal) to negate the presence of the dominant white society in the United States. To be viable, American education must reflect the values of a multi-ethnic society. For the black student, such an education should help the individual cope with the white world without either alienating him completely from it or making him subservient to it. It is not enough for black studies to affirm personal dignity, self-identity, and intrapersonal integration. Without the proper skills and intellectual competence needed to successfully enter the larger society, one's personal confidence and pride will not long endure. LaMar P. Miller, education director for the Institute of Afro-American Affairs, New York University, suggests that the following two referents be used in making decisions about such black studies:

117

Attention should be paid to (1) contemporary society, its institutions and social processes as they apply to the experience of blacks, and to (2) black heritage (i.e., an objective, scholastic inquiry into the history of the black man in America).[25]

The black heritage is not an integral part of the curriculum in institutions of learning. Blacks' contributions to the growth of America are not made known by adding black children to traditional primary readers, nor by the existence of a black faculty and administration. It is, however, in part contingent upon these variables. But it is primarily dependent upon a curriculum which is cognizant of the heterogeneity of the population and appropriate educational programs around this diversity. To the black child, the black heritage should nurture both a positive self-image and a positive orientation to the cognitive skills with an emphasis on improving the quality of individual and group life that becomes a river that flows into the broader culture. The black experience in its totality should facilitate the building of a prosperous, integrated community.

The danger in developing in isolation an alternative system of education for blacks based on heretofore unrecognized ideologies, values, and norms is the danger of perpetuating the "miseducation" of American youth. A monocultural education, be it white or black, is an incomplete education which may too easily breed racism, hostilities, misunderstanding, and rigidity. One's self-integrity and identity may, indeed, flow from the respect, cultivation, and practice of one's cultural heritage, but prior to and above culture is humanity. "Man's dignity comes from being human—not Negro, Oriental, Caucasian, American Russian."[26] To be proud of one's culture is laudable; to be preoccupied by it to the exclusion of knowledge and appreciation of other cultures is a threat to the very existence of one's own culture. White America, obsessed by the "melting-pot" myth and its version of democracy through conformity, has experienced such a threat. Cultural pride must be tempered by cultural criticism; that which is invalid or anachronistic within a culture must be rejected.

This writer deplores the unfortunate conditions existing in the United States which legitimize the suggestion of a monocultural education for the minority communities. Despite the apparent necessity of implementing such an educational program, there is a very real fear of further polarization and alienation within the larger society. Perhaps our hopes lie in an approach which emphasizes one's culture as part of the total human experience, an approach through which an individual's worth is identified by his humanness. Freedom and equality do not demand uniformity; they do, however, require a respect for differentiation within the latitude of humanity.

CHAPTER 4

DEMANDS ON SCHOOL POLICY:
DECISION-MAKING IN
THE INNER-CITY SCHOOLS

WITHIN the last several years America has witnessed a marked increase in the amount of interest and concern for race relations. Many individuals and groups are concerning themselves with this problem. Not since the days of the Civil War has the question of race and our democratic institutions been of such widespread concern as it is at the present. One has merely to examine the titles of recently published books, and magazine and newspaper articles to be convinced that researchers and scholars are now directing their energies toward solutions to the race problem in America.

Rapid development of technology, urbanization, and lost communication between blacks and whites have weakened the sense of social responsibility in our society. A few of the many problems our society is plagued with are: the interest of members of the inner-city community is no longer defined by the community; urbanization has weakened the influence the community can exert on the lives of its members; and the fact that there is a loss of common goals and a divided allegiance.

No group of educators alone can define social purposes of education or share its policies apart from a consideration of the ideals and aspirations of the public upon which education is dependent for support. This is mainly because value conflicts in America have increasingly made it difficult to identify and sort out the fundamental implications which new directions have raised for the future of race relations in the United States. What is needed is a way to identify explicitly the basic underlying causes of value and culture conflicts; the first order of business in discussing racial problems should be to identify the causes of social value conflict.

A close examination of the contents of some of the recently edited volumes permits a second inference about the present state of racial unrest in urban American society. One cannot help being struck by the fact that there is substantial disagreement among contributors on such matters as the most pressing problems for study, and the relative usefulness of different research findings or ideological views. The use of such concepts as "racism," "liberal," and "conservative" conveys a misleading image of a collection of social and cultural values and beliefs with some general agreement among interest or pressure groups about the final say about the reconstruction of our society, its shape, and the building materials to be used to bridge the "deep moat" between races. On the contrary, it is argued that different interest groups are working from vastly different sets of architectural plans and that many are unsympathetic toward the activities of other contributors.

The diversity in approaches to a solution to the racial crisis in public education on the part of persons representing different interest groups does in itself constitute a serious problem in heading off further disintegration in race relations. It is important to be explicit about these differences, in order that discussions of current value issues and racial crises in public education can start from a common frame of reference or at least from a recognition of the differing frames of reference employed.

An Overview of the Situation

Inasmuch as I accept the view that an examination of culture and values can, in many ways, make a highly significant contribution to the solution of racial problems in inner-city schools, the culture of the students, and their educational, social, and economic values have a tremendous influence on

121

educational policy. Understanding the problem of values and culture differences, I believe, is crucially important not only in developing relevant programs for the inner-city pupils' education but also as a matter of deep and widespread social significance and attitudes in the community.

The importance of this concern and its effect on educational policy and curriculum is by no means peculiar to me. A little over twenty years ago, one of America's most distinguished social scientists, Alfred L. Hilliard, commented: "A distinguishing characteristic of the present stage in the development of history is its pervasive and acute conflict of values, a fact to which almost all thinkers agree and almost all contemporary social events attest. Insofar as the concept of values enters every human act and decision, and insofar as disagreement on values ultimately endangers the continuance of civilization, the resolution, or at least the clarification of this conflict may claim to be the most momentous task of our time."[1]

In having been conclusively established elsewhere, the rudimentary history of disagreement on values permeates a long record of gradually intensifying racial and cultural conflict in democratic America. More than ever before, these epithetic problems of conflict in valuation are upon us. The present racial and cultural crisis situations in America and public education are such that an inquiry into the value conflicts in patriotism and loyalty to America should not be ruled as being out of order, or irrelevant to broad human concerns.

In America, it is possible for us to hold certain values which often—according to our mental convictions—are incongruent with the American democratic and educational values we believe in. We may not be aware that we harbor contradictory norms, or that we misuse a certain one in a particular situation that contradicts other ideals that we support. Nevertheless, because of the complexity of our society, complacency is becoming more difficult for us to maintain because certain values can be acquired in many different ways. For instance, the familiar dichotomy of "rural" and "urban" concepts of community life or inner-city and suburban community life, shading into each other, often creates a combination of emerging educational values that conflict with one another when making policy decisions on community affairs.

Although there is no method yet devised which can measure accurately values or how they are partaken, it is purported that almost all persons come into possession of their moral ideas unreflectively; and such ideas are not usually changed even after we become mature.[2] We may become, because of the immense influence upon our mode of thought and feeling, habituated to the same contradictions that everyone else around us practices.

To illustrate this point, it is possible that a child growing from infancy to adulthood in a social environment of fairly intense and relatively uniform values, where all of his younger and older associates hold and express the same judgments of valuation on American democratic principles, may form firmly entrenched beliefs—some of them overly idealized—and may automatically accept without questioning such beliefs and behavior that should be very difficult to reshape by the time he reaches adulthood.[3]

Once an adult, as long as he remains in his respective social sphere not knowing what people of other social strata think nor the values by which they rationalize their conduct, his own interpretation of American democracy is unchallenged. But when he moves from one social stratum to another, for example, from inner-city to outer city, or when he comes in contact with the ideals and points of view on democracy or equal educational opportunity contrary to his own, conflict may occur, and he may adopt various forms of mental gymnastics, such as compartmentalizing his life in his effort to achieve peace of mind.

Myrdal's entire study, *The American Dilemma*, in attempting to examine the democratic values of patriotic Americans, indicated that most Americans tend to associate certain democratic principles with relevant attitudes toward what Americans should value as ideal.[4] According to Myrdal, there exists in the structure of American ideals a fatal contradiction in so-called primary and secondary values in democratic belief. For example, during public events when the national anthem is sung, we insist that certain democratic principles—to which we attribute the highest virtues—be assimilated by all citizens without qualification. But conversely, some Americans will not acknowledge that a segment of the American population is denied full equal opportunities such as social prestige, a relevant education, and economic gains. This seemingly paradoxical situation—the inconsistent habit of thinking and acting—is prevalent in America today.

The American creed, itself, contains conflicting ideals. If almost everyone in the entire country practices a certain inconsistency—say, nationalism and brotherhood of man—then in many ways members of our society almost inevitably acquire incongruent habits as they grow in the American culture.

The late Ralph Linton wrote in a similar vein but stressed the interrelationship of culture and values from an anthropological perspective. He stated that when two societies or cultures are in the process of fusion, the conflict in values is reflected in the personality of the individual.[5]

Moreover, this is the situation we are experiencing; our society is still trying to assimilate and integrate diverse norms from many races, from many eras in history, and from every part of the world. The end our society strives for, and the means for achieving it, places in doubt our ability to unify our democratic society into one social whole.

Value-Culture Influence on Education

Today, Americans are not conscious of their discordant values, their conflicting viewpoints of democratic action, and their beliefs about other ethnic groups which are internalized almost automatically.

In our democratic society we have many social groups, organizations, and institutions where we are exposed to values in numerous ways by different agents of socialization. The school, the community, the peer group, the mass media of communication, to name but a few, are institutions where we can absorb values which negate or bestir those held by our immediate family.[6]

Embedded in these entities can be contradictions and normative problems of the first magnitude of which many youths, as well as adults, do not seem to be aware. That is, many institutions exhort a philosophy of togetherness and exhibit a pretense of wholeness, but none really exists.

Secondly, modern advances in communication have drasti-

124

cally changed our society so that unless we learn to integrate our value systems, reflectively, we will inevitably acquire one that is more complex and more conflicting. By means of the radio, television, newspapers, magazines, and even business correspondence, today, we take on the conceptions of a wide variety of beliefs about the inner-city and its value to our democratic society. We are exposed to the ideas of interest groups like the organizations for, or against, racial integration; organizations opposing low-income houses in the suburbs; the emerging subcultures; the black inner-city community; and new life conditions resulting from technology.

The substantive role of the institutions, if they are to serve the needs of the people as well as strengthen society, should be one built around logical, meaningful action in which social institutions are in harmonious relation; and more important, where there is agreement on fundamentally intellectual and democratic postulates.

The argument at this point is that there is little harmony among American institutions and that there is a marked absence of agreement upon interpreting and teaching democracy which involves fundamental conceptions of the nature of human personality; the relation of individuals to society; the character of human motivation; the content and basis of human rights; the function of government; the meaning of liberty, equality, fraternity; propriety in human affairs; and the ultimate goal of living the "good life" in a democratic society.

One other part to this problem is that we are caught in a transitional era in which conceptions of the old order and race relations are not yet dead and the emerging principles of the new integrated society are not yet developed. The most important reason for this is the ever-increasing rate of scientific and technological change which characterizes our society and has created an "educational gap." On each side of the "educational gap," members in our society perceive the other as being guided by opposing values, with each group insisting that their values are proper and just. Adults fear that young people are lacking in values or have adopted new values that are not wholesome. Conversely, young people insist that adults' value beliefs are misguided and are out of date. Both adults and young people, at times, are accusing each other of being unwilling to adhere

to some moral principles. Both accuse each other of being un
willing to compromise. In other words, the American people
tend to develop two ways of thinking—one a product of the
past, the other the product of actual conditions of modern life

Social change influences other values, including society'
individual and group attitude toward change itself. The
American society has become splintered into special interes
groups; these many segments of society have developed thei
own standards, values, and interpretations of American ideals
It is not surprising, therefore, that the individual may find
himself articulating empty rhetoric on some American ideal
on a high level of valuation, but violating these principles in
actual practice in social and economic relations with others.

In this quandary we are able to empirically acquire a range
or sphere, of what can be known by observing firsthand for
ourselves the plight of people and their material possession
and passions. From this cultural stimulation, these experiences
however small, increase the potential for further change.

Add still another catalyst—modern education—and we find
the individual's value system becoming more and more complex
Education and learning have their effects—maybe good, maybe
bad—but effects they do have. In the case of desegregating
schools, the very fact that a culturally disadvantaged and an
affluent child are integrated into a new learning environment
can have an impact on what each values as democracy. The
point is that we now are brought into contact with a wide
variety of begetting values. In desegregating schools, how does
one teach history, or any social science, when there are white
and black pupils in the classrooms? The real quandary may lie
in the fact that the teacher, himself, is against integration.

We are caught up in a society consisting of vast invisible
connectors and do not see the inconsistencies and contradiction
of our values; we are no longer certain about the meaning of
democracy or about using democratic means for a democratic
end; and we are swept along by forces that we do not under
stand. Our sense of social direction, in short, is atrophied; and,
therefore, we develop a life style of conflicting values, in which
we live, work, play, and learn our ideals.

The number of possible combinations of inconsistent values
within us, as illustrated in various situations, is almost infinite.

The following illustrative examples of possible conflicts will make clear some of the democratic principles, as expressed on the level of generalizations, and how they are qualified by contrasting ideas and conflicting values.

1. We are *all* equal, democracy is based on *equality* we (Americans) believe in freedom, justice, and equality for *all* Americans.

But: Black people must not be permitted in schools with white people. Blacks must stay in their place.

Question: How can we believe in freedom, equality, and justice and at the same time confine black Americans in our society to a designated place?

2. Individualism, independence, and self-reliance are basic ideals that America must preserve and are embedded in the Bill of Rights.

But: If an individual expresses an opinion different from that of the group, chances are he will be ostracized.

Question: How can we believe in individual differences, but discipline people for voicing a different point of view?

What makes it psychologically possible for us to live by contradictory rules in our society? First of all, we achieve a measure of peace of mind by various psychological tricks that are not painful, such as compartmentalizing our lives. That is, we play the different games of life—businessman, family man, religious man, social man, integration man, economic man, political man—by acting first on one set of principles and then on another, according to the game we are playing and avoiding a conscious awareness of our inconsistent behavior. Almost everyone in our society tries to conform reasonably well to so-called moral ideals on Sunday, but practice something else through the week. On Sunday, our churches are usually packed with "God-fearing" people, but on Monday—look out! We wall off our life into compartments with such soundproof materials that in our roles as "Economic Man," or "Domestic Man," we never hear nor recall what was said on Sunday in our role as "Religious Man."

Not only are the contradictions to be found among sets of principles in these different activities, but the more general principles that apply to all compartments are torqued according to the situation. Such democratic principles, for example, as equality and freedom—usually presumed to be universal because they are supposed to apply to everyone in a similar manner—are given one meaning when applied to a certain group or race, and another meaning when applied to a different group. The contrasting interpretations of the democratic principles, compartmentalization of society and personality, can lead to undesirable consequences. For example, it is possible that such a loosely woven, ambiguous, and incongruent set of values can be used to justify discrimination against individuals and even against collections of people on the basis of such things as social status, religion, sex, race, jobs, and equal educational opportunities. Through our inconsistent behavior, we value openly a show of patriotism with one set of principles with no concern for how this outward display mirrors inconsistent inner feelings.

This type of flexible living is viewed as living on different planes at various times, different levels of morality and patriotism. Values on the different planes correspond to different degrees of generality of moral judgment. Some values are made to apply to human beings in general; others, only to upper class, lower class, blacks, women, students or foreigners. Again, some values have general and eternal validity; others are valid only for certain situations. Since the more general and timeless values are considered to be morally higher than the more specific ones, people generally try to present the more specific values as inferences from the more general values.

In the course of actual day-to-day living, a person will be found focusing attention on the valuation of one particular plane of his moral personality—and leaving in the shadow, for the time being, the other plane. Most of the time, the selection of the focus of evaluation by the individual is plainly opportunistic.

Furthermore, in operating daily we may act, depending on the situation, a certain way at one time and a different way at another time simply because the beliefs which dictate the actions do not show themselves in opposition until we are confronted with decision-making. Or we may fail to see inconsistency by assuming that the incongruent actions do follow consistent beliefs but become modified by the variations in this situation. This type of behavior is "situation ethics."

128

We interact with others who also act on contradictory principles. Most often, we merely play our compartmentalized role for which we are programmed and proceed happily until someone points out our inconsistencies. Then to preserve our self-respect, we resort to all kinds of rationalizations and explanations. Thus, as a result of innumerable contradictions in our civilization, we have developed a "general numbness" of moral perception and an insensitivity for inconsistent action. We use every trick possible, though we may not be consciously aware that we do so, in our struggle to keep conflicts off our minds—rationalizations, convenient blind spots of knowledge, instant ignorance and mutilation of our beliefs about social reality.

Because many of us perform most of our activities, including our thinking, by habit and routine, there is little occasion to examine critically the basis of our ideals, especially the interrelations of these ideals as they are confronted in different compartments of living. Unless we are realistically conscious in our effort to bring order, clarity, and consistency into our valuing, our lives will be lived in a society of democratic confusion.

Furthermore, until modern man is fortunate enough to avert the horror of subjective interpretation of democratic principles, he will not become resonant to the problems that plague our inner-city schools and society. It is not fallacious to assert that pervasive and deep conflicts in democratic value have characterized our society. The problem of restoration of integration and cooperation among American beliefs in values and purposes that should direct our conduct is one of the deepest problems in modern life.

Although we learn from conflict, what has been neglected is a national mission with consistent efforts which point up the real void in subjective interpretation of democratic values. In our society, we have reached a point where Americans in large numbers, larger than ever before, should become more actively involved in the preservation of our democracy from irretrievable disaster.

Black and White Conflict in Patriotism

American democratic society, in relation to the rest of the world, is caught in the grip of a profound racial crisis which can be resolved, apart from a revolution, only through education and mutual understanding. Unquestionably, since the days when the civil rights struggle began, the question of loyalty to the American government and our democratic institutions has generated a widespread public concern to the vexing problems of race relations in these United States. Educators, intellectuals, legislators, and literary writers have presented numerous plans and programs to the public for educating Americans in an effort to improve race relations. Havighurst and Neugarten, in describing the condition of our society, see the American scene as one faced with the ever increasing problem of intergroup conflict, a problem that exists in various forms and various degrees of intensity.[8] There are conflicts between economic groups such as management and labor; and between religious groups such as fundamental modernists within denominations; and between different denominations. Some Americans of one skin color are hostile to Americans of another skin color and try to prevent them from moving into their neighborhoods and encroaching on what they consider their territory.

There is an abundance of literature that describes the cause of racial conflicts, the racial unrest sweeping the country, and the abundance of conflicting beliefs and values being propagated by innumerable groups and factions. There is a challenge to authority, and institutions are on trial. Each in its own way is concerned about the loyalty of all Americans; public schools and institutions of higher education have entered a degenerative stage, and many are accused of not educating students to embrace American values. Scholars, students, and community groups alike across the nation are prescribing proposals for action to counteract these charges. Many of these proposals are superficial, and many conflict with one another.[9] The efforts to restore order, clarity, and some degree of consistency in a democracy should logically be contingent on the willingness of Americans to behave as patriotic citizens and not on proposals and programs. Until Americans are able to identify explicitly the basic underlying causes of racial unrest which in many ways can be attributed to value conflicts, it is virtually impossible to appraise the significance and wisdom of further programs to achieve an integrated society.

The problem of racial integration and cooperation between

majority and minority members of society and their belief in democratic values and purposes that should direct their conduct is the deepest problem of contemporary American society. We, today, are in desperate need of a way to adjudicate racial conflict without endangering the very existence of contemporary civilization, as well as any opportunity to advance whatever American values we want to conserve.[10]

As stated earlier, such principles as equality and freedom, usually presumed to be universal because they are supposed to apply to everyone in a similar manner, should be resolved.

Individuals and groups who believe that everything will turn out all right if we can just muddle through for a certain time with a compensatory program, that democracy will somehow prevail no matter what, are implicitly holding to a watered-down version of Hegelianism. The consequences of such racial conflict in America are now uniquely dangerous because of rapid means of communication. A major racial confrontation in one region of the country can reverberate throughout the entire social structure in a matter of minutes.

Even if modern man should be fortunate enough to avert the horror of a race polarization and the less obvious, but no less real, danger of social revolution, there are other compelling forces which force him to examine his values and the intellectual operation by which he comes to know or to have them. For almost every American professes to believe in equal opportunities for all; but, let someone try, through a proposal or program, to obtain integrated education through busing and curriculum reform for desegregating schools, and we can expect to find people rationally bring forth a host of seemingly democratic principles to support a denial of this concept.

Because there exists, continuously, conflict in our interpretation of democracy, what is needed is to emphasize the importance of being consistent with American ideals, because certain paramount democratic principles of social relationships in our society are at issue. Respect for the individual person, respect for law and order as this is hammered out on the anvils, respect for legislation that seeks to equalize opportunities for the disadvantaged in our society—all are essential to social planning in accordance with democratic principles.

A society built on democratic principles, then, should insist that its members exemplify consistency in rhetoric and action toward each other and demonstrate all the tolerance which democratic principles demand if they are to be free of dogma or contradictions.[11] No group or individual should have the inherent right to interpret democracy for others.

Recently, we have been differing over the wrong things; instead of examining the consequences of our action to see what democratic principles we are conflicting over, we rage about the validity of our rights as an individual and the prospectus we propose. Some groups or individuals who believe in the strict interpretation of democratic principles as a way of solving our differences are accused of being authoritarians and undemocratic. Conversely, other groups, or individuals, reverse the picture, saying that those who do not believe in the high-level democratic principles are irresponsible, un-American and are sometimes labeled Communists. We label too freely, therefore, dividing ourselves into camps, each with its own interpretation of democracy and each in its own way accusing the other of being un-American.

Democratic ends demand democratic methods for their realization. The practice of consistency demands that means and ends cannot be separated. To a great extent, to be consistent warrants an understanding of American ideals; and they must be lived. The feeling and attitudes that are fundamental to a democracy must be worked out in everyday activities if they are to become real to the individual.

In conclusion, these analyses constitute a fruitful examination of the problem of value conflicts in democratic principles and some slight contribution toward better resolution. If all Americans undertook consistency in all beliefs and values, in accord with American ideals, instead of isolated paths, it would follow that a considerable number of social and racial problems in public education could be resolved. For, with ideas held in common, there is the possibility of collective action, and a "social foundation" for our society that involves more than the verification of democratic principles—a foundation which entails validation of normative rules and reconsideration of educational decisions and policies as an integral part of all the processes for the reconstruction of beliefs and attitudes. This is possible if each citizen draws his beliefs and values from a common core and consents to accept certain matters of democratic belief and value already formed. A principle of authority, therefore, already exists; and it will be established in the moral fiber of our society.

If we share as our common holdings the values of our society, we may create an enriched life in which all Americans may participate with some degree of consistency and dignity, and we may create future citizens who possess the techniques and the temperament to carry out our democratic life with order, clarity, and consistency that should make the burden of life more tolerable.

A Quest for Community Control

In recent years, the terms of debate and the range of alternate solutions concerning inner-city educational problems have shifted dramatically. "Integration," "decentralization," "compensatory education," "community control"—these and other slogans suggest quite different approaches to educational problems. Complicating the whole matter is a growing belief that the bureaucratization of inner-city schools has made many city systems so ossified, so large and self-protective that they cannot efficiently change to meet new conditions and cannot correct their operation by learning from past mistakes. At the same time, many observers see no viable alternative to present inner-city public school systems and point out that many of them have, in fact, adapted to new conditions. In any case, some redistribution of power among community residents, administrators, teachers, students, and parents seems to be inevitable.

Behind much of the public's repeated outcry over public education in the cities lies the belief of many people that the school systems have failed to be responsive to the needs and feelings of the community they serve. Seeing that, this turmoil over public education is echoed around the country; the question of how these services have failed the people and how they may be made more relevant to the people is upon us.

In almost every area of public education, the need for greater community involvement has been recognized. For

133

example, as stated in Chapter 2, the federally funded program, Titles I, II, and III of the Elementary and Secondary Education Act of 1965, reflect the government's concern for direct participation of the poor in developing community educational programs.

This organization of local community agencies suggests a dissatisfaction with highly centralized city bureaucracies which do not provide the kind of service and responses to local needs. No more than any other city agency has the inner-city public school system escaped this demand for decentralization through increased community control. The demand for community control and the resistance to it have been great. The pressure built up by this development has been manifest in public incidents— a symbolic act by the inner-city black community that wants to have the board of education more representative of its interests and educational needs.

There can be little doubt today that the inner-city black community is aware of the school crisis. This minority group is aware and asking the local educational and political leaders to do something about improving the quality of instruction and education in their schools. Some responses to the educational crisis and the demands of the black community have been for the inner-cities to develop plans for decentralizing the schools, developing school sub-systems and other community-involvement programs. At the same time, the community people have been moving toward another plan closer to what might be called "community control of the schools."

The *Education News* summarized the present decentralization debate this way: "In education, decentralization has become a red-flag word. Like neighborhood school, freedom of choice, federal control and national testing, the word evokes more emotion than definition. It means different things to different people—more power for the Black-separatist militant, less power for the entrenched White school board, headaches for the school superintendent who perhaps used to think racial integration was the goal of all but status quo whites."[12]

The criticism of the inner-city public schools exerted by the black community is that public education is not directed toward the best interest of the community served, particularly the inner-city black tenement. Harold R. Isaacs states: "The crisis

134

now wide open in American life is a concatenation of long-unsolved problems of poverty, the cities and race, each set formidable enough in itself but woven all together now in a single massive tangle of issues, demands and circumstances. Of the three, the most critical is clearly race. To see that this is so, one has only to imagine what our present national condition and state of mind would be if our poor, especially in our city slums, were not so largely Black. Without the problem of race, we would be facing demands of the kind this society has shown itself matchlessly able to confront and solve. It is the demand that we finally resolve the place of the Black man in the American society that makes this the potentially mortal climax of an issue that has been with us since the founding of the Republic."[13]

Since racial crisis permeates inner-city public education institutions, it is unreasonable to expect that much progress will be made merely by appealing to the majority in the interests of equality for the minority.

To firmly establish this point, it is only necessary to talk for a few moments with anyone who has spent much time working to achieve equal educational opportunities through the existing political structure.

Even the most avid advocate of decentralized educational control finds it difficult to explain how public education would be better if every community adhered to the dictates of the dominant culture. Consider, for example, the recent confession of Kenneth A. McDonald, chairman of the Washington State Board Against Discrimination: "I find, as a white man, that after 10 years of this I've about had it. I can't talk to whites any more. I'm sick to death of exhorting and pleading with these prejudiced whites. I'm sick of being an entertainer. I'm sick of going down on bended knees to school boards, city councils, legislatures, group meetings. I'm sick of it because they have not and are not going to pay any attention."[14]

If the black community cannot hope to gain meaningful educational programs relevant to their needs by appealing to the good will and sympathy of the white majority, the attainment of this goal depends on their gaining and exercising much more control of their community.

Decentralization and greater community control of the

135

school will come in spite of the many problems connected with the concept. It will and must come on the demands of inner-city people to change the environment in which they now live and the inadequate schools their children attend. Such an environmental change will bring the institution of the school along because it is one agency that cannot operate in a vacuum.

This argument seems very clear and straightforward, yet there is something very disconcerting about it. We have already indicated that inner-city public education is now directed by school boards who embrace the life-style and culture of the dominant culture. This is clearly unfortunate, but is the situation as it exists—the dominant culture controlling inner-city education.

Inner-city public education, believe it or not, is an institution in American culture, and like all institutions, it should have a reciprocal agreement with the culture as a whole, in that, to a degree, education determines the educational system. The norms which are visible in the dominant culture simply reflect patterns of norms present in the larger society, while inner-city educational norms are neither incompatible with nor complement those which dominate American society. The purpose and process of education should not, if it is to meet needs, be divorced from the culture it is to serve; for education is an integral part of the culture. Furthermore, the process of education should not be a single-minded transmission of knowledge, for "when we talk about culture, we touch upon the values we live by, the definitions of the desirable and the right that gives meaning to human existence."[15]

There is no longer a single purpose or process of public education. Today, each community seeks its own means to a democratic end. The black community should be no exception. What is in the best educational interest of the dominant culture? What is in the best educational interest of the democratic society? Who should have the right and the responsibility to define this interest? The fallacy in this type of thought should be clear.

One of the major areas in inner-city educational debate today concerns whether the school's function should be to reflect black culture as it is, or to reconstruct it. Therefore, it is necessary to become committed on the question as stated, for

136

this dichotomy is real. It seems reasonable and appropriate to say that, up until recently, inner-city public education has perpetuated those aspects of American society which those involved in the educational enterprise feel are worthwhile and has not perpetuated those things which are disliked by those responsible for the educational system.

One major difficulty here is that the responsibility for inner-city public education is controlled by professional educators and the elected lay members of school boards who have the legally defined responsibility for the inner-city schools. Many ideas which might be seen as a step forward in the inner-city by the school board and professional educators may be seen as evil by the community served. Nevertheless, it seems clear that by selecting certain things to be taught and rejecting other things, the inner-city school, under this control, does, in actuality, reflect and alter the culture. The question here is: What are the criteria used for this selection? The first step in answering this question is to uncover some of the major norms which exist in inner-city schools.

There is little reason for believing that the inner-city school boards and professional educators can arrest the tendency toward community control by themselves. It is also unlikely that the black community in American culture which exercises educative influences will, in the near future, be willing to correlate its educative efforts with those of the school board and professional educators. I have already indicated that the educative influence of the dominant culture is incompatible with the inner-city school; and there is no reason to assume that the incompatibility will cease, as long as black culture is not an integral part of institutions of learning.

Given this situation, there are few easy answers or recipes which will indicate clearly what the school board and the black community can do about it. However, it seems reasonable to assume that a culture, if it is to survive, must have clear-cut goals which are a direct manifestation of inherited values. An inner-city educational system also must have a set of goals which reflect important values. This is a paradox, if education is supposed to reflect the culture. Many educators have suggested that a concept of public education for the inner-city can find a source of stability in performance contracting. This argument for control of education asserts that the growing, evolving "disadvantaged child" be made the center of the educational enterprise, through performance contracting. This is not the wish of the teacher. This concept of inner-city education contains an assertion which is at present unwarranted—that the process of adaptation with long-range goals and special types of transactions logically contingent to desirable learning outcomes toward which the individual can strive result in increased stability and security for the individual. But extra materials, while necessary, are not sufficient to compensate and make a radical difference in the education of blacks.

There is, therefore, no justification in seeking for "disadvantaged students" contracted education where business firms take over teaching students unable to attain normal grade levels. What are teachers paid to do? Is it possible that teachers do not get the control over course matter that can be written into contracts? Certainly, there are others in our society which, if given a chance, can help the inner-city pupil acquire a system of priorities which will provide him with a sense of direction and stability—an inner-city, community-controlled school system. Naturally, this system should grow and change as the individuals develop. It should not remain unchanged, but be given a chance to serve a vital function of putting inner-city black kids on an academic track that runs into the open society. It should, however, provide them with some personally valid criteria for the acceptance of some changes and the rejection of others. The inner-city child, like most children, is one who accepts the folkways and mores around him without questioning the assumptions or consequences of what they observe. We cannot (and should not) provide inner-city pupils with the same direction and educational values which traditionally have been provided to previous black generations. We should provide them with explainers through community control of their schools, which will enable them to see into the educational values that pervade every aspect of their community and environment.

Community control is as practical for the inner-city public schools as it is fundamentally for people anywhere. We may remind ourselves that in a middle-class community, the parents and community leaders exercise a great deal of informal control over their local schools. Through parents' associations and through easy access to the administrators, they can produce change.

Though the bitter struggle for community control of the Ocean Hill-Brownsville schools in New York City and the controversy surrounding this experiment has aroused great fears in the headline-reading public, less publicized experiments are demonstrating that the inner-city community can indeed improve its lot by handling the entire job of planning, policy-making, and managing a program. Even the brief history of the subsystem says with some clarity that community control is practical, can work, and is absolutely necessary to the establishment of viable schools. Individual teachers and administrators must have the autonomy to act as adult professionals plus the additional money to make change possible. It is equally clear that there must be a great deal more involvement of parents and community people, perhaps not to the extent of total control, but at least to the point where they feel they have a real voice in what happens to their children and some honest responsibility. The most important thing of all, however, is the simple knowledge that it is possible to operate first-rate schools in the middle of the black community.

Political Influence

One indication of the difficulties involved in working out solutions to the inner-city racial crisis has been registered in the behavior of aerospace officials who several years ago often talked about applying the skills, concepts, and talents of personnel in that industry to solve the problems of our cities. After a closer look at the inner-city setting, however, many of these officials ceased proclaiming that the industry should move to apply its vaunted "systems analysis" approach to racial and related problems in the cities, and some publicly admitted that the totality of problems created by urbanization—racism—individualism in the United States is likely to prove much more complex and resistant to solution than the simpler task of going to the moon.

Nevertheless, today, any effort to identify the major issues around which controversy is now swirling within the black community in attaining equality, must start by recognizing that the ghetto is more than simply an inner-city low-income neighborhood whose citizens tend to be economically destitute.

To what extent is it realistic to expect that strengthening "parallel" or separate institutions without simultaneously striking at the root problems of segregation and exclusion from the wider society can really bring about major improvements in the black community? Arguments on this issue appear most frequently in debates over how to respond to the educational, social, and political needs and other basically economic manifestations of the racial inner-city crisis.

On the one side, the argument is made that government as well as business leaders should concentrate on stimulating economic growth in enterprises owned and operated by ghetto residents, on providing jobs and monetary assistance for the poor and needy, and on underwriting the establishment of community corporations to redevelop the ghetto.

It is undeniable that economics and politics cannot be separated in any strict way. It is also a safe presumption that business leaders and groups not only have more pervasive influence in the general community but also have far greater access to the "tension points" of the decision-making process.[16] This is not to say, however, that these groups and individuals exercise such power and influence so continuously that there are no opportunities for others to participate. In our large inner-city areas, social change takes many forms and is a response to a variety of different pressures. Local boards of supervisors, for example, are sensitive not only to the ballot box but also to a wide range of influence, persuasion, bargaining, and power in which a multitude of private groups and organizations play a decisive part from one day to the next.[17] It is in this area that a disproportionate amount of power may be wielded by some groups and individuals rather than by others. To talk of community decision-making, therefore, is to recognize that some of the most crucial "public" decisions are neither public nor private.

If one takes such a pressing problem as the inner-city school system, it is clear that the shape and direction of a community's educational program is not simply the result of an electoral choice or even of a public administrative decision. It is also the result of intricate relations between public officials, the board of education, minority racial organizations, teachers' groups, neighborhood groups, and many others.[18]

The politics involved in the inner-city school along with their corollary social and economic repercussions become clearer if we consider that our inner-city difficulties require a more intensified, coordinated attack than is embodied in our present policies and politics. For example, we will never be able to utilize the technology of mass construction in housing if the field continues to be dominated by scores of small builders, each one responsible for a few units a year. Erecting thousands of housing units within a relatively compact area leads to chaos when construction is not integrated with industry, education, transportation, health services, and other life-support systems.

Furthermore, the degree to which politics and economics are interrelated with an obviously onerous effect on the inner-city school can be seen in the logic dictating private school aid. In the past two years, for example, at least six states have passed laws providing substantial general aid to private schools, and similar bills are pending in half a dozen other states. The New York State Commission on the Quality, Cost and Financing of Elementary and Secondary Education, better known as the Fleischmann Commission, in examining ways to support financially public and non-public schools in New York stated: "Shared time and dual enrollment of pupils in both public and non-public schools seem permissable under the Federal and State Constitution, and we recommend that the right of a local district to experiment with such plans be clarified by legislation if necessary."[19]

This new concern by state legislatures for non-public education is a response to a well-organized Catholic lobby and to simple arithmetic: by supporting in part the education of children in non-public schools, nine-tenths of which are supported by the Roman Catholic Church, they can avoid supporting in full the education of the same children in public schools. As it stands the Supreme Court has already reviewed two lower-court decisions on comprehensive state aid to non-public schools. Both of the decisions have been tested for their constitutionality on First Amendment grounds because they

141

provide for the purchase by the state of "secular" educational services for children in private schools.

It is not hard to see why many of the people opposed to easing the separation of church and state have focused so closely on the First Amendment issue and its underlying principle of insulating the political process from religious factionalism. It is, after all, the fact that this insulation has worn thin that has made the statutes possible. Preserving the "wall" between church and state is indeed a basic problem. But purchase-of-secular-services agreements have educational consequences that are perhaps even more important.

At this point, one cannot help wondering that, ideally, these laws might prove a powerful force for equalization of educational opportunity, for stimulation of wide experimentation in both public and non-public schools, and for development of new schools that will provide greater diversity in education, particularly to that of the inner-city schools.

Moreover, to fully understand the impact of politico-economic decisions on education, and that of the urban area in particular, one must consider the competitive aspect of state and local taxation. In New York City, there is a concentration of high incomes unequaled anywhere in the country. Nearly 20 percent of all internal revenue is collected in New York State. Thus it would appear that the state of New York, which levies an income tax, could easily have the very best schools in the nation. The difficulty is, however, that many high-income persons and corporations would move if tax rates were raised substantially. This seems to be the reason why it is often a fallacy to criticize states and communities for not raising taxes; if they did so, they would lose people and business to areas less concerned about education. The need for, and justice of, federal taxation for education would thus remain even if there were substantial equality in wealth and revenues among all states and school districts. The fact that a federal tax cannot be evaded at the expense of children in a particular school district is one of the most compelling reasons why we must move toward an educational system financed by the federal government.

The state of New York's big city school boards—New York City, Buffalo, Syracuse, Rochester, and Yonkers—agreed that their school systems have taken a step backward and that the only long-range answer for them is full state and federal funding of the public school system. But, while they were able to agree on their long-range goals, the delegates could not reach some agreement on what type of aid to seek from the state and federal government. However, the envisioned takeover of the full cost of education by the state is not expected for at least several years. Nevertheless, the governor of New York's Fleischmann Commission has recommended full state funding, which inflames the crisis in public education.

The New York State School Boards Association, which smaller rural and suburban districts control, opposes full state funding because they fear loss of local control.

The city of Rochester delegates and the State Education Department delegates disagree with members of other cities, who want to continue to seek federal aid that must be spent for special programs. For example it is argued that such categorical aid is destroying school systems, for cities are required to spend the aid only on the disadvantaged and only in addition to programs offered for all school districts' students. It is suggested that the cities stop being willing to accept "categorical aid" and work for general aid, which can be spent indiscriminately.[20]

Many black as well as white leaders, however, do not agree that economic strategies in themselves are nearly enough to overcome the problems associated with ghettoization. On the one hand are critics such as Helen Safa who believe that black Americans must build up separate cultural institutions and a strong black identity if they are to function effectively in a modern society: "The ethnic solidarity for Negroes must be based primarily on sentiments which are pro-Negro rather than anti-white. The Negro needs to develop a sense of racial pride and identity and to reject the inferior status imposed upon him by white society. . . . Separatism goes far beyond the aims of the integrationists, who aimed primarily at the assimilation of the American Negro by raising his socioeconomic status in the larger society. Separatism attempts to establish for the Negro a sense of racial pride and identity which has long been denied him in American society."[21]

On the contrary, critics such as Bayard Rustin believe that

separate economic development, if pushed too far, is a chimeri-
cal fantasy because it does nothing to reduce or eliminate the
isolation of the segregated from the larger society: "Separatism
is valid neither from a psychological nor a political point of
view. Dr. Kenneth Clark has recently argued that 'There is
absolutely no evidence to support the contention that the
inherent damage to human beings of primitive exclusion on
the basis of race is any less damaging when demanded or
enforced by the previous victims than when imposed by the
dominant group.' . . . Even if separatism were psychologically
sensible—which it is not—it does not make political sense."[22]

The central difference of opinion here is *not* concerning
whether black Americans should deny the existence and values
of black culture or should oppose assimilation into an
amorphous national culture which leaves an individual with no
secure sense of his heritage or identity. It is not illogical to
argue that stress should be placed on the study of black history
and culture or that black Americans should hold to distinctive
black customs and still conclude that strengthening economic
and/or cultural institutions in the ghetto is not in itself likely
to be a sufficient route to the attainment of quality education.

Nor does the disagreement center on whether black-con-
trolled community-development and employment programs are
important, indeed indispensable components in any comprehensive program which might stand a chance to improve the
lives of people in the ghetto. It is not necessary to believe that
self-determination within the ghetto will cure all or most of the
evils attendant upon ghettoization in order to agree that community control of schools can make public education more
responsive and hence more effective in serving the needs of
black people.

Disagreements involving the adequacy of primarily educational programs in combatting poverty, the feasibility of
economic self-sufficiency in the ghetto, the desirability of cultural nationalism, programs for stimulating the development
of black identity and black pride, and related matters have
been and are being widely discussed in a variety of sources.
Although the points of view expressed on these topics almost
always are strikingly unaccompanied by practical ways to alleviate the social crises in public education prognosis in regard to

the course and termination of a disease which might help one choose among them, persuasive political, social, and/or historical arguments often are used to great advantage on each side of each disagreement.[23]

In conclusion, public education, and particularly public inner-city education, has a referent in the quality of education as well as in its financial basis. The qualitative referent is an education in which the search for truth is carried on regardless of what empires topple, interests collapse, or heads roll. Without this, inner-city public education is a delusion, as dangerous as the notion that mere government ownership of the means of production will automatically result in their operation for the public welfare instead of for private interests. The socialization of a service at any level of government is no automatic guarantee that the service will be performed in the inner-city black community's interest. In all probability, there will not be a real attack on the racial crisis and despair that the inner-city schools reflect so long as no effort is made to integrate the "categorical aid" and "general aid" from state and federal government, influences that affect the inner-city school socially as well as economically.

It is important to note that there are some distinct differences between decentralization of schools and community control, especially related to the concept of "decision-making and shared power." Decentralization plans have mostly addressed themselves to dividing a large city system into smaller districts or subsystems. The residents of these local districts would then have some input through the principle of community involvement. Community control of the schools moves closer to a "shared-power concept" by giving direct decision-making authority to the community people. According to Dorothy Jones, community control requires not only a change in the matter of who makes the decisions at the top but also a complete change in the relationships of professional with professional and professional with community. Community-control is defined as the power to make and enforce the following decisions:

(a) Expenditures of funds—local, state and federal.
(b) Hiring and firing of all staff—including training and re-programming.

145

(c) Site selection and naming of schools.

(d) Design and construction of schools—awarding and supervising of contracts.

(e) Purchasing power—for books, supplies, equipment, food services, etc.

(f) Setting up of educational policy and programs.

(g) Merit pay to staff—increments and salary based on effective performance alone.[24]

The implications of this power thrust tends to wedge a new type of interaction between the board of education and the black community. Such stated goals imply that the black ghettos are committed to control their own community schools and have moved toward outlining their areas of responsibility.

If public education in the inner-city accepts the challenge of these changing times in school organization, it will be necessary to improve the disintegrating school—black community relationship we presently have in the inner-cities. This means for the educator that we must acknowledge the need for a new relationship with the black community in shaping educational policy. It also suggests developing new programs to assist the community people to understand what the problems are in making educational decisions that affect the lives of children and cost millions of dollars. What it means, however, is that school boards must realize the functional role the people in the black community can play in developing meaningful, realistic, educational programs, when their know-how is blended with professional education.

The inner-city educational programs must pursue excellence without compromise. For too long, inner-city children have tolerated a disadvantaged teacher and a disadvantaged curriculum. We cannot continue to make administrative placements and design programs that have an unexplainable "commitment to educational retardation" of disadvantaged children.

Finally, decentralization and/or community-controlled schools should not develop programs that will foster segregation. Indeed, there is nothing inherent in either of the reorganization plans that must create additional ghettoization and segregation in education. The history of our country has spoken on what segregated environments do to the hearts and

146

minds of black and white youngsters. The task of the professional educator is to see that our plans have the ingredients
that will help all racial groups to build cultural identity, racial
pride, and to provide an opportunity for each to do his own
thing.

If educators are serious and the community people will
do their part, perhaps the task of improving our inner-city
schools can be accomplished.

CHAPTER 5

THE INFLUENCE OF
SOCIAL AND AFRO-AMERICAN
STUDIES

MOST teachers teaching in inner-city schools engaged in modern educational programs maintain that older traditional ways of teaching must be supplanted by learning resulting from careful research in education in other disciplines—the interdisciplinary approach. It is known, too, that this transition is difficult. However, the complexity of urban civilization and the diversity of persons and situations with which he must deal demands of the urban teacher an especially rich background in both liberal arts and in professional studies.

He must have an adequate background in the behavioral sciences in order to understand the children he will teach. To be effective, a teacher in an underprivileged area needs an understanding of sociology, anthropology, and psychology to have some insight into the values and the goals of children and families from these areas. For too long, educators have attempted to fit the underprivileged into the curriculum instead of fitting the curriculum to the underprivileged.

The task of teaching in inner-city schools is truly formidable. This is well known to everyone who has studied the city schools by observing them and reading the professional literature. The results of hundreds of serious studies of the educational problems of black Americans have made unmistakably clear the fundamental inaccuracy of any conception of education which does not include the need for individual and group differentiation. The tasks which teachers cannot escape as easily as their critics are those of matching learning experience to the needs and abilities of the pupils. This is the function of schooling which has been implied most frequently in the recent series of attacks upon the schools. However, at the present time, the only situation in which sole attention is given to minorities is through specialized compensatory education programs.

Multi-purpose mass education is not the invention of educators. Their role has been chiefly that of guiding its development in response to public demands for more and more variety in the school curriculum. By implication, at least, the public has rejected the idea of education that includes adding to the curriculum Afro-American studies. Afro-American studies were and still are studies regarded as appropriate for black students only, an opinion to which a good number of educators would take some exception.

In contemporary American education, it is necessary for teachers to continue to plan subject materials to serve differences in individual interest and needs. Indeed, the organization of the multi-purpose curriculum that includes Afro-American studies, has barely passed through the earliest stages of its development. Much is still to be learned, and much remains to be done, about the dual problems of arranging sufficient variety and flexibility to accommodate the complete range of minorities' educational interests and needs. Neither the subject matter nor the training of teachers for inner-city schools are as yet adequate to satisfy the known interests and needs of black pupils. There is a need for such program development within existing disciplines.

When programs are planned for teachers who work with inner-city children, emphasis should be on giving teachers new attitudes, new methods, and new subject content. True, teachers, particularly those who lack experience teaching children who fall short of the middle-class societal standard, need to improve their understanding of black inner-city children and their problems, but they need far more. A program to increase teacher competency must be geared to training in subject matter relevant to their pupils (oftentimes new subject matter) and to appropriate methods of teaching. Further, the program must improve teachers' feelings, values, and beliefs about themselves

149

and their relationships and responsibilities to the disadvantaged. Teachers of the disadvantaged must be retrained in both attitude and methods in an on-the-job situation in the classroom in which they are working with children, not in some university classroom listening to a professor lecture on poverty.

In an effort to discover or illustrate various facets of curriculum change and the effect these variances have on the learning process, numerous innovations and/or demonstrations, which will be described later, are suggested. These programs have significance for the total educational program of the inner-city. In effect, there has been a breakdown in implementing what is known about learning and the learner. Curriculum change that develops programs utilizing and encompassing the strengths of the local community is the humanistic approach to urban problems. As the program is described, one will notice that those facets proving most effective in established projects and programs will be used as a focal point for demonstration and innovation.

Advocating the educational philosophy that curriculum consists of experiences in which the evolutionary quality of our world is represented through the curriculum—experiences external as well as internal to the confines of the classroom—curriculum then becomes the intermediary and liaison agent between reality and the learner.

The curriculum in inner-city schools should emphasize what consumer habits might get a buyer a little more for his money; explain clearly what the pattern of local social services is, and how one takes valid advantage of those services.

Within the framework of this definition of curriculum, in many of these programs there are components reaching beyond the confines of the university. An examination of authoritative resources lends strong support to the inclusion of the development of a university-public school partnership in realizing the objectives of education.

The profound changes in the institutional life of our democratic society and the ferment in the economic and social life led blacks to begin to think harder and harder about education. The actual conditions under which blacks lived and the changes they worked and fought through the civil rights movement prompted them to look more critically at the kind of education they saw about them and to visualize an education that would be more appropriate to the times. New outlooks on life and the black community caused some to bring their ideas to bear upon educational goals, content, and practice. Traditional educational outlooks were reflected and asserted in traditional conceptions of education; whereas the poor, who saw no value in the traditional concept, began to argue for a newer and more relevant concept of education.

Moreover, the primary responsibility and the shape of inner-city education across the nation has largely been the function of institutionalized boards of education leavened by the dominant beliefs and ideas of the middle-class whites who control the educative process. Chapter 3 described some of the main cultural patterns and institutions that provided the setting in which education for black Americans operated. These gave character to the organization of communities and the framework of education for the inner-city. Before the heart of the aims, curriculum and methods of inner-city education can be understood adequately, however, the texture and context of the prevailing ideas and motivations must be briefly sketched. This chapter seeks to describe some of the most important current approaches through the subject matter of relating to inner-city culture and pupils.

Among the most prominent topics in education today are the special programs for the education of the disadvantaged students. Whether such programs will be judged in the future to have been effective and efficient cannot be determined at this time. But whatever the final evaluation, it is reasonable to assume that programs with emphasis on social studies will be cited among the most involved courses in these programs.

The importance of social studies in the education of the inner-city black student rests upon a number of points, some of which have already been discussed at length in educational literature. These points amount to the recognition that the content of social studies classes includes the social and economic skills necessary for participation in the total society. Also, social studies as a field of study is perhaps broader and includes a greater number of subjects than any other single academic field.

Furthermore, the field of Afro-American studies is broadly conceived as a cross-disciplinary area focusing on the experience of people of African descent in the United States. African-American studies is related to the major disciplines of social and behavioral science and humanities. Therefore, Afro-American studies, being broad in base and multi-disciplinary, necessarily identifies with the division called social studies. Moreover, Afro-American studies (black studies) is merely social studies from a black perspective.[1] Because of these similarities and interrelations, it is possible that the social tools of social analysis, focusing on the contemporary situation of the black community, can be found in social studies.

Social studies is not just a required skill subject; it is one of the content areas in which the deliberate teaching of values is both inherent and inescapable. This is particularly true for such subjects as sociology, civics, and all social studies courses dealing with citizenship. Whether the word *value* is used with reference to either aesthetic standards or to social standards, the social studies teacher deals with values in his teaching. In fact, the very selection of the materials and topics for study is done on the basis of values; and, subsequently, the teaching of the selected materials and topics is influenced by the values of the teacher, his students, or the community.

A rationale for this study can be found in the attack on persistent ignorance, poverty, and disease, first undertaken by the United States outside its own borders. For example, it was only after the Peace Corps had been successfully established (1961) and implemented in many of the more remote parts of the world that the Great Society (1964) was formally proposed and large sums of federal money were made available to attack the same problems at home. The reasons for this sequence of actions are by no means entirely clear, but one possible explanation is that it may be easier to distinguish and acknowledge the presence of disquieting circumstances and conditions in an alien society than it is to do so in one's own. In other words, they are seen more broadly and deeply than are the peoples with whom the observer's eyes are more familiar.

The notion that social studies might be able to make a contribution to the black community and black students emerged as soon as the basic educational problem of these students was recognized as one of cultural differences rather than of innate nationality or racial traits.

Furthermore, the community style of life of the black ghetto student often poses major problems for the teacher who comes from another culture. The teacher's lack of experience or training makes it difficult for him to serve as any academic agent in trying to relate meaningfully to the inner-city student. From one point of view, it is the teacher who is in a culturally disadvantaged position because his style of life is different from the community to which he is trying to relate.

The primary purpose of indicating a relationship between culture of the community and social studies teaching is to make teacher and pupils alert to the role that the community plays in teaching and in learning. In short, pointing out relationships between the principles and methods of social studies and the teaching of social studies to culturally disadvantaged students aims to build or strengthen *cultural awareness* in the teacher. Cultural awareness includes not only a sensitivity to the influence of the students' cultures on their classroom attitudes, behaviors, and performances, but also, a sensitivity to the influence of the teacher's culture on his classroom attitude, behavior, and performance.

The educational process is defined and viewed in many ways. For example, one can view education as a process designed to preserve or transmit a culture as nearly intact as possible; to renew or revise an established culture; to replace an established culture by introducing a new one. Actually, because a culture is so complex and because some of its elements are constantly in a state of flux, none of these three views of education can be regarded as a totally pure nor completely successful process. Nevertheless, one of these three views generally predominates in the educational goals of each society.

Social scientists agree that the core values of a society must be the core goals of its educational system. Otherwise, the young members of the society will not internalize the norms of the culture, i.e., the cultural goals, the motivations to secure and express the goals, and the ways of attaining them. If the cultural norms are not internalized, the social orders cannot be maintained, and the culture also disintegrates.

Therefore, whichever view of the educational process is favored by a society, the purpose is to produce change in the individuals. Ordinarily, it is the young who are most often and most steadily exposed to education. Social scientists, along with child psychologists, regard the early training of a child as the start of his education; this early training is generally called *socialization* and includes not only the socially approved behaviors dealing with the child's own bodily needs and functions but also the appropriate behaviors for dealing with other members of the society. In this latter area, as the child begins to learn his culture through the socialization process, he is really beginning to learn a system that includes a complex set of contracts for regulating interactions between people who have motivations and thought patterns that are both like and unlike his own. Only as the interacting members of a society know and abide by this "set of contracts" can any society function as a unit. Thus, the cultural norms provide the means by which individuals may both retain their own individuality and interact effectively with other individuals in their society.

Education, however, also includes the more specific preparations for participation in the adult life of a society. In this sense, too, education can be viewed in different ways. In primitive societies, education may be a relatively informal process in which the young learn how to hunt or fish or grow food simply by watching, imitating, and assisting their elders. In contrast, modern industrial society assigns the task to cadres of licensed professional educators who are to perform their duties in specially provided locations at prescribed times. In both of these cases, however, the young who undergo the experience of education are expected to change by acquiring certain knowledges and skills that the society regards as important, i.e., which reflect social goals. To the extent the young learner gains knowledge and masters those skills, he is accepted by the society and permitted to participate more fully in its life as he approaches adulthood.

Therefore, education with its accompanying changes is sometimes spoken of as a kind of growth or maturation process. However, like physical growth which is influenced by ecological factors, educational growth is influenced by the social ecology in which it occurs. Education is growth, but it is directed growth along the lines intended by the society. Further, since education is growth, emphasis will be placed on black studies and social studies as means of change to direct the growth of inner-city pupils. However, the general problem is the *social distance* between the white teacher and the black community. But the question remains, Can social studies or black studies most effectively serve as an agent of change for black students?

Fundamental to the work of any successful change in a human being is respect for his culture, and especially for the culture in which the student is reared. Clyde Kluckhohn, in "The Student of Values," holds that *values,* like *needs,* are universal and that they lie at the very heart of all cultures. He makes the point, however, that whereas the same basic values are identifiable in all societies, they are differently weighted in the societies. Broadly speaking, he says that any given value is "a selective orientation toward experience, implying deep commitment or repudiation, which influences the ordering of 'choices' between possible alternatives in action. These orientations may be cognitive and expressed verbally or merely inferable from recurrent trends in behavior."[2]

He also states that values restrain or channel impulses in terms of what a group has defined as wider or more enduring goals. Values are "images formulating positive or negative action commitments, a set of hierarchically ordered prescriptions and proscriptions."[3] Among the most important characteristics of values are the following:

(1) They assume distinctive forms in different cultures;

(2) They have a tenacious tendency to persist through time;

(3) They are not merely random outcomes of conflicting human desires.[4]

Since the process of education ordinarily includes the knowledge that cultures, and the values upon which they are based vary among groups of people, it would seem that an understanding of and the need to relate to the inner-city pupils and their culture is warranted. Daniel A. Prescott in his 1958 Horace Mann Lecture discusses the fact that the American society is one of plural cultures.[5] He notes that when each child enters school at the age of five or six, he has already internalized the concepts, attitudes, and behavior patterns of his own family and neighborhood. Therefore, in an elementary classroom, many culturally different patterns may be represented, and by the time students reach high school, the likelihood of diversity is even greater. Furthermore, by adolescence, students have probably begun to question the values of the various societies in which they were reared, as well as the values that the school has promoted as desirable.

The pluralistic nature of student backgrounds possible in a single social studies class is made quite clear by Prescott's delineation of six major, culturally different sets of learnings that students have when they enter school. He lists the following major sets of differences that the child has already basically learned when he enters school: (1) those which concern behavior appropriate to his own sex; (2) those which reflect his immediate environment, whether urban or rural; (3) those which are regional in their influence, whether the region is natural, political, historical, or geographical; (4) those which have ethnic or national origins, whether such origins lie in his own family or his neighbors; (5) those which spring primarily from the social class of which the family is a part; and (6) the caste category in which his biological inheritance places him.[6]

Prescott's emphasis on cultural background differences is presented here because it is one of the important psychological factors that influence what a person learns. Prescott's statement is of great significance to any teacher. He says: "Learning is far more than stimulating a child by stating a truth in his presence. Learning depends upon its having the kind of significance for him, the inner meaning, that will make it worth remembering."[7] In other words, what a student learns is related to what he has already internalized, to his background experiences, and to the value system by which he has learned to live.

Therefore, when an inner-city teacher undertakes the concomitant role of educator, he needs to consider thoroughly the following elements of the situation: (1) he must determine what cultural change he is trying to induce, whether all elements in the change process have equal priority, and, most importantly, why the cultural change program is being undertaken; (2) he must take into account his own attitudes and beliefs about the change, as they are determined by his personal beliefs about the change, as they are determined by his personal experience, his social and cultural background, and his professional experiences and qualifications; (3) he must ascertain, as far as possible, for each of his students, the personal experiences, the social and cultural background, and the educational experiences and qualifications that may influence their participation in the change being undertaken; (4) he must, on the basis of the above factors, define what constitutes each student's cultural disadvantage in a social studies class and determine the extent of the defined disadvantage both in terms of the dominant society and of the individual student as a member of a subculture; (5) he must always keep in mind that as a social studies teacher, and therefore probably as a member of the American middle-class, he and his students most likely regard what occurs in a social science class from quite different cultural perspectives. That is, ethnocentricity is ever present on both sides of the desk, and it assumes many forms in the classroom of a pluralistic society.

For the social studies teacher to meet all of the above requirements completely can require the expenditure of a great deal of time and energy. However, if the interactions in a "culturally homogeneous" classroom are complex (and few teachers would dispute this assumption), it must be emphasized that the social interactions in a culturally heterogeneous classroom are infinitely more complex. Failure to be aware of any one or any combination of the complexities can seriously limit the social studies teacher's proper function.

Felix M. Keesing, in listing what he calls "some of the important general propositions" of applied anthropology, includes ones that are particularly relevant to the social studies teacher's role as an agent of change.[8] In reading Kessing's principles, the teacher is urged to keep in mind what has been said earlier in this study about his own inclination toward *ethnocentricity*, and the fact that he, too, operates on the basis of a value system quite likely to be different from that of his culturally different students. This point cannot be stressed too often, because unless it is constantly borne in mind, the teacher may do both himself and his students an injustice by attributing frustrations and failures to the wrong causes. Consequently, little is likely to be done to correct or compensate for the real causes, and the frustrations will probably be compounded, to the dissatisfaction of all concerned.

The White Educator in the Ghetto

It has been a number of years since "educators" first showed a comprehensive concern for disadvantaged (i.e., non-white) youth in the inner-city classroom. In 1961, Conant wrote an interesting and controversial book entitled *Slum and Suburbs,* followed in 1962 by *The Culturally Deprived Child,* which was followed in turn in 1963 by a collection of essays entitled *Education in Deprived Areas;* these three books began the "movement of educators" to observe, study, analyze, and dissect their "newly discovered" non-white minority-group pupils in the inner-city setting. This "victim analysis," as one educator aptly describes the research by teachers of their non-white students, has produced a mass of data to date on the "victim" but little on the victimizers or the social relationship between teachers and pupil. For example, in the 1960s many labels were applied to the inner-city pupil resulting from research studies, projects, programs, such as culturally deprived, culturally disadvantaged, culturally different, and educationally disadvantaged. Each of the labels emphasized a slightly different facet of the problems confronting educators.

I suppose it is not strange that white teachers have been teaching in the black, Puerto Rican, and Mexican-American ghetto for the past twenty years or more, yet have not really established a true rapport with most of their students, let alone the adult in institutions of a particular community. It is as if the white teacher does not wish to recognize the difference between his non-white pupils—such as the social and racial intellectual distinctions and his own social, urban, and racial background.

Even today with all the manifest concerns for minority youth and the type of education they should receive, many white classroom teachers in inner-city elementary and secondary schools from New York, Chicago, and Los Angeles really do not know or hesitate to admit that they did or now do discriminate against their non-white pupils.

This is mainly because most white teachers go into the ghetto with little conception of what to expect. True, many teachers take a sociology or anthropology course in minority-people race relations, but this is like studying an automobile engine by book without actually working on the "real thing." There is a common misconception among those who prepare teachers for the "ghetto experience" that a field-experience course where one visits the ghetto, like one visits the local zoo, with a healthy supplement of readings about black culture, history, etc., will prepare the teacher for the task of dealing with pupils who live in a different subculture or more precisely one of a different caste.

The type of training now going on throughout the inner-city areas of our society is geared to the white administrators and teachers who directly relate to non-white pupils. These in-service workshops and seminars attempt to "make" the white educator see himself in terms of an outsider looking into another world much like the anthropologist who studies the economic activities of a particular tribe in Africa or Asia without acquainting himself with the culture of the people he is examining. In other words, many white educators think they understand their non-white pupils because *no problems* have accrued, while all the time they and their pupils have been intentionally ignoring one another's existence.

In 1969, race and human relations seminars were made to introduce white teachers to the subcultural existence of their predominantly black students. This was done by bringing in black speakers who then proceeded to put the majority of teachers in a state of cultural shock. A similar program is discussed in *Time* magazine (September 19, 1969, pp. 44-45).

A detailed analysis of such "racial sensitivity" programs for teachers might be appropriate at this point in our discussion. The initial session deals with the teachers reporting their attitudes toward minority-group pupils and evaluating the particular learning environment as they personally know it. This approach enables each member of the workshop to voice his opinion on the school and race relations from his personal experience. This also brings out individual and group prejudices and beliefs about non-white students.

The next step is to bring in representative members of other community institutions such as the mayor, police chief, welfare agency personnel, businessmen, and clergy. Their discussion of race relations from the viewpoint of the non-educational institution exposes the teacher to possible different interpretations of institutional racism if it exists.

At this point in the workshop, teachers and other representatives from the white community have discussed the problem of race relations and the actual or potential existence and causes of institutional racism—but from the white point of view. At this crucial moment, a black human relations resource person is brought in to discuss racism in the white community as seen by members of the black community. In other words, the supposedly thorough analysis of prejudice and discrimination, seen by the white teacher as non-self-contradictory relative to his own "humanistorian" relations toward non-whites is shattered by the remarks of the black man. A sort of racism in reverse develops because the teachers are now looking at society and its institutions from the black minority viewpoint. Heated debate usually ensues, as most whites do not realize that they are ethnocentric in their evaluation of non-whites in general and the ghetto school in particular.

Now the workshop can turn to a more realistic analysis of prejudice, discrimination, and the teacher. The mechanism of prejudice can be explained through the use of representatives from the particular community in which the workshop is located, and then regional and national examples can be examined. Discriminatory practices in the school can then be related to specific prejudices held by the representative institutions of the community. A discussion of de facto and de jure segregation would be appropriate at this juncture in the course.

By this time, many teachers will be questioning the racial practices of both the school in which they work and the community in which they live, that is, if they grasp the significance of individual and institutional prejudice. While the white teachers are reflecting on "their" treatment of black students in the school, a black teacher who is a human relations resource person is introduced to discuss his reflections on the white educational process. This consists of informing the teachers that they have been guilty of perpetrating a feeling of white superiority in the curriculum that reflects the castelike relationship of the white and non-white world. Examples are drawn from history and literature to show that blacks have been eliminated from their place in American life.

This discussion is followed by an analysis of the curriculum and the counseling system of the ghetto school. The resource person tells the workshop that they have been guilty of "brainwashing" the black student into thinking he is inferior to whites by telling him that he has to learn "white ways" in order to succeed academically. If the black student acquiesces to his white teachers and their "think white," he still is in for a rude shock when graduation from secondary school approaches. At this time, the white vocational counselor usually informs his "white student in black skin" that he should avoid certain occupations because blacks cannot obtain these positions. Thus, the black who quietly and even largely mastered the white learning process learns that he is not accepted even if he plays the educational games by the rules!

The workshop by this time is usually worked up into a high emotional state as most teachers do not realize or even want to accept the fact that they have been "brainwashing" their black students into not just the white life-style but also a middle-class school system that many times conflicts with the racial-class orientation of a great number of ghetto inhabitants.

During this emotional period, the topic of racism can be appropriately introduced. The teachers have been exposed to both white and black racism and are in an excellent position to comprehend that it is a dehumanizing process that is not one-sided. The initial feelings of uneasiness exhibited by some teachers in recollecting their treatment of black students, the anger in the inadvertence of the "traditional" school curriculum in dealing with the problems of disadvantaged youth, and the distaste that are expressed in community attitudes toward minority youth will be brought to the surface, exposing the unconscious imprints of habits and predispositions.

Once the workshop participants are made aware that prejudice exists on the part of white teachers and non-white students, some progress can be made in explaining the position of the school in a changing society that has experienced both civil and political disorder that is to a certain extent racially based and motivated. The concepts of separation, integration, diffusion, and assimilation can be dealt with more realistically as the teachers should have some idea of what these terms mean to an individual who has suffered the personal agonies of living in a castelike system of racial inequality.

The last segment of the workshop concerns itself with the teacher as a change agent, in other words, what the teacher can accomplish in the school to bring both herself and the non-white student closer together in the pursuit of educational goals that will destroy the inferior status of non-whites predominant in American society. This task is, by far, the most difficult, as no easy solution is available. Possibly the workshop's chief benefit is making the white educator aware that racism is real and affects him even if he passionately thought he was not racist nor teaching a curriculum that in part did nothing to help destroy institutional racism.

One should not assume that these in-service workshops, which are seminars for teachers in race relations, are going to alter the status quo in the educational institutions. After all, one exposure to racism and its effects on society does not alter attitudes and opinions that have been built up in a lifetime. If experience is part of being educated, we have learned our lesson from the Southern desegregation experience that prejudice cannot be legislated out of a community by using the school as a vehicle for social change.

In some cases, these workshops and seminars only attract those who are interested in race relations. Those who do not wish to know about this social problem do not take part or, if mandatory, "close their eyes and cover their ears to the facts." Further, the teacher who shows concern and enthusiasm in the program is likely to be the teacher who is most responsive to the needs and problems of her non-white students. One is also faced with the realization that a number of white teachers in the ghetto schools either are indifferent to the needs of their pupils or are waiting for their transfer to a "better school" (i.e., white), which comes automatically if they are "certified" teachers by the bureau of teacher personnel of the board of education.

Turning now to the attitude of teachers toward their non-white, and more often than not, disadvantaged, pupils; teachers' attitudes toward minority-group youth are to a great extent due to class-linked values. Thus, overt and covert racial prejudice and discrimination may be associated with teachers' personal values—attitude and social class difference.

If one accepts the premise that much of the prejudice and discrimination of white teachers in the non-white ghetto school is due to class differences, then one can reach some tentative conclusions concerning teacher-pupil relationships. First, a generally unconscious negative attitude prevails which interferes with successful teaching of minority youth, all other things being equal. Second, blame is often placed on the parents, the ghetto environment, and the child for classroom problems. And last, a more negative education of minority group results, thus completing a vicious circle from which the teacher cannot escape. However, the primary objective of the workshop is to assist teachers in broadening their perspective through examining alternatives for facts before drawing conclusions based on values that can have a direct effect upon their teaching effectiveness and performance. The specific objectives are:

1. To instruct teachers in how to maintain a certain amount of objectivity in making judgments.

2. To help teachers understand and recognize others' preferences, likes, and dislikes.

3. To help teachers analyze one's own preference and its motivation.

4. To enhance, through reflective thinking, past experiences and problems and generalize to probable behavior in similar future situations.

5. To engage teachers in activities where they must:
   a. demonstrate willingness to listen,
   b. record mentally and understand with order, clarity, and consistency others' positions,
   c. avoid the temptation to give others answers that may appear to be socially acceptable or individually advantageous.

6. To help teachers discover the neglected meaning which particular social concepts and expressions are given through the ways they are used in different contexts.

7. To help teachers lay bare unrecognized logical inconsistencies which result from the uncritical use of language when teaching.

8. To help teachers uncover conceptual blunders and to lay bare erroneous lines of reasoning which result from failure to understand how language is being used in a given situation.

9. To help teachers explore the dimensions of racial terminology and to gain a clearer understanding of the relationships between thought, language, and reality, and thus to broaden the basis upon which their beliefs are grounded.

10. To help teachers clear away pseudo-problems and questions that exist only as a result of confused and unclear conceptions.

Teaching Afro-American Studies

The inclusion of Afro-American studies in the modern curriculum should serve both black and white Americans: black Americans in terms of cultural heritage and identity; white Americans in terms of an exchange of knowledge and understanding, black and whites in terms of order, clarity, and consistency on racial and cultural differences in democratic America.

Afro-American studies is one of the most significant concepts to emerge out of the civil rights struggle by black Americans. W. E. B. DuBois envisioned something very much like it as the goal of Negro colleges and universities of higher learning. In writing of his own endeavors, he stated once, "The main significance of my work at Atlanta University during the years 1897 to 1910, was the development at an American institution of learning of a program of study of the problems affecting the American Negroes covering a progressively widening and deepening effort designed to stretch over the span of a century."[9] In 1942, DuBois challenged Negro colleges to assume control of scientific investigations into the condition of Afro-Americans, not, as he put it, "for the purpose of creating a Negro science of purely racial facts, but in order to make sure that the whole undistorted picture is there, and that the complete interpretation is made by those competent to do it through their lives and training."[10]

Though the idea of Afro-American studies is not new, it has recently captured the imagination of educators and institutions of higher learning. It is now being written about in the press

164

and talked about at meetings, conferences, and conventions. Recently, the annual convention of the National Council for the Social Studies included in their program many sessions on Afro-American studies.[11] This interest in Afro-Americans alone, with the efforts of black students to expand the existing disciplines by adding to the curriculum materials more relevant to the black experience, is part of the idea, as is the pressure which students and some faculty are exerting for more profound changes in the cultural orientation of their institutions. The suggestions for implementation range from minor adjustments in the content of existing courses to the establishment of massive research projects for the creation of new knowledge, values and beliefs for all students (black and white) about the realities of social and cultural life of black Americans.

Though the concept of Afro-American studies was influenced by the history of "oppression" and cultural exclusion from outside of the black community, it derived its essential vitality and its compelling urgency from black people, from its responsiveness to the internal needs of the black community. Therefore, Afro-American studies has had a strong and positive impact on black students because of its potential for resolving a series of dilemmas with which the black community is confronted, and which prevent that community from achieving what it would perceive as its own fulfillments.

For example, the talk about decentralized schools is talk for a branching of the centralized system; talking about new role relationships; a new kind of educational philosophy; a new role for students and for parents; new values and beliefs and really building humanity into the educational process.

Black people see Afro-American studies as a process of learning how to effectively educate black people; to incorporate deep within themselves a pride in being who they are. In short, the concept of Afro-American studies can best be appreciated from a black perspective.

In arguments for Afro-American studies in institutions of learning, the needs of the black community are often expressed in rhetorical terms describing oppressive dependence on white cultural modes and blacks' being culturally excluded from white institutions and curricula. This exclusion is often emphasized to the neglect of black desires for black autonomy, the desire

165

for a sense of sovereign black dignity in whatever world the black man might choose to call his own.

The desire for black autonomy, for black control of the environment in which black people live, has its primary source in black private self-perception, and is only secondarily reactive to institutional exclusion as full participants in a democratic society. The internal problem within the black community is the problem of distinguishing between the need to affirm autonomy and the need to put an end to dependence, between the conceptualization of long-range goals and the implementation of short-range goals, between the potential for black unity and the reality of black diversity. Carmichael and Hamilton conclude: "We blacks must face the fact that in the past, what we have called the movement had not really questioned the middle-class values and institutions of this country. If anything, it has accepted those values and institutions without fully realizing their racist nature. Reorientation means an emphasis on the dignity of man, not on the sanctity of property. It means the creation of a society where human misery and poverty are repugnant to that society, not an indication of laziness or lack of initiative. The creation of new values means the establishment of a society based . . . on free people, not free enterprise."[12]

The faculty committee on African and Afro-American Studies, Harvard University, reported from their research that "what the black students want is an opportunity to study the black experience and to employ the intellectual resources . . . in seeking solutions to the problems of the black community."[13]

W. E. B. DuBois, in "The New Deal for Negroes," suggests the teaching of social science, giving trained teachers time and funds for investigation and the publishing of the findings to be used by social reformers.[14] The division of social sciences he had in mind included economics, psychology, sociology, political science, anthropology, sociology, and history to give students unified knowledge in social trends. This was to be a core of social studies in Negro colleges and universities. The *Journal of Negro Education,* in summarizing DuBois's proposal, stated in an article:

"Briefly, Dr. W. E. B. DuBois's proposal, agreed upon by the presidents of the land-grant colleges, assumes, first, a core of social studies in each of our Negro colleges and graduate schools. It assumes that by internal administrative and staff efforts, these may be internally unified and coordinated for a joint, continuous attack upon the problem of the study of the Negro population in the area surrounding each college. It assumes that, pouring into a central headquarters, yet to be designated, for review and analysis by a central board, yet to be chosen, there would be a continuous flow of raw data and completed studies. It assumes central coordination, synthesis, and report of these studies. It assumes that by great increase in knowledge, sound and rich and full, we would have materials wholly convincing as to the needs of the local, regional, and national Negro population. It assumes that with this knowledge, we could so increase our wisdom as to be able both to make Negro higher education very much better than it is in all aspects, and we would have the facts at last on which to base valid requests for support from foundations, individuals, and local, state, and national government. By knowing what the problems are, we could know also how to arrange them in priorities and further, much better than we know now, how to attack them each in turn with some expectation of success."[15]

From the *Journal of Negro Education's* summation of DuBois's proposal, DuBois envisioned the Afro-American studies program for black institutions to be taught by black scholars. However, today, with the ever-increasing number of black students enrolling in predominantly white institutions of learning, with the desegregation law, and with public schools demanding that the curriculum be blackened, many problems have been created. In predominantly white universities, blacks are demanding that these institutions add to the curriculum materials relevant to the experience and lives of black people.

What black students want from school today conflicts with what the white institutions can offer in the way of a learning experience. In trying to meet the black demands, in white-orientated institutions, for change, we find in the area of curriculum development possible conflict between long- and short-range goals for black students; between the model of the Afro-American program (i.e., should the program be for blacks only?) and the current revisionist efforts of white institutions.

It was DuBois's belief that to make intelligent and academic changes, the depths of the black community should be probed

167

to develop meaningful guidelines for change, as he put it, "by those competent to do it through their . . . training."[16]

Although the DuBois proposal has excellent utility for the aspirations of Afro-Americans, times have changed enough toward the integration of institutions of learning to invalidate his approach. As a possible alternative, the development of integrated materials in social studies is warrantedly asserted. The chief objective of the integrated approach through social studies is to bring together in a problem-oriented course different perspectives on cultural and social issues. The purpose should be to develop a high-quality, respectable course of teaching and learning in the area of Afro-American studies; to provide students and faculty, both black and white, an opportunity to develop deeper appreciation and understanding of the contributions of black people to American culture; the many and varied problems of a multi-racial society; the social and psychological difficulties embodied in second-class citizenship; the pain and suffering endured by black Americans in black ghettos over decades of social and economic ostracism; the effect of racism and racist institutions on America's growth and development; and to assist students in acquiring the information and attitudes necessary for living and working effectively in a multi-racial environment, hopefully, arriving at a meaningful concept of education that includes the experience of all America. This is quality education. Furthermore, it has been stated earlier in this chapter, that African-American studies is related to the major disciplines of social and behavioral science and humanities, and, Afro-American studies being broad in base and multi-disciplinary is the same as social studies, but from the black perspective. Therefore, if this is valid, the social tools of social analysis, focusing on the contemporary situation of the black community in America, are applicable for intellectual inquiry through the Hunt and Metcalf model described in *Teaching High School Social Studies*,[17] and by Massialas and Cox, in *Inquiry in Social Studies*.[18] The model they propose for teaching is appropriate for the teaching of Afro-American studies. In short, just as the authors see no problem in teaching history reflectively, as no different from the problem of teaching in social studies, the reflective method of teaching seems appropriate for the teaching of Afro-American studies.

The use of the reflective teaching model should be the primary pedagogical method in studying the contemporary life of Afro-American people, integrating the curriculum with black perspectives and reconstructing the social and behavioral science disciplines in the social studies classroom.

The interdisciplinary classroom should be a research-oriented class, a classroom of inquiry, a teaching-learning classroom, and a focal point for reorganization. But its most comprehensive function will be the creative one of generating the intellectual apparatus; the new values; the new myths, concepts, and criteria; the models, policies, and procedural guidelines which must inform and support the reconstruction of the curriculum. DeVere E. Pentony, in describing the role of black studies, states: "An emphasis on blackness, black dignity, black contributions, and black history will provide whites with new perspectives about the black man and woman. In turn, these new perspectives may indicate what clues of behavior and guides to proper responsiveness are necessary to enable whites to relate to blacks in something other than a patronizing or deprecating fashion. Through black studies, there may be opportunities for whites to enrich their understanding of the black man and thus, perhaps, to build more meaningful bridges of mutual respect and obligation. Moreover, if the truth can make blacks free and open, it may also force the whites from their ignorant stereotypes of the black man and his culture."[19]

The dilemma of the black rhetoric can have excellent utility for group discovery in the social studies classroom by using the reflective method of teaching. By using the pedagogical model of reflective teaching, students and teacher in the class should be able to clarify and understand in an orderly fashion the black rhetoric and achieve new insights on the black community situation.

When teaching a value-laden situation in the social studies classroom, the teacher can use reflective teaching to bring values and beliefs out in the open for discussion, creating conditions under which students will think and examine their values, express how they feel, and examine the valued beliefs of others. It will be the teacher's job to create conflict. Above all, the teacher in the social studies classroom should, on a continual basis, deal with the emotion-laden issues as a part of the education process. The student experience should be the origin of the basic tool of learning, "the key vocabulary." By emphasizing the value of experience, the teacher can channel natural destructive forces into creative outlets. This approach to teaching is particularly relevant to the teaching of black history for the way in which it recognizes and utilizes the cultural differences of the students in a creative fashion, and for the way it enables the student to focus on material which he, himself, is to learn. Thus, the interdisciplinary class can be a center that produces new insights about reality and a major device for dissemination of that knowledge, and places in perspective the legitimacy and worth of the experience of black people.

Many problem-centered activities should occur in the interdisciplinary approach; if not, the teacher should create some that the group can engage in using the reflective thinking model. For example, the group can be required to experiment with a pedagogical problem, such as: How does one meet the problem of teaching history when racism on the part of both white and black students is evident in the classroom? Whose bias do you project?

These types of dilemmas are inescapably essential to the understanding of the black position. In the interdisciplinary classroom under the guidance of a teacher skilled in reflective thinking, the class should be able to seek clarity and understanding on these positions.

It can help students apply their skills as an integral part of the educational process and integrate into the curriculum—throughout the curriculum—concern for the black position.

The interdisciplinary classroom is a deliberate and systematic effort as a part of the education process to help black and white communicate on social issues, to deal rationally with irrationality, to deal intellectually with conflict, and to examine crisis and conflict in constructive ways.

For the interdisciplinary social studies class to be meaningful for all, its inception must be entirely free of the corroding effects of extraneous influences to reflect without distortion the new human truths that are discovered through the committed participation of the students. It is from this premise that structural principles must undergird these courses: freedom from outside influences, committed responsiveness to the devotion to learning, and the rational resolution of differences.

It is hoped that in planning such a class, it should be academically sound and respectable, with students required to take a limited number of hours in the center to meet academic requirements. In this respect, the Afro-American studies will be an educational program for all students—a program which reflects and contributes to the vitality of the students' experience and which is relevant and responsive to the reality of black students' needs; which respects all students' values in the broadest cultural terms; promotes the self-determined growth of the students; liberates the mind and mobilizes resources for the development and promotion of the pedagogical model of reflective teaching for order, clarity; and consistency in integrating the curriculum. Teams of black and white are the ideal models of teaching social studies—Afro-American studies. This concept enables social issues to be taught from the black as well as from the white perspective, which the students observe. This way, they are able to understand the social issue from both perspectives, and if they desire, they can synthesize the two, thus broadening their own perspectives. The specific purpose of the "I Spy" team approach and reflective teaching in the interdisciplinary center is to liberate through rational discussion students' potential ways of fulfilling a number of kinds of potential: political and social potential, through training for social change; intellectual and cultural potential, through development of the critical faculties and creative abilities of the students; and to establish the relevance of the reconstruction of the public school curriculum.

A Curriculum Idea:
For Developing Integrated Material

This curriculum idea, being exploratory in nature, is designed to develop a set of procedures for use in the teaching of Afro-American studies in conjunction with social studies. The aim is to describe a set of curriculum procedures, centered around the case study approach to integrating the existing curriculum, which would:

(1) Allow a teacher in a predominantly inner-city black school to use and integrate whatever talents she finds among her students around a common focus, and

(2) Enable her to teach, for example, black history by allowing her students to "do" history as a historian does history.

It is expected that a more positive identification with his own culture as well as a real contribution on his part to the collective understanding of that culture will improve the student's self-esteem and thereby increase his willingness to learn.

The first phase of development in a three-phase project should involve the collection of primary source materials from historical antecedents of the black experience and contributions in American civil rights organizations and of supplementary materials such as data on population and economic trends. This material should be organized according to historical and pedagogical criteria. Out of this organization, general principles and procedures should be developed which will then be initiated to test the procedures in the schools; and later, if this is successful, the last phase should undertake to train teachers in the use of such procedures.

The terms *case study* or *episode* are used in this instance to refer to the social techniques used in analyzing traditional social studies materials and black studies. Much of the case study material used in the schools presents to the student someone else's written description of a situation or problem, and it is then the student's task to weigh alternatives and to suggest resolutions. The procedures to be developed in this study differ by virtue of the fact that the materials will be presented to the student as data from which he will be asked to formulate his own meaning in his own way. In this sense, he will act as the perceiver of problems as well as the resolver of them. When the student notes, for example, that a particular historical figure took X as his course of action, the teacher would help him see that X was taken in preference to Y and Z, which were also available. The next question would then be, why X? From an inspection of the material, the students would determine both the chronological sequence of events and the factors—economic, social, political—influencing this choice.

In order to develop successfully such a set of procedures, a number of considerations are relevant. One of these is the nature of the material to be introduced. The historical period must not extend over an extraordinary length of time; otherwise the sheer task of discovering the sequence of events will overshadow any attempt to discover the relationships among them. The number of major personalities involved in the movement must have some definable limit which students will be able to handle, and the geographical arena of the movement's activity must have a similar limit. Further, any change in the movement's concern, direction, or strategy must not be subtle, but dramatic and obvious. And the movement must relate to the student's own interest and culture. These limitations would suggest that the material used in the development of such procedures be related to a specific and recent organization (or related organizations) with a specific leader or group of leaders. They suggest also that the organization has come into existence because of a specific event. However, given certain limitations, the particular organization is less important than the insight that teachers might gain into the arrangement of similar material and its use in the classroom. Given such insight, they could easily substitute other material.

Another important consideration is the ability of students to deal with material in this particular way. This consideration should be seen first in light of the actual abilities which students bring with them to the classroom, but it would be well to remember that conceptual skill is only one kind of ability. Nevertheless, the ability level of the child suggests that the age level of the group must be considered and also that instructional techniques must be developed in order to teach the skills needed for an undertaking of this kind. Instructional technique will be discussed in a later section. It is important to stress, however, that the aim should not merely be to use the skills which children have already developed for the solving of the problems issuing from the case study, but also to use the study in order to improve and develop skills.

The short-range goals have more meaning in light of the long-term goals of the project as a whole. They are as follows:

1. To decrease the distance between the culture of the home and the culture of the inner-city black schools.

2. To introduce important black personalities to black

children as models, suggesting that they too can be effective social agents, and thereby presenting to each child a view that, through his efforts, the world is open to change.

3. To improve the self-esteem of the black child.

4. To develop a setting in which skills and learning are meaningfully employed, and to show the students how social science techniques can be related to their own life situation.

5. To use this setting for the improvement of the "acquisition" of skills.

6. To provide more concrete career models for black children.

7. To develop a new concept of discipline for children in inner-city schools.

It should not be expected that all children will approach the case study in the same way or with the same set of skills. Meaning can be found and expressed in a variety of ways. One of the major objectives of this project is to establish a set of procedures which will enable a teacher to use any skill found in the classroom which can add to the meaning of the material under consideration.

The fact that, at any given moment, a wide array of different skills will be in operation means that a great deal of planning and coordination must go into the preparing and managing of the class. At one session, for example, some children could be working on population and employment charts; others could be writing or dictating historical accounts and deciding how such charts have relevance to them. Still others could be working on methods of duplicating the study in print; and some could be working to express the material visually through woodcuts. Much of this planning will have to be done by the individual teacher considering the unique qualities in the classroom and the limitations imposed by the physical setting. However, as the materials and the procedures are developed and later tested, it should be possible to provide some minimum guidelines to indicate what aspects of the project could be successful under given sets of conditions—for example, because of limited time, space, and the various resources of the school which extend beyond the classroom into the community at large.

At this stage in the project, however, it is of primary

importance for the teacher to develop a set of procedures which will enable the students to do the case study. In order that the teacher may be able to test these procedures at some later date, it is also important to develop a set of materials which will enhance testing. Hence, the following steps are recommended:

1. Data about the community, organization, etc., must be collected. This entails not only library work, but also other resource materials.

2. Supplementary materials, such as population, income distribution charts, newspaper accounts, must also be collected.

3. The material must be organized in such a way that it could be used as the starting point for a case study. General categories, under which each piece of material is to be placed, must be established, and then the material must be sorted. Also, a record must be kept of the reasons behind each selection so that when the material is later reorganized, others can see the historical connections, contradictions, and inconsistencies which are being perceived.

4. The materials must be inspected and sorted again according to their relevancy and interest to the pupils. Each item must be inspected with an eye to the level of competency needed to deal with it, and some items will have to be rewritten or simplified. Also, decisions will have to be made about the kinds of clues such children need in order to make the desired connections, and then these clues will have to be invented for them.

5. Background information on "black social studies" will have to be provided in order to set a context for the case studies, and decisions will have to be made about the materials to be included and how eventually they could be taught.

6. Smaller exercises in problem-solving techniques and in cooperation will have to be planned or developed. In this area there are a number of games which should be useful, such as Prisoner's Dilemma, individual, institutional, and structural racism.

7. The problem of timing will have to be thought through with great care. If different children are to be doing different kinds of things, it can be expected that some activities will be of longer duration than others. In order to avoid the chaos

which this situation could provoke, some relevant tasks will have to be planned in which children can participate when their own work is finished.

8. Techniques will have to be planned to overcome or to rechannel both the hostility and the frustration which will arise in children at various occasions as they undertake such an inquiry.

9. A decision must be made about the grade level at which such material could be introduced. This will depend greatly upon the nature of the material and the level of skill needed to assess it. The general rule which would guide such a decision would be that, given the ability of children to handle such material, it should be introduced in the lowest possible grade. It would, however, be difficult to conceive of such an inquiry being undertaken before the sixth or seventh grade, and it may will be that it will be undertaken on a higher level.

10. After the materials have been collected and arranged, the teachers should decide on how to synthesize the materials into the existing disciplines. That is, whether it should constitute a unit in the social studies curriculum, or whether there are possibilities for total integration.

Why Do Social Studies—Why Not Just Teach It?

Schools have generally accepted a responsibility to teach certain conceptual skills to children. Among the most obvious are reading and number skills. In addition, other kinds of subject matter such as history and social studies have occupied a traditional place in the curriculum. History and social studies, however, are different order subjects which can be called "skills" only obliquely. They are in fact subjects which take on meaning only through the application of other skills.

If we abstract all of the conceptual tools which a person brings with him to a historical event, that event takes on the form of a happening which bears no recognizable relation to other happenings. The relationships become recognizable when cause-and-effect patterns appear, and the appearance of such patterns requires the application of abstract skills to the event. Hence, for example, the happening of Martin Luther King in

176

Montgomery or in Chicago becomes meaningful only in relation to racial concepts formed because of economic, political, and psychological factors, all of which are illuminated by charts and graphs which allow a student to compare and contrast certain aspects of the happening and to see a pattern and a logic behind a number of happenings.

It is frequently the case, however, that the teaching of history is modeled after the teaching of reading or numerical skills with the teacher attempting to find and convey something which is unique to history alone. When this occurs, the student is presented with a series of happenings, each identifiable by a given name and number, e.g., 1776, George Washington; 1941, Franklin D. Roosevelt. While there may well be a logic to the historian's chronology, the logic does not come across to the child in the classroom. When such teaching does take place, the effect is that the child continues to view the world as a series of unrelated, disconnected happenings, and there is developed in him a passivity towards a world which appears either irrationally governed, or, as more often is the case, governed by the principle that the good guy always wins.

In the United States, the history and social studies curriculum has generally had a dual purpose. Besides attempting to teach factual material to children, teachers in these areas have been commissioned to Americanize the child by establishing a certain attitudinal response. The result has often been a highly inflexible subject matter which has had little relevance to the world of the child as it is lived in the home and community and society.

Rather than the subject matter of social studies serving as the ground for the development of abstract skills, it too has been imposed and enforced by a rigid discipline unrelated to either the interest of the child or the material under study. In the haste to "Americanize" the student, any factors which conflicted with that task, such as his own ethnic background and struggles, were conveniently overlooked. Sometimes this endeavor has been successful—an emotional feeling for country has found its way into the student's life. However, patriotism of this kind, besides being bought at the expense of cultural identity, has developed in the student a feeling that social studies is something ready-made and passively received. This means that the student develops little sense that he may impose his categories upon historical data and also that he develops little ability to test his ideas against the data. The long-range effect is to make him extremely receptive to any notion that may happen to get his hearing. When the general attitude of inner-city children is considered, it is clear that the passivity that such an approach develops merely reinforces an attitude which is already present.

Many inner-city public schools have not taken into account that the "open society" appears closed to many black children. The emphasis in the classroom is frequently upon a limited number of conceptual skills, and it is quite clear that some skills are "better" than others. The argument advanced for teaching such skills is that they are the requisite keys for opening society's doors and for obtaining its rewards. Yet for a student who does not have such skills and who believes, for one reason or another, that he cannot attain them, this emphasis is just so much more proof that society is closed to him. Granting, however, that such skills must be taught, it makes a great deal of difference how they are taught.

Except on rare occasions, the emphasis in the inner-city public schools on language skills assumes that the Anglo-Saxon mode of grammar is the only viable one. But for most black children, the Anglo-Saxon mode is irrelevant. It is used neither in the home nor in the black community. When the school assumes that this is the only valid mode, it not only creates difficulty for a student who may be fluent in another mode, but it also passes an implicit value judgment upon his own background and cultural training. It would be very difficult for a child not to feel the force of such a judgment. Yet, J. L. Dillard has shown that in many instances the black dialect exhibits a consistency of grammar which is overlooked by those not extremely familiar with it. This is a consideration of which teachers should be made aware. For a teacher to assume that most black children are more articulate than classroom evidence would indicate is a sound assumption. Furthermore, many of the personality disorganizations and decreased mental functioning occurring during a child's school years may well result from the disparity between the home and the school culture. Thus, a curriculum idea is envisioned to develop techniques to enable the child to communicate the meaning of the material in a style and a form which is comfortable to him. It would then be the teacher's task to show the students that there would be some value in communicating these findings to members of the dominant culture and then to direct them in the study of a linguistic style which that culture can understand. Here, no value judgments should be made about the merits of one style as opposed to another, but each would be seen as a tool, the worth of which is to be determined by the object to be worked on.

It should be possible not only to look upon one form of language as a tool among other tools, but also to look upon language itself as a tool among others. Usually, however, the schools emphasize verbal modes of communication to the sacrifice of others, and this is the failure which even black studies, taught in the traditional way, makes. When a child comes to school without such skills, the demands made appear to be too great and his chances of success too small. Thus again, the adult world is perceived as closed. Yet verbal communication is only one way to establish and express meaning. For something to have meaning suggests that someone is able to make sense out of it and is able to share that sense with others. It does not prescribe the mode of sharing beforehand. For a person to perceive meaning in something suggests that he is able to fit something which is initially unknown into something which is known. The headline, "Yanks Whip Indians," would, for example, suggest one thing to the sports fan and quite another to the uninitiated foreigner. To discover or to communicate the meaning is to highlight the context of a statement or an event, and there are a number of ways in which they may be done. Verbal communication is only one of them. It is probably the case that people learn by a combination of telling, showing, and doing, but that for any single individual an emphasis on one is more effective than an emphasis on the others.

If it is true that schools do emphasize the value of the verbal mode of communication to the sacrifice of others, then it is probably also true that some children are being stunted unnecessarily. Nor does a heavy emphasis on vocational training completely solve the problem, for the performance of a task is not the same thing as seeing value in the task performed. It is for these reasons that in developing this curriculum idea for implementation, the teacher should include in the design the

179

use of as many skills, talents, abilities, and interests as may be present in a given classroom.

Acquisition of Skills and Discipline

The emotional and social attitudes of the inner-city child have led us to discuss the use of skills, but schools also have the responsibility of helping a child acquire and develop skills. It is wrong, however, to make a great distinction between the use and the development of a skill. A child learns to swim by swimming, and, to some extent, he learns to read by reading. Of course, a child may learn to swim poorly, but if *he* is to understand that he does swim poorly, some situation or reference must be present to indicate that his present level is inadequate. Similarly, if a child has no reason to read, he has no reason to attempt to improve his reading. Moreover, in a general sense, it may be argued that a child rarely acquires a significant skill in school which he does not already possess in some form. A baby of eighteen months has a repertoire of behavior indicating a communication design calculated to elicit an anticipated response. Moreover, basic calculation skills are apparent even earlier as the child moves his hand to the rhythm of a song or follows his parent in repeating first one and then two taps on a table. The task of the school is not to place a skill in a child, but to provide a reason and an opportunity for him to improve upon and elaborate skills of which he is already possessed. Skills and attitudes toward skills are developed in many ways; a rigorous, demanding, highly structured teacher is only one of them; children usually learn as much from their peers as they do from their teachers. A skill exercised by one child on an object valued by another becomes a desirable tool for the other which he may seek to possess. Assuming that a case study can be introduced properly and assuming that children place value in it, there is a strong possibility that skills of various types will be accepted by students who previously saw no use for them.

When skills are discussed, it is important to think also of the vocational aspect of education. When the black child views the "open society" as closed, this view includes the way he

180

perceives future vocational opportunities. The absence of a father means also the absence of a vocational model, and when the father is not absent, his work, being often a series of jobs rather than a vocation, is often difficult to describe. Contrast this to the world of the middle-class white child who knows where his father works, what his father does, and what his father's friends do, and who then only has the problem of choosing one vocation from a multiplicity of models. The failure of many courses in vocational training could well be as much the result of limited vocational models as it is of limited employment opportunities.

In any event, if schools are willing to open up the styles of communication which are acceptable, they may also be willing to open up the techniques which could be used to express them. While the case study approach does not rest upon such a willingness, it does lend itself to it. Television and film are examples of some of the techniques which a case study approach lends itself to. Here, dramatic talent relies heavily upon mechanical, electronic, and artistic skills, and each one of these demands much planning and discipline. Moreover, such equipment provides the student with a visual record of his successes, failures, and progress. The cost of such equipment is no longer prohibitive for a school.

The above guidelines are merely suggestive alternatives to developing integrated curriculum materials. They should be developed as further attempts to emphasize the active side of learning. Motion pictures and television, for example, are not strangers to the classroom, but they are most commonly used to transmit information to children and hence demand as little activity as a spelling drill. There is, however, much value to be gained in translating a prose form into a dramatic form, and there is equal value in the planning and cooperation that must go into the expression of that form through a technological media. In middle-class schools some of these purposes have been served by theatrical activities, and these could be used in inner-city schools as well. Yet TV and film still have the value of providing a visual record of the student's behavior, of his successes and his failures, and also of providing him the opportunity to repeat the production and eliminate his failures. The importance of this in inner-city schools cannot be overestimated.

For the inner-city black child, failure is a major part of his life. The concept of failing is to him a much less viable one than the concept of being a failure. The former suggests some chance for success; the latter does not. It has been shown that children with low self-esteem are less able to recall their past failures and, therefore, we may speculate, that they are less able to learn from them. Praise is certainly one method of aiding such a child, but unless he sees some reason for the praise, its effect will be short-lived. Video and film are visual records of a child's progress, and if students are technicians as well as actors, such techniques are also statements of the value and interdependence of a wide range of skills.

It should be clear that the curriculum idea described herein is partly an attempt to change the concept and the practice of discipline which is often found in the inner-city schools. It is not infrequent to find teachers in such places assuming as their major task the maintenance of quiet and order, and taking their stance with a rod or a paddle as the symbol of that task. The only viable argument to support such activities is that either the students are incapable of learning or else, they are incapable of learning in any other way. Yet the success of some inner-city schools practicing other forms of discipline would belie such arguments. Some teachers seem to assume that such discipline is an end unto itself, preparing the students for the harsh realities which life has to greet them with. They see such discipline as a prerequisite for working in the world and for developing the concomitant attitude which allows a child to meet the disappointments which the world has in store for him. Yet there are a few teachers who feel that their task is not only to train the child to work in our democratic society, but also to teach him to work with society. And here, too, discipline is required, but it is a different kind of discipline. The difference comes from believing that children must simply bend themselves to the will of society or believing that the child must bend so that society will bend itself to his will. It is the difference between seeing society as something which is closed or as something which is open to human choice. The imposition of discipline makes sense only when the tasks the child is expected to perform and the skills he is expected to acquire are seen by him as irrelevant to him. Children, inner-city children included, can engage in even the most rigorous drill when they perceive that it has meaning for them. This is the only way one could explain a child standing on a line for three hours and throwing a ball into a hoop, oblivious to the fact that he has missed his lunch.

The black, inner-city child is too often placed in a classroom where discipline is seen as an end in itself and which, therefore, is always the first resort of the teacher. Probably, traditional discipline will never be completely absent from the classroom. Even when it is not exercised, children know it is there, and, when used wisely, it is a valuable asset to both teacher and student. There will always be work to be done, and the rights of those students who want to do it must be protected. But this should be the only reason for the use of this kind of discipline, and when it is used as a substitute for meaningful work or study, then it is misused.

Insofar as the material presented in the inner-city school is irrelevant to the child, such discipline will be the rule rather than the exception. We should not assume, however, that the skills a child must acquire and the materials through which they are acquired must be irrelevant to him. There are just too many instances where this does not hold true, and these instances range from mentally retarded children making and selling their arts and crafts work in a school to the intellectually gifted student building a computer. The aim of this curriculum idea is not to eliminate discipline in inner-city schools, but rather to explore a way in which it might become a last, rather than a first, resort.

Thus, the curriculum idea is to develop a process of education and preparation which stresses social studies and Afro-American studies; an inductive, problem-solving approach to the learning process. As implemented, the curriculum, courses, and the reflective method of instruction should proceed in the context of the educational process in which the pupils are actually engaged in the direct observation, integration, and application of information, knowledge, and skills in the classroom. This approach results in an integrated curriculum that crosses black and white cultures and that analyzes the culture and society. For example, topics such as freedom, alienation, imperialism, nationalism, racism, democracy, tyranny, and black power can be studied and analyzed. This curriculum idea is

183

appropriate for the classroom format, sufficiently valuable as part of the pupils' "general education," relevant to the inner-city pupils' environment, and appealing to their interest and curiosity.

CHAPTER 6

INNER-CITY EDUCATIONAL
PROBLEMS: MODELS
AND STRATEGIES

A CRITICAL aspect of the contemporary attack on inner-city public school problems is that it has been organized largely in terms of theoretical models which direct improving efforts at the individual student rather than at the improvement of the community. Such models explain the problems of inner-city schools in terms of the deprivations and disadvantages experienced by many inner-city children. Accordingly, efforts to deal with these problems have focused on the individual student under the strategy of compensatory education.[1] The task of the school is that of trying to compensate for the failure of the home and neighborhood to develop needed skills and attitudes. Models which center the attention of educators on intercommunity relationships, that is, those which obtain between the school and conditions in the community, rarely have been utilized.[2] Hence, the possibility of organizing the school's improvement efforts by strategies which are directed at community conditions and problems is generally not entertained.

The wisdom of entertaining intercommunity models is suggested by the fact that compensatory education programs have not yet demonstrated conclusive educational gains.[3] In part, this may simply reflect a failure to organize the evaluation of such programs so that the gains which had been made could be shown. The use of control groups in a carefully designed evaluative program would help to clarify this question. But there is also reason to believe that compensatory education programs are combatting the symptoms rather than the roots of many of the problems which burden inner-city schools and communities.

There are many community conditions which have been correlated with academic and behavioral problems of inner-city students. Poverty, slum-housing residence, unemployment, cultural deprivation of parents, racial discrimination, and father absence have been shown to be related to school attendance, academic achievement, IQ scores, pupil retention, and other educational outcomes.

Furthermore, it has been established that academic and behavior problems occur more frequently among lower-class students than among middle-class students.[4] Thus, schools in the inner-city areas can expect a high proportion of students with such problems unless steps are taken to assist them in seeking solutions. In recognition of this, some educators have predicted that the proportion of black students in inner-city schools with academic and behavioral problems will increase rather than decrease in the next decade, despite the establishment of numerous compensatory educational programs.[5] This conclusion is based on an interpretation of current demographic trends related to the increase of multi-problem families in the inner-city. If this prediction is sound, then the inner-city school can anticipate a constant supply of dropouts unless some effective action is taken toward these problems.

The popularity of the culturally disadvantaged models and other individualistic models which deal with individual characteristics hinges partly on the assumption that the educational institution is virtually powerless to alter conditions in the community. Viable alternatives to the extreme position of powerlessness are available, but they are not apparent in most individualistic models. Intercommunity models, which formulate the problems of inner-city schools and students in terms of the latter's relationship to certain external conditions in the community, are needed. Several such models will be proposed here. Their emphasis is on producing changes in the kind of education contrived for the inner-city students and the better use of existing institutions. The models are a new dedication of teaching and human service to the black community.

Revolutionary changes are taking place in our inner-city communities. Public institutions of learning are experiencing the full impact of these inner-city changes in insights, in values, and in philosophy of education. Many of the programs and projects implemented in inner-city schools in the past no longer seem adequate, and recent school desegregation programs have made possible the doing of things which were not feasible earlier. For example, the plan aimed at integrating the public schools across the nation is purported to bring significant changes in the community and to enhance quality integrated education. According to these reorganized integrated concepts, many white children will be learning with black children for the first time. Many teachers are overly concerned about the desegregated program and uncertain about their efficiency and effectiveness in the classroom with minority-group members. In order to prepare for the school year, many teachers attended workshops in human relations, formally conducted by city school districts, and informal workshops with representatives from various community groups, especially in the inner-city. There is a hidden assumption that a curriculum appropriate for the dominant group would have similar values for the black minority group. But, it is also reasonable to assume that some educational goals and objectives of the program are not relevant to the needs of the blacks.

In specific areas of concern, integration of the school seems to emphasize and focus on logistical matters such as busing, time schedules of buses, separation of junior and senior high schools, and the effects of shifting classes. Very little, if anything at all, is being said about curriculum reform and the preparation of teachers who are expected to interact in the learning environment with an integrated class and transmit to one culture the ideas and feelings of another. In general, teachers across the nation are not being trained to work in this kind of situation. Thus, a viable step toward achieving racial harmony and accord central to quality integrated education is not only the cultural integration of the student body, but in addition, the conceptual integrating of knowledge.

Young blacks and many white pupils in high schools across

the country are demanding recognition of ethnic studies in the school curriculum, pointing out the fact that it is excluded. One general conclusion can be drawn from analyzing these so-called integrated curricula; there is an urgent and immediate need for curriculum development. Integrated curricula in inner-city public schools have and are operating on the basis of weak and short-term planning; most tend to plan their curriculum by ear; procedures for studying and developing a meaningful curriculum are *ad hoc* and are created to meet crisis situations devised on the basis of *hunches* and *intuitions*. Little is known, with any degree of order, clarity, and consistency, about the actual antecedents, conditions, and processes by which black culture is diffused. The key factor inhibiting comprehension and consistency is the absence of an effective educational offering in the broadest sense of the term.

Likewise, major universities' and colleges' teacher education programs continue to train teachers to teach in traditional classrooms, assuming that in such a setting the skills needed to teach in integrated schools will be acquired. In a sense, the arguments for integration which so many professors have put forth for the public schools have not been extended to their own universities. Whether the future teacher chooses to teach in an inner-city urban, rural, or suburban setting, whether she enters an integrated class or a class with all black or all white students, it should be clear that she probably will not be equipped to teach if her own education has been carried out in racial isolation. The best teachers are the translators to one group of the ideas and feelings of another, and this role cannot be served if a teacher does not have a keen awareness of what those ideas and feelings may be.

Realization of this in some cases has led to an unnatural expansion and modification of the curriculum in an attempt to make the program offerings applicable to specific crisis situations through alternative approaches, but what is needed as a vital segment of inner-city schools are programs that are broad enough in their perspective to include and address themselves to the need of the black community, provide human services to the community, train prospective teachers aspiring to teach in the inner-city and, finally, programs that can contribute to the refinement of curriculum ideas to enhance the effectiveness of inner-city public education.

For years now, scholars have researched and written about the academic deficiencies of blacks and proposed ways to enhance their cognitive and affective models for a broader educational experience, for self-awareness, and for an understanding of their functional role as integral entities in institutions of learning. Others have introduced new machines and materials which are purported to change attitudes, in addition to teaching skills, and have researched programmed materials which are supposed to influence students' behavior and strengthen their character.

However, it is apparent, in contemporary times, that these methods of demonstration and practices are ineffective. We cannot illustrate a positive attitude to inner-city students and then have them practice it. We must acknowledge that teaching in urban or inner-city schools is a different art from teaching suburban children, and the fundamental goal of inner-city education today should be to provide learning opportunities for them as individuals. The complexity of the inner-city society has led to the realization that we can no longer afford to continue to use the same pedagogical techniques, methods, and models.

The Need for Reform in Teacher Education

One fact, I am sure, evident to all of us, is that we desperately need to redefine the concept of teacher education in institutions of higher learning. However, because of the incredible lack of research throughout programs on this subject, we can only dimly perceive the direction such innovation in teacher education might take. Consequently, I would like to share my perspectives which might expand teacher education into a full dimension and propose an alternate way to train teachers. But first, let me stress my tentative argument for a new direction and meaningful reform.

In a modern society, education is necessary to enable our youth to adjust socially as well as achieve academically. Starting with the beginning of democratic ideals, equal opportunity to

189

learn and achieve has come to be a necessity for success and social adjustment. The history of the development of the earlier concepts of schools and teacher-training programs demonstrates an attempt to maintain equilibrium with demands for change in society and schools. Also, teacher-educators have tried to keep pace with the changing needs and ideals of our technical, material, and non-material cultural advances. During these periods of transition, emphasis on the function of our schools shifted from the subject matter to the pupil as the center of attention, with little, if any, innovation in teacher education.

In recent years, in institutions of higher learning, teacher-educators have been prolific in almost every way possible, attempting to improve the method of training prospective teachers. For example, institutions are conducting experiments in teacher education with various projects and programs such as contact and get-acquainted programs to increase student-teacher participation in community activities. This involvement in the community is purported to help prospective teachers develop a profound awareness of the community problems and school needs. Despite these attempts to redefine and advance teacher education, parents and organized interest groups have begun to react with rage as if they were not securing adequate returns for their investments of patience and taxes for what they were getting from teachers and the school.

To many of these parents and pressure groups, the school is the place where an aggregation of pupils gather to learn, and the teachers' functional role is to move pupils toward meaningful goals and toward the ability to grapple with a complex society. If these things and others are expected of a teacher, the limited experience and exposure they are getting place them in an unfavorable position. If teachers are to be held responsible for the pupil and contend with pressures with multidimensions they should be prepared to be more than "perfunctory servants" of parents, who are wrathful about inadequate teachers and appear destined to go their way. Many of these parents are suggesting that the school should be controlled by the local community. Some are thinking about setting up their own educational system with community control. Regardless of these inflamed attitudes and their ambitions, they cannot carry out their mission without the involvement of teachers. Teachers

190

are contained in the school as a part of the ritual, they are recipients of all the forces to which the school and society is subjected, and they are effective change agents when adequately equipped with knowledge and experience. In short, at the present rate, the status of teacher education, unless brought into proper perspective with the changes of the prevailing contemporary conditions, tends to suggest that public education will be shattered by disruptive charges from without by pressure groups before it has time to accommodate itself from within. The tragedy of all of this is that too many teacher-educators seem reluctant to respond to the demands for reform in teacher education.

Allen and Mackin, describing educators' loss of voluntary movement to innovate, stated:

> Teacher education has long suffered from a severe case of paralysis. Whereas American society has been undergoing massive changes both technologically and socially over the past ten years, our teacher education institutions, for the most part, have stood idly about, watching society pass them by. Innovations have been verbalized constantly, but have rarely been acted upon. In fact, the dichotomy between talk and action has been so great as to embarrass the most innovative of our profession. Educational journals, in an effort to disseminate information about brilliant new programs, appear to have deluded many of us into thinking that real change in teacher education is sweeping the country. Thus, rather than adapting to contemporary educational needs, most teacher educators comfortably maintain their antiquated programs, content that the publicized work of others will help camouflage their own inactivity.

In a less cogent manner, a critical aspect of teacher education is that it is organized largely in terms of theoretical models and does not direct improving efforts at the preservice level for prospective teachers, or their ability to deal with the realities of the schools. Many of these programs in attempting to revolutionize teacher education have virtually disregarded the value of broadening the cultural background of prospective teachers through early school experience. In examining some of these programs, one can find meager, outdated, unilluminating and sometimes grotesquely misleading guidance for prospective teachers. Such shortcomings arise, not primarily from the paucity of materials, but apparently from the indifference in the type of preparation. The inquiring future teacher would naturally assume that these sources, which stress social and cultural conditions and experience in the school, are major contributions on what to expect.

Although academic and methods courses alone are assumed to be insufficient, the necessity of a broad social background of education is being realized. I argue for a modification of the traditional teacher-training program as opposed to discarding it completely. Therefore, I advocate that in order for prospective teachers to grapple with our changing schools, educators revise their teacher education programs to meet with the requirement of exposing student teachers early in their preparation to the perplexities of our modern schools. The position is that the traditional programs do not show a broader view of understanding of public schools for prospective teachers. This assumption has several bases in fact. For example, student teachers have often stated upon completion of the limited practice-teaching experience in the traditional programs, "I wish I could practice-teach longer," or "if only I could do it over again." Students who wanted to correct and improve on their past practice-teaching experience before starting a teaching career were unable to do so. Should student teachers be limited to a predetermined concept of what every prospective teacher should know?

Perhaps the most compelling need is for priorities in teacher education. In the teacher education movement, we must keep our sights on the fact that teacher education must change with the times and the needs of prospective teachers. I propose that teacher education provide early school experience for future teachers by assigning them to public schools their freshman year. This approach can add to their basic preparation for a teaching career. Ehlers and Lee brilliantly describe the importance of teacher education. In quoting from the Rockefeller Reports on the proper education of teachers, they write, "No education system can be better than its teachers." They state further: "To a great many people this means that the most crucial consideration to all is the nature of the education and training teachers receive. Here it is felt lie the primary inadequacies, and here the most essential reforms must be instituted."[7]

No other enterprise is as important to the future welfare of our society as that of the training of teachers. We may reorganize school systems, revolutionize courses of study, increase salaries, insure pension and mass endowments, but we cannot raise the standard of education unless we improve the preparation of the teacher.

In a contemporary society with all its perplexities, the teacher of children and youth, although not the sole instrument through which a society may consciously control its future directly, determines in great part both the extent and degree to which sound fundamental ideas pervade, unite, and move a society. In our society a teacher is one of a few public figures who on a continuous basis interacts with pupils academically for a large part of their life—from early childhood to young adulthood. Why not enhance this interaction by lengthening the practical experience prospective teachers have with pupils? If pupils are to receive guidance and direction through new experiences, and teachers are to interact with them in transactions of cultural and social crisis in the school, teacher-educators should consider the impact prospective teachers can have through this early exposure to school problems. Teacher preparation that includes the integration of earlier practical experience can increase beginners' perspectives on what teaching is all about and enhance the vital and reciprocal relationship between understanding the working of the school and the culture of the pupils. This approach can bring prospective teachers into the vital current of events and make them closely responsive to the criticisms and aspirations of the people they serve.

I conceive teacher education to be one's encounter with reality, or whatever particular problem is under consideration in the schools; and one's attempt to cope with that problem and ever-changing reality.

In other professions or career fields it is recognized that students' involvement is not limited to the theoretical approach. Students interested in the medical profession are involved in other aspects of their chosen field which are relevant to their studies, i.e., they walk the wards in addition to studying surgery and medicine in classrooms. These students gain practical experience by having as a part of their preparation exposure to activities, duties, and responsibilities in the hospital, and other related areas, in addition to reading about them in textbooks. This exposure is assumed to quicken their understanding and adjustment when they begin their career.[8]

In a field such as law, practical experience in the workshop (the courtroom) is integrated with study of the theory. The same holds with other careers, such as geology, oceanography, and anthropology.

This is not to despise method or theory courses which are essential; empirical exposure and theory—they are both important and necessary, but they are different. I do not believe that future teacher needs can be fully met without a meaningful experience in the school.

It is something which has been read or heard without paying much attention to it or seeing much meaning in it, suddenly acquiring meaning and coming to life, because of the kind of experience to which it is related. Field experience for teachers is necessary for the full and fruitful study of diverse cultural values and school problems if the cultural education of teachers about the school and society is to be complete. Seen in its many manifestations, teachers deal with an infinite number of subjects, many in which prospective teachers can be discerned. Early school experience, for teachers, if well planned, might do something to meet the most serious demands of our schools.

For future teachers to have a diverse practical experience with the various pressures and problems of public schools is a way of understanding the theory, for without such experience full understanding is practically impossible. If teachers are to be agents of change and deal face-to-face with social as well as academic problems, teacher-educators must acknowledge an approach which has been almost ignored. That is, a continuous but modified interaction between a cross-fertilization of theory and practical experience.

If it is true that the future of our society depends on its schools, too much emphasis cannot be laid on the kind of teachers produced. In our modern society we should be educating for a new world with new responsibilities, values, ideals, and purposes. Therefore, the direction of the teacher education program must not only be toward the refinement of teaching techniques, but better understanding of the new world and its problems in order to mold the minds of the new generation.

No doubt we are living in an age of specialists and specialization, but teaching as a career warrants prospective teachers to have the type of training and experience that put their preparation in a wider social setting. Many incumbent teachers today are so deeply engrossed in theory that they are unable to see outside of it, and consequently their social outlook is lacking. Knowledge of what theory says is necessary, but the teacher is only acquainted with it when he experiences the relationship between it and the real situation in the school.

Therefore, in order to bridge the gap, the fundamental thing in teacher education is for prospective teachers to be placed in public schools their freshman year as non-certified teacher aides to see the significance of what they are to do and study for academic growth and development.

Teachers must be trained to be at home in the ever-increasing culture of our time. They should be trained to have a knowledge of the culture of our time. They should be trained to have a knowledge of the culture in the community, for they are society's agents for transmitting this culture and values in the form of organized knowledge to youth by making them sensitive to the world of ideas and social change. The teacher must have that intangible "something more than preparation of process." That "something more" should be early experience and exposure to the community and school ideas which make possible an intelligent adjustment to new situations.

Laying the Foundation for Early School Experience

There is general agreement among some teacher-educators that the educational problems of the disadvantaged pupils have become a challenge for teachers. Such presupposed problems as lack of motivation, retarded cognitive behavior, and their disaffection for education poses problems for teachers in inner-city schools. Despite innumerable academic studies, there is precious little relevant information available concerning what teachers should be doing to help disadvantaged pupils achieve academically and adjust socially. Anyone who has taken the time to visit inner-city schools knows that even the most experienced teachers are not very good with disadvantaged pupils. Many inner-city teachers readily admit—if that is the proper term—that they have not had the training to deal effectively with this type of pupil. If meaningful educational goals are to be achieved by disadvantaged pupils, the level of competency for prospective teachers should be raised to handle these problems.

During the past decade, teacher-educators attempted to improve the training of prospective teachers interested in teaching in the inner-city through an interdisciplinary approach that included more relevant courses of sociology, anthropology, and an intern semester of inner-city school experience. The assumption was this type of preparation enhanced future teachers' ability to deal with disadvantaged pupils' problems. Student teachers were encouraged to participate not only in the school, but in the community as "participant-observers" to acquaint themselves with problems that propagate in the school.

Scholarly critics of teacher education have acknowledged the importance and functional significance of early school experience for prospective teachers. Kenny, Bartholomew, and Kvaraceus, participating in a regional conference on teacher education, proposed that early experience should be an integral part of teacher preparation. The following factors emphasizing early experience were reported:

1. Beginning in the freshman or sophomore year, students interested in becoming teachers should work with children as teacher aides, teacher assistants, tutors, or recreation aides through school and community-based programs. A case study of one child involving discussions with the child's teacher, as well as home visits, would be an easily planned introduction into the practical realities of teaching.

2. Early experience should be more than simply "learning about"; it should involve the student in serious efforts to provide genuine services.

3. A community "live-in" experience should be made available for all students in those communities which present a social context different from the student's

own social background. This exchange should be multi-directional with students moving freely from the inner-city to the suburbs to the country, if feasible; and among all possible socioeconomic, ethnic, and racial groups.

4. Experience should be planned for all grade levels, to allow the students to get a first-hand view of the general development of the child.

5. Observation of, if not direct contact with, children with special problems—the mentally retarded, the physically handicapped, the emotionally disturbed—should be provided.

6. The experience of student teaching should be subjected to immediate analysis and evaluation for the student's own use in learning about himself as a teacher. Videotaping, demonstration teaching through role playing, student observation of other students are some ways in which a dynamic evaluation program could be developed to effect a continuous interaction between the student teacher and his teaching coach.

7. The bulk of the teacher training time should be spent on the actual scene of the future teaching. The schools themselves should become the college laboratories and it is there that the teachers of teachers should be located.

8. Student teaching assignments should be the result of a joint decision of the individuals concerned—the student teacher, the college coordinator, the school administrator, and the supervising teacher.

9. The student teacher should be treated as a full member of the professional team, contributing as much as possible within the limits of his professional skills and abilities.

10. The student teaching experience should be as long as possible—a year, ideally, and remunerated, particularly if it is set up as a fifth year or internship program.[9]

If teacher-educators accept this concept of teacher training as being viable for all prospective teachers, it follows that institutions, in setting up a program to involve student teachers in school and community affairs their freshman year, make a serious mistake if they consider only a limited concept of early school experience. In other words, the program should be a balanced one. If properly planned and implemented, a program of this nature can result in a new dimension for teacher preparation that provides the best opportunity for the integration of theory and practical experience to produce a more efficient and capable teacher. However, any attempt by teacher-educators to formulate a program with emphasis on early school experience should be done with caution to avoid weakening the curriculum. Also, if such a program is planned, it should be with the awareness that the particular needs of the community to be served may demand that the existing program be altered. but that such alteration should not jeopardize the creditability of the institution, and the student teacher's eventual certification.

A Conceptional Model for Reform in Teacher Education

All of the activities that are provided for student teachers by the teacher education program constitute its curriculum. It is assumed these activities contribute to the full development of the future teacher. It is, therefore, important that in redefining teacher education consideration be given to the kind and organization of learning activities which can be provided. In doing this, teacher-educators must take into account the nature of the early school experience and its function in the curriculum.

The purpose of this section is to describe a conceptional model as a way to reform teacher education to include early school experience. First, if such a program is contemplated, some procedure should be coordinated within the institution whereby all prospective teachers register initially in teacher education, and be advised by teacher-educators, the usual practice for elementary education but atypical of secondary education students in some colleges and universities.[10] Second, an arrangement must be worked out with public school administrators whereby prospective teachers are assigned to public schools in small seminars. The seminars should contain three major sources for exposing future teachers to school and the community—the seminar teacher-educators, the public school teachers, and the pupils. The major part of the student-teacher experience should be in the practicum seminar serving to integrate a number of subject areas. Groups of no more than twelve or fifteen student-teachers should work closely with seminar teacher-educators on relevant projects in the school and community. Such projects could include work as tutor, working with certified schoolteachers, and community projects. Additional faculty members assigned to the school seminar should meet with this group of student teachers to help them think through and articulate the problems they encounter. For instance, faculty members from the sociology and anthropology departments can meet with prospective teachers weekly in the school seminar to help them relate their work to the larger question of education's role in society. The faculty members might also devise a list of readings and a course syllabus which would help the seminar teacher-educator deal with the issues that this area involves.

Ideally, the visiting faculty member should be an integral member of the seminar teams, where the teacher-educator and the visiting faculty member along with the student teacher combine early school experience with theory in the seminars. This approach to teacher preparation is an alternative to the traditional teacher-training concept. It is assumed to be viable as a full dimension of teacher education that facilitates the preparation of prospective teachers' understanding of school problems. It is envisioned as a motivational device that can contribute significantly to the success of the future teacher; that provides them an opportunity to reflectively examine what transpired in their transaction in seminar discussions. Included in their preparation for discussion should be descriptions of the subject matter content, teaching processes, and their assessments of the relationships among teachers, pupils, community, and themselves. It is conceivable that teacher-educators can utilize this information in the seminar discussion, often relating it to their own teaching. Although the seminar activities are integrated with the early school experience, the supervision of the prospective teachers' actual practice-teaching experience can reside with competent teaching assistants.[11]

The cooperation of the public school teacher can be an essential element in the process of helping prospective teachers assigned to the school. The teachers can explain areas of teaching difficulties and offer useful information about public schools and pupils.

The seminar should stress an inductive, problem-solving approach to the learning process. The courses and method of instruction should proceed in the context of an educational process in which the prospective teacher actually engages in the direct observation, integration, and application of information, knowledge, and skills in the seminar. However, several criteria should be paramount to a program of this nature. For instance, the curriculum should focus on topics of contemporary American culture and society that are important to teacher education, appropriate to seminar format, sufficiently valuable as part of the prospective teacher's "general education," and appealing to their interest and curiosity.

Prospective teachers interacting with a team of professionals in the public schools can see teaching and learning in action. This early supervised contact if arranged properly allows the future teacher to observe what a pupil does, what a teacher would expect of him, and what a teacher does to make a pupil's school experience more useful. The idea is to expose prospective teachers to the duties and responsibilities of public school teachers. To heighten the future teachers' involvement, teacher-educators should encourage student teachers to discuss their experiences and observations in the seminar and to make suggestions and even critical contributions about their early school experience and observations.

Thus, the guided seminar discussion can provide an immediate opportunity for the future teacher to think and discuss school experience and seminar assignments, while allowing student teachers to relate course content to their own experience. This exchange of such ideas in the seminar by student teachers and professionals can become an important part of curriculum development. Shared ideas can be synthesized to serve as curriculum foci. It is assumed that prospective teachers would gain an understanding of pupils' academic needs and provide valuable insight on the way children see programs and the reasons why they do not respond to them.

It is very important that the teachers selected for this program also have open minds—not closed to a student, or to a prospective teacher—criticizing something seen in the classroom. Complete interaction among the teacher-educators, the teachers, and the prospective teachers is essential.

In summary, this alternate approach to teacher education includes a number of planned transactions for both the teacher-educators and prospective teachers. For instance:

1. Earlier supervised contact with schoolchildren and/or development of curriculum materials.

2. Guided seminar instructions related closely to the work with children and materials.

3. The discussion and evaluation of important social issues with groups of pupils and faculty.

4. A close working relationship with teacher-educators, teachers and pupils.

5. Group sessions examining the importance of personal values and community needs.

Much has been said about early school experience and its place in the teacher education program. The outstanding objective of the concept of teacher training is for prospective teachers to receive full benefit from their years of preparation. Teachers must do more than learn stereotyped factual data. They must supplement a progressive acquisition of theory with personal experience in creative work in the school, thus, a worthwhile approach in teacher education that provides for the prospective teacher systematized extra professional preparation and experience by blending early school experience with theory. Through this approach it seems sufficiently feasible to meet the expected course requirement of the traditional program and reform teaching training. I believe students interested in teacher education learn most satisfactorily when they are trained to interact in the school, for a lack of personal acquaintance frequently results in misunderstanding.

Matching Resources to Needs

During the past decade, many federally financed programs have been implemented in a multi-faceted approach to assisting the poverty-stricken families and inner-city schools of our nation. Though billions of dollars have been spent, some wisely or otherwise, the results have not been as visible or far-reaching as had been hoped. In the area of education, the large variety of federally financed programs has not provided the anticipated results to any great degree. Experts in various aspects of education, on both the local and national levels, have made great pronouncements of future successes, yet the outcomes bear witness to the shattering of their dreams for those students who are classified as the dispossessed.

The complexities of the problems facing inner-city education are somewhat staggering, yet there must be a reasonable means of resolving these problems on a logical basis. First and foremost, educators must assess the existing problems carefully and face the realities regarding those problems that are related directly to education, within the schools, and also those that are a function of the community at large, such as equal housing and job opportunities. Secondly, those problems that are on a continuum of the school-community relationship must be identified. Once these problems have been identified and assessed, a viable plan for attacking them can be established and put into action. In the past, it has been commonly assumed that covering the problems with money would make them disappear. The results of this assumption indicate the naivete of it!

It is contended that what is needed most is a human commitment to success, based on interpersonal relationships, and supported by the financial means to effectively implement the actions needed to meet the assessed problems of the inner-city community of which the schools are an integral part.

Higher Education and Community Development

Student-exchange educational programs in some degree are going on with countries all over the world. Many of the nations involved are well established and mature, and others are currently emerging into nations, including industrialized and non-industrialized societies, large and small nations, and highly varied cultures, races, and religions. The human talent and aspiration on which this educative interchange rests know no national boundary lines. These programs focus on national development, on economic and technological advance, and on the training and education of manpower for rapidly changing societies. They involve ordinarily long-range planning, combined with immediate urgency, emphasizing a developmental approach in education as in other fields of endeavor. They emphasize economic advancement, but with it, also, an urgent rise in literacy and the quality of educational leadership.

Institutions of higher education, thrust toward the inner-city community, with their resources, faculty, and students, can have a tremendous impact on the development of the inner-city core. With these resources, institutions of learning should accept the challenge and responsibility of human leadership by providing support and direction to help the inner-city community learn to value knowledge and work for its pursuits and, at the same time, award academic credit to students. They can provide service to the inner-city community that enables the inhabitants to develop those qualities of the good life, and self-supporting skills of which they are capable. The advantage of such a scheme is that it can obviate the necessity for growing government involvement in community affairs and be of some benefit to the community toward developing a "self-help" attitude.

The pervasive impact of education upon American inner-city society, without doubt, has become one of the foremost challenges of institutions of higher education. More than before, the resources of colleges and universities are seen as a means of solving inner-city problems.

Although the need for greater institutional and student involvement in the inner-city community affairs is clearly apparent, there has not hitherto existed a comprehensive human service compendium in this new and challenging direction.

Institutional Goal

Being aware of the enormous gap between institutions of higher education and the community, and the substantial shortfall of community action projects and programs for the poor, I propose a multifold offering of human services by institutions of higher education to inner-city communities that involves service not only for the intellectual and physical, but for the moral development of the inner-city community and its inhabitants.

Our institutions of higher education, being among leaders in educational, cultural, social, and economic opportunities in many ways can, with their resources, meet widespread student demands for valid practical experience for human service majors, training, and research at all levels from kindergarten through adult education.

From many sources, we have learned that all life is educative, that democratic institutions of higher learning must become definitely concerned with the improvement of community and human living, that the major areas and problems of life should give direction to the curriculum, and that functional education does not require active participation in constructive academic-oriented activities. All of these emphases are dominant in modern educational thinking today.

Henry David Thoreau, who, almost a hundred years ago, questioned and remonstrated with people in his day realizing how shallow are the roots of an experience not planted in the soil of everyday community life, when confronted with describing a functional educational experience for students and their contributors to the community at large, was asked: "You do not mean that students should go to work with their hands instead of their heads?" Thoreau replied: "I do not mean that exactly, but I mean something which he might think a good deal like that; I mean that they should not *play* life, or *study* it merely, while the community supports them at this expensive game, but earnestly *live* it from beginning to end. How could youths better learn to live than by once trying the experiment of living? Methinks this would exercise their minds as much as mathematics. . . . Why, if I had taken one turn down the harbor I should have known more about it."[12]

By interacting in the inner-city community, faculty and students can strengthen the institutional relationship and, at the same time, enhance greater understanding in developing and implementing programs with a common goal. The educational philosophy underlining the thrust of the institution into the inner-city community is to bridge the "deep moat" that separates the institution of higher education and the community by moving human service courses and programs that are relevant to the inner-city. The thrust should be twofold: (1) The offering of extension courses in social and humanistic sciences in the community. This academic offering is envisioned as a way of directly relating students' classroom learning to relevant realistic problems and situations; (2) The offering of human service courses; those which focus on the inner-city environment can append practical field experiences to the curriculum.

In order to become truly effective, the courses should be organized around fundamental inner-city needs, both individual and group, and inner-city community life processes and problems. This type of offering can provide extensive service opportunities for students and community inhabitants.

What is envisioned are programs whereby learning as well as teaching become the central focus, with each participant receiving the opportunity to progress at his maximum capacity. Translated into technical parlance, this is a fusion of the sporadic efforts with which the institutions of learning have been buried in recent years. It is an attempt to blend and unify social-economic, industrial and vocational needs of the inner-city community with academic and tangible services of faculty and the institutions of learning.

The type of education needed in a changing world includes the usual skills of a literate citizen, the social skills which permit the student and non-student to engage in productive social action, and coping skills which allow the learners to cope with the known and unknown, engaging in the continuous learning process demanded by our evolving world. Our current educational system is designed to maintain excellence in a static society, viewing learners collectively.

The effectiveness of any society must be measured against its members' needs and responses, and activities of the human service to the community must be determined by their value in facilitating the learning process for all. The ultimate goal should be autonomy in learning participants.

In the human service offered to the community, students should engage in activities of interest to them, exploring new areas and reinforcing weak skills. The activities should be problem oriented, involving the students with hands-on experience using a wide range of media. The faculty's job should be to help the individual students engage successfully in these activities, structuring the learning situation and guiding the development of the literacy, social, and coping skills of each community participant through that learner's success. The activities may take place anywhere within the reach of the student and the participant, both within the school and the community.

The Community Program

There can be no satisfactory solutions to ghetto social problems and no propagation toward meaningful growth in citizenship unless inner-city youth be permitted to measure themselves against actual situations requiring decisions and action in cooperation with others. The process of social education, as well as cultural growth and civic achievement, must fulfill itself through mutual counseling and intradependent action between the youth of the inner-city community and the students and scholars of the university, matured by a greater experience. Through such action and counseling, youth of the inner-city community can benefit by the knowledge and experience of the university scholars, and, at the same time, the students and faculty derive the advantage of seeing the situation of the inner-city community through the eyes of the young people upon whom the community, and university of the future, must depend. Hopefully, this would inspire and motivate more inner-city youth to strive for higher education and also enlighten the university scholars to inner-city pupils' real potential.

It is envisioned that the impetus of the human service program should work through a steering committee and subcommittees in which there is representation from various groups in the university and community.

The committee members should be representatives from the inner-city community, students, alumni of the university, the faculty, parents of the youth, and representatives from the social, civic, municipal, religious, and fraternal organizations, and social service agencies in the community.

All programs proposed for the community should be planned in conferences of these committees, and a community advisory council should act as a coordinating agency for the program. In these conferences and in the community advisory council, full recognition should be given to democratic principles and procedures. Pupil and student members of the committees should be allowed to express themselves freely on all matters. Likewise, members from the community should not only be permitted to speak on all subjects, but should be encouraged to enter freely into discussions of policy-making. The desire is to create not only a knowledge of the community and institution of learning itself, but also the type of leadership that can meet these needs.[13]

In the "communiversity" program, certain phases seem to be more important than others. Educational, social, and economic assistance, for instance, are of major importance in a heterogeneous community like the inner-city. A phase of the program emphasizing intercultural education should become a vital part of the human service work in the institution and in the community. Likewise, because certain sections of the community are laden with much poverty and very poor housing, which handicaps the development of the community, the campaign for better housing and community health improvement is urgent and should also become an immediate concern of the human service program. If we take education to mean that process whereby changes in behavior are induced, then the new thrust of the human service involvement in the community should have this as one of its goals.

It should be the desire of the human service program to become a clearinghouse for the needs of the community. In order to do this, it could set up several service agencies within the community where anyone could bring any problem on which help is desired. These newly created agencies should acknowledge the fact that they will not be able to solve all problems, but for those problems beyond its scope, the agencies hope to identify the logical source within the university for "immediate action" and solutions. For example, a few of the things the Human Service Office can assist with are listed below:

1. When requested, the institution should help to plan programs for social or public meetings, assisting pageants and plays, and should cooperate with them in conducting these activities.

2. When requested, it will help locate resources within the university who can assist in matters such as planning the interior arrangements and decoration of homes, furnishing recipes, menus, health suggestions, and in planning clothing for the family, etc.

For example, the Home Economics Department can help make clothing for members of a needy family as class projects. It can help plan interior decorating, menus for various types of meals and parties; and can furnish students to help in carrying out the party if desired. It can design costumes and can lend them freely to churches and other organizations in the community. The home economics staff can conduct each year a mothers' class in sewing, cooking and homemaking.

3. The Human Service Office could furnish help in poultry raising, gardens, tree spraying and pruning shrubbery, planting of flowers and landscaping.

For example, the Horticulture Department can test seeds for germination, give information and assist in flower growing, bulbs, shrubbery, spraying, etc. The Veterinary Medical Science Department can provide assistance in the care of poultry, dogs and pets. In fact, it is possible class projects can be conducted in the community with homeowners and others involved.

4. There can be a special department to help with the planning of home or church weddings. Sometimes this department simply remains in the background and gives advice, while other times it may be asked to take complete charge and make all arrangements. Students can be given credit for this while they gain experience.

5. Identify within the university appropriate resources who can furnish cost estimates for prospective home buyers.

6. Identify students and staff who will volunteer (intangible service) help to church organizations, families, and individuals.

For example, compute taxes, do household accounting, make out public statements and balance sheets, do mimeographing and typing, print programs, prepare public notices for paper, etc.

When a question is asked or information is requested, and answers for which are not immediately available in the Human Service Office, the information section could dispatch such questions through coordinated channels to the appropriate source. The Information Office should be able to answer any bona fide question if given time, provided that the answer or solution is available. These efforts and institutional resources make up a utilitarian program efficiency in home management, but also provide opportunities for social intercourse. In brief, the Human Service Office should try to help the community solve any problem that may confront it.

Academic Programs and Assistance

There are several general categories into which programs can be implemented by the human service program that could be for academic credit.

For example:

1. *A Volunteer Program.* Volunteers can make a real contribution in the War on Poverty, even on a part-time basis, if appropriate leadership is provided. Home-economist volunteers joined by graduate assistants can offer weekly classes for a group of recipients of Aid to Dependent Children. This could include teaching how to improve diets, efficiency in homemaking, consumer buying habits, etc.

2. *A Program of Intercultural Education.* This program can be designed to systematically improve attitudes and relationships between children of diverse backgrounds attending the public schools.

209

3. *Adult Education Program.* This program should be developed in the community by affording opportunities to non-professional adults to increase their competence, by encouraging and assisting organizations and agencies within the university concerned with adult education to develop program activities and to work together in the interest of the community.

Because adult education contributes directly and immediately to increasing the competence of adults who are affected by, and can influence many aspects of, social change in the community, a program of this nature warrants major attention in our efforts to deal with community problems.

The goal should be an adult education program designed to enable all segments of the community to participate. Recognizing the economic and social disadvantage that has occurred, the university can meet some of the problems with an adult evening program. Each semester it can offer some classes in general education subjects, business, management, etc.; some for credit, some not.

4. *Tutorial Programs in the Community.* Students and faculty can work with community youth, helping them with reading, mathematics and English, drafting, etc. This program should be staffed by specialists in education and social and human relations.

5. *Field Service Program.* This program should be supported by the liberal arts college offering a number of vocational professional studies in education and business administration. Students and faculty should work on community organization agencies. They should be supervised by a staff member of the agency and a coordinator for the Human Service Office.

6. *Social Analysis Program.* This program should be a mission-oriented community project that awards credit primarily for community work with the requirements of academic study. The program should be an approved course of an experimental or interdisciplinary nature with students working with community agencies and

indigenous organizations, rather than initiating their own program.

7. *Community Summer Program.* A program sponsored by the university in cooperation with the community awarding credit primarily for community work. This program can present an opportunity for university summer graduate students and community people to explore different facets of a community and become actively involved in a number of projects which the community sees as beneficial to its needs. For example, the Neighborhood Youth Corps (NYC) or the summer recreation programs.

The program, if initiated, should be implemented on a small scale at first in order to overcome obstacles that may occur, for the initial attempt must be successful. Programs of this type depend on the confidence which is established between the institution and the community.

Once the programs are implemented, a staff coordinator could be assigned to assume the responsibility of overviewing the program operation. This is in line with the ultimate goal of the human service program director to appoint staff members from the community to actively participate in all phases of the program offerings. The staff field coordinator should be required to keep in touch with the director, submit periodic reports, check attendance, and collect the final evaluations. He could be a liaison officer between the human service and the community programs, providing information, following up requests, and supervising whenever necessary. The coordinator gains an overall picture of the program and its significance to the community. His interpretation or feedback to the community can do much to develop the enthusiasm to enhance future programs. His observations can be of great value to the human service director and the various community factions.

The Guiding Principles of the Human Service Program

—The "communiversity" social service program should be expanded when need for it is shown.

211

—The cooperation of the university faculty, staff and community leaders should be enlisted after a complete, unbiased presentation of the situation has been made of the people requesting assistance.

—Help from all available communities and outside sources should be solicited and utilized.

—Discussion among participants should be conducted on a frank and fearless basis.

—Both direct and indirect modes of attack on community problems should be utilized; every area of the neighborhood and school life should be explored for the contributions each can make in helping to solve the problems.

—The members of the steering committee should not be discouraged by apparent setbacks, minor or major disappointments, as the program progresses.

—As much knowledge as is available and practicable should be brought to bear upon the problem by the university and community which will engage in its solution.

—The active programs proposed should attempt to include as many of the community people as possible.

—In addition to a long-term program for handling the situation, a plan for dealing with emergent cases in the community should be devised.

—Cooperation among the various faculty and community representatives to the steering committee should be freely and enthusiastically given in implementing the programs.

—Meeting of the steering committee should be regular and conducted within acceptable parliamentary procedures.

—The "communiversity" social service program, when new dimensions are proposed, should include items looking toward the social and economic improvement of the area in whatever ways needed, utilizing existing agencies and organizations for the purpose.

The Needs of the Program

In order to develop the human service program into a full dimension of inclusion for all as a laboratory of social education there must be a "change of heart."

In spite of the stumbling blocks of federally funded programs in the inner-city, and the stumbling blocks with inner-city community groups, institutions of higher education should accept the challenge.

However, a program of this nature at the college and university level requires stimulation from a committed administration, not just the occasional and temporary attention of selected individuals. If the human service program is to be a functional program, major attention is necessary, adequate funds should be appropriated to achieve meaningful goals at the level of expectancy, and additional staff members should be appointed. Adequate endowment from the university can enhance the director's efforts to strive for the expected level of efficiency and effectiveness.

The human service program should be a total university-community program, and caution should be taken whereby the inner-city community leaders are not saddled with the responsibility of trying to keep the program striving in the face of institutional coolness and reluctance if the robust human service program is to survive in institutions of higher learning.

The precise dimensions and potential of a human service program have only been touched upon here. However, if the program is to be developed and refined, the strengths of its administrators and faculty must be drawn upon.

Summary

The human service program is an entity in which community and university people should be interested. Therefore, the university and community should swing open their doors freely, inviting hearty cooperation in the common cause of a better community for all; a plant for promoting neighborliness and common brotherhood of common interest for group cooperation on the part of the university and community.

What is envisioned are programs whereby learning rather than teaching become the central focus, with each participant receiving the opportunity to progress at his maximum capacity without regard to the relative capacity of his peers.

Translated into technical parlance, the human service approach is a fusion of the sporadic efforts in which the university has been buried in recent years. It blends a unified social-economic, industrial and vocational need of the community with academic and intangible services from the university.

Community Control Academy

When we speak of the inner-city, its social and educational problems, we often think of the black community, but seldom do we react to the new school of thought and perspective envisioned by the black community. The new school of thought is that of creating a black identity and community control. This is an effort of the black community to explain itself and not to be explained. This is part of the traditional pattern of a higher ethnic first generation, a second generation that "denies everything," and a third generation that has overcome its inferiority complex and seeks cultural ties and identity. The recent rekindling of black ethnic feeling is largely a result of the black sense of the invasion of their community by other ethnic groups to educate them.

The obvious facts should not delude educators, administrators, and curriculum reformers in making educational policy for the inner-city schools. The community wants schools with the essential quality of providing an education that enhances the identity of blacks, with black studies as an integral part of the curriculum. The black community is sensitive to the functional role of white teachers in inner-city schools. Though not totally committed to this extreme view, it is important to note that the black community thinking is not in conflict with other ethnic group thinking and concerns for their community. It points with accurate reflections on history to other ethnic groups and ghetto courses they took to give themselves self-confidence and control of their affairs. By devices of community control,

214

they achieved the status from which they were accorded the esteem on the basis of which they were more fully assimilated equally into the general institutional framework.

The aim of inner-city education should be to create a system in which the resources of the city are intimately integrated with the educational process at the community level. The problem of the best education for blacks emanates, in large measure, from whites' thinking of the inner-city child as being one who desires to be bused. The inner-city pupil is thought to be mobile because he is perceived as being disadvantaged.

The effect of this simplistic overgeneralization creates a major social problem by leaving the concept disadvantaged so vague; the general public perceives every city school with a significant proportion of black pupils as a school for the disadvantaged. According to Kenneth B. Clark, "The problem of education in the urban ghetto seems to be a vicious cycle: if children go to school where they live and if most neighborhoods are racially segregated, then the schools are necessarily segregated too. If Negroes move into a previously white community and whites then move away or send their children to private or parochial school, the public school will continue to be segregated. If the quality of education in Negro schools is inferior to that in white schools, whites feel justified in the fear that the presence of Negroes in their own school would lower its standards. If they move their own children away and the school becomes predominantly Negro, and, therefore, receives an inferior quality of education, the pattern begins all over again.

"The cycle of systematic neglect of Negro children must be broken, but the powerlessness of the Negro communities and fear and indifference of the White community have combined so far to keep the cycle intact."[14]

Although there are many obstacles to creating a new form of integration, and although many different arrangements tried on a sporadic basis have not been successful, for example, compensatory education, limited busing, to name but a few, it should be clear that until a new way of conceptualizing school integration in the city is developed, it will be difficult, if not impossible to reject the demand for community control of schools.

What, then, are the consequences for community control?

Well, inner-city children will inevitably go to school with children from their immediate neighborhood. It is surprising that a large number of Americans regard this arrangement as an absolute good for the white community, but a "no-no" for the black community. There is also a widespread belief that keeping the inner-city child in his immediate environment creates psychological difficulties for him. While this is not improbable, neither is there overwhelming evidence that the consequences of busing are uniformly desirable. So much mobility has recently been tried with the inner-city child that it can be said we really do not know what the consequence of community-controlled inner-city schools would be. Even the best seed has trouble growing up in alien soil.

Underlying the whole argument of school integration that characterizes the American school is a concept of uniformity in children. Such a concept, despite all disclaimers, presupposes a commonality or similarity among children which simply does not exist and could never exist. Although we recognize that there are wide intellectual, cultural, and personality differences among children, we essentially mass-produce a curriculum for all children. Teachers and administrators are not insensitive to differences among inner-city children. Indeed, they are probably more sensitive to the range of these differences than any other group. However, the present educational structure in the inner-cities' schools on which the school system operates does not provide for this variety.

Many inner-city teachers are bruised by any suggestion that the inner-city schools ignore cultural, social, and intellectual differences among black pupils—the point, for instance, which the school has attempted to accommodate a wide range of differences. But these arrangements always operate within the overall assumption that pupils are there to be processed. We have tried off and on, over the last half-century, a tracking system that funnels children into castelike classroom groups in terms of some measure of aptitude. A reflection on the tracking system brings to mind what Louise Kennedy calls "Union Rooms," stating: "Even in communities where it was finally difficult to establish separate school buildings for Negroes, the authorities have developed what have been called 'Union Rooms.' In these 'Union Rooms' are placed all the Negro chil-

216

dren in the school, irrespective of grades. The resulting situation is that while the White children of the school are distributed in grades, usually one grade to a room . . . the Negro children of varying ages are grouped together regardless of school grade."[15] Such a system is simply a way of refining the classroom, essentially leaving its basic structure unchanged. Obviously, this has not changed, nor has the method of teacher assignments been altered to any great degree. Similarly, systems of flexible scheduling make greater varieties or combinations of pupils possible, but again, even flexible scheduling systems operate within the present structure of the school.

Thus, changes in learning in the inner-city school system depend, in part, on the extent to which the concept of inner-city educational mass misproduction can be criticized, evaluated, modified, or even completely abandoned. This latter point, of course, raises all kinds of disturbing questions of political and social nature. Such questions would not be disturbing if the present inner-city school system of organization were capable of meeting the challenges of the black community that face it. But it is difficult to see how the city school system, in its present form, can produce the social and cultural changes that are essential for the inner-city. It is also obvious that no meaningful large-scale changes within the inner-city school system will take place so long as the change occurs solely within the boundaries of the educational system itself. Anyone, for example, who has visited the schools in the suburbs and city, can hardly regard this idea as revolutionary. The community-controlled school in the suburbs is a standard part of the educational system. What I propose is that the notion of school integration be modified and that the notion of inner-city community control of schools become a central concern in organizing inner-city pupils in relation to learning opportunities. Moreover, the whole notion of a fixed curriculum for inner-city schools must be abandoned. If one retained the idea of fixed curricula, he would create essentially the same kinds of learning experiences that exist today in inner-city schools.

I will adopt the concept community academy—meaning a place in the creative learning environment, in which we may assemble any size group, of any age, with the purpose of producing certain kinds of educational changes in black pupils as quality products. In order to create such community academies, it is necessary to have—as, in fact, I think the black community does have—a reasonably clear notion of what constitutes the educational problem of the black community. What I am proposing is that community academies be designed specifically to overcome these deficiencies, but that no one community academy attempt to produce all such changes.

One of the primary goals of education in American society is to teach children how to interact as equals with one another in ways that are consistent with our democratic principles. This noble American ideal, as we all recognize, is only partially achieved in desegregated schools. It has been, for a long time, difficult for blacks to achieve in the inner-city school systems as they are now constituted. However, advocates of integrated schools who have observed recent attempts at desegregation must be appalled by the fact that integration is largely a matter of moving pupils of different cultural or ethnic background—in particular, blacks—into the same building. Once there, these groups are inside these buildings; however, they rarely interact socially in ways that are likely to lead to the development of social attitudes that, in fact, do integrate the various ethnic groups. Nor do the pupils in desegregated schools, whatever their ethnic origin may be, learn to relate to each other in a way that will make them members of the kind of society that is clearly going to evolve in this country.

We are confronted with a major crisis—to integrate or segregate. For many years now, integration has been the major theme. We fail to acknowledge that desegregation and integration are not synonymous. If we look logically at the two concepts—integration and desegregation—we will find that desegregation is a legal term that is legislated and must be carried out.

In other words, desegregation is a law. On the other hand, if we look logically at the term *integration,* it is a social concept that is governed by the individual, that is, the system or the democratic process is the democratic spirit with high regard for individual rights.

Integration involves social interaction, social transition, communication, mutual respect, and cooperation. Integration and desegregation do not mean the same thing. Black pupils in desegregated schools are academically and socially excluded from academic affairs, from the curriculum to student affairs. The only black voice to be heard in the purpose and process of education is in exclusively black affairs. Having no black values in the traditional curriculum with the exception of black studies only serves to perpetuate the status quo.

If integration is to be our goal, why place inner-city pupils in environments where the curriculum stands between them? I do not believe that mixing pupils heterogeneously in desegregated schools accomplishes the purpose of integration, but brings about racial antagonism that further inflames the racial crisis in public schools. Nor do I believe forced busing for blacks and whites alike accomplishes the goal of an integrated society.

Although I can only dimly foresee what a community academy can do to foster the goal of integration, I can forecast what its essential characteristics must be. It must be an academy in which inner-city pupils are far more active than passive. It is an environment in which social interaction and learning are the major forms of student activity. It is an environment in which a variety of teaching methods is used, from role-playing to group therapy sessions, from lectures and discussions to whatever method stimulates learning. Within the academy, the purposes of instruction should determine the type of learning environment that is created in the centers, and also the members of the inner-city community should organize around the creation of the centers to create a community school concept as an independent unit designed to achieve a specific educational purpose.

It is conceptualized as a community-controlled individualized instruction program, earlier known as the Dalton Plan and the Winnetka Plan that we call today "the open classroom," "school without walls," or the "world of inquiry." This concept was developed in the eighteenth century by Jean-Jacques Rousseau.

However, in 1920, Helen Parkhurst instituted a concept of the Rousseau thesis called the Dalton Plan, which allowed pupils opportunity for individual development. Like Rousseau, it was her belief that children should be permitted to concentrate on their activities over longer periods of time, in accordance with a strongly motivated interest, under conditions

219

of a flexible schedule which varied from day to day. The Parkhurst concept was "a simple and economic reorganization of the schools whereby pupils and teachers function to better advantage. . . ."

The three underlying principles of the Dalton Plan were:

1. The principle of *freedom*. This does not mean that the pupil may do as he or she likes.
2. The principle of *group interaction*. Making the individual an intelligent participator in the life of his immediate group—democratic education.
3. The principle of *"psychology of a point of view."* A child, she explained, "never voluntarily undertakes anything that he does not understand," but he involves himself with "pursuits which he can understand," and, "in initiating his own pursuits he looks at a thing from all angles and he plans to carry out his objectives."

It is here where teaching and learning should move rapidly from the role of the teacher as dispenser of knowledge and controller of learning to the role of guiding and managing learning activities. There is nothing new in the desire. What is new is the ability to do it. For years now, blacks have been raging that the schools were not relevant, and they were labeled "dropouts." Today, the same concept of education is referred to as individualized instruction. For the first time, the philosophy of individualization and learner responsibility and the means of accomplishing it exist together. Needed now is the human transformation to permit and guarantee realization in the inner-city black community.

The community-controlled academy can be a complex learning resource facility where can be had almost any kind of learning experience. Formal classes for *presentation* should decrease sharply—such things will be learned individually or in small groups from multiple media (books, printed materials from computers, films, sound tape recordings, video tape recordings, television, computer programs, etc.). Teachers should spend their time analyzing learning difficulties, giving guidance, conducting seminars, and so on. More of the time of the student should be unscheduled or self-scheduled. The learner will be learning to do what he will do all his life—learn.

The reasoning underlying this proposed approach is that the inner-city schools face tremendous problems in educating black pupils, and the city schools in their present form cannot solve these problems. Nor are these problems exclusively the domain of the schools. They are problems of the total inner-city environment. Therefore, the solution to these problems must be achieved by the community as a whole.

Thus, the community-controlled academy should be an integral part of the broader inner-city community, and the present concept of inner-city schools, as buildings in a geographic location, be abandoned. This concept of community control is envisioned as the way to eliminate many of the educational difficulties faced by black pupils simply because the system of education would be properly geared to the achievement of its local as well as society's objectives. At the same time, the notion of bending blacks to slots of comparable units of educated people created by the dominant culture would, in large part, be abandoned once and for all.

I am well aware that an immense amount of research and development in the inner-city community needs to be done to test what kind of community-controlled academy can achieve significant educational purposes. Nevertheless, the following community-controlled academy is proposed. Such a program has not been tried in the black community, where a community academy involving parents and teachers and children in the community is specifically related to the achievement of significant educational goals, for credit. Given this concept of a community-controlled educational system of this character, what is achieved within could be enlarged, broadened, deepened, and inserted into the open society. Such is the type of concept of inner-city to which public education must turn if the inner-city inhabitant is to achieve educationally and accomplish the goal of a truly equal integrated society.

The community academy should house the activities for formal and informal educational experiences for administrators, teachers, pupils, and parents. The fundamental purpose of the academy should be to provide opportunities and experience that, hopefully, will result in desirable attitudes and motivation for quality education. Both teachers who have had limited formal preparation in inner-city education, and parents who have not attended institutions of higher learning, should have the opportunity both to study about the local community and have experience with new ideas, new methods and materials, as means to an end of ghetto pupil educational deficiencies.

It is envisioned that the faculty of the academy can be a consortium of competent individuals from the local high schools, colleges, and universities. The academy should be a place of inquiry, critical thinking, and a center of teaching and learning that moves participants in the direction of greater individualization in education, and of increased learner responsibility.

It is the belief that an effective educational academy in the inner-city community can provide the inner-city child an excellent opportunity to assess his chances of success in public schools and higher education and at the same time be beneficial to his teacher.

Inner-city community members participating in the educational academy need to experience innovative ways of learning. They need to learn to be responsible for their own learning activities, to choose what they want to learn and by what methods. They need to have full opportunity to study about and put into practice, the newer methods, when possible, in the classroom. Finally, they should be provided maximum assistance with learning by the teacher.

Furthermore, the educational community academy is conceptualized as identifying participating academic potential and capability and guiding their development. It should be a large facility where pupils, adults, and teachers can work, either individually or in small seminars, carrying out assignments or pursuing personal interests. Faculty members should prepare units of instruction or materials for the participants to use in the program. An opportunity to learn and a choice of opportunities and means of acquiring knowledge should be an important feature of the academy. The academy must be both attractive and challenging. It should exemplify the life-long learning ideal and facilitate the development of more mature levels of behavior as well as self-actualization.

Special instructional areas should be provided for social

studies education, humanities, anthropology, mathematics education, value analysis and clarification, reading and language arts education, and any other courses requested. Each area should have model seminars in which the methods and approaches suited to that area are taught. The actual content of each of the disciplines should be an integral part of each participant's program. The model seminars should be designed and equipped for the special areas, but also highly suitable and used for other classes. Each of the special academic areas should have workroom display sections.

There are four general categories into which the community academy should fall:

1. Well-developed multiple courses in field work.
2. Formal program courses designed to consist of single classes centered around a specific subject for academic credit.
3. Informal program courses designed to consist of single classes centered around non-academic credit.
4. Programs designed in community work that are primarily formal and/or informal.

The following are examples of educational courses or subjects proposed. If coordinated with the local colleges and universities, there is the possibility that community academy participants can receive academic credit for community work.

—Field education instruction
—Academic-oriented courses relevant to community needs
—Community service courses
—Individual or independent study courses

The educational objectives of these courses should be:

1. To address community needs for an educational experience relevant to the work that they are doing in the inner-city community.
2. To meet the responsibility to provide the resources necessary to community groups in the process of im-

plementing change so that these groups can make decisions concerning the direction of change, as desired.

3. To extend educational opportunities to inner-city adults who ordinarily would not be able to afford it.

4. To bridge the "deep moat" of cultural and social barriers which exists between the community and members of outside communities.

5. To enhance an in-depth comprehensive study of community structure, process, and problems.

Humanistic and Race Relations Center

City boards of education have long realized that their decisions affect the inner-city community they serve as a whole and that their continued success, in part, depends upon the support of people they serve in the inner-city community. The increasing number of inner-city community organized interest groups certainly play a part in making the board of education conscious of their social role. Furthermore, the inner-city community inhabitants are important, for their confidence and support are indispensable for their success.

The ethical responsibilities of the humanistic and race relations center proceed beyond the protection of narrowly economic or self-interests to one of genuine social leadership. This novel idea can bring radical change in personnel attitudes and beliefs, effect shifts in community development plans, and set new trends for the future.

The best way for a humanistic and race relations center to cultivate a social consciousness is through a study of the liberal arts and sciences conceived as those areas of knowledge which enlarge the understanding and deepen the insights of people, especially citizens in the inner-city community it is to serve, both with regard to individuals themselves and their social relationship to the community.

The boards of education should insist that teachers utilize community resources to invigorate their experience and understanding in order to vitalize the school, give depth of meaning to instruction and training, and provide for direct, as well as vicarious, learning experiences. It is projected that this approach will point the direction for activities and programs of quality for the inner-city pupil.

The inner-city is a microcosm of human experiences. Within it is the continuous process and related problems of making a living, exchanging ideas, securing an education, adjusting to people, and meeting individual and group needs. Therefore, the center should be organized around order, clarity, and consistency in understanding the community's physical setting, condition, class and caste structure, organized interest groups, climate of opinion, needs and problems as these and similar factors affect the school and the type of service it renders.

The role of the inner-city school, again, should be a cooperative one with various service projects of a genuinely civic nature. In a center of this nature, participants will discover that the community has a need for their talent and services. Therefore, teachers should become actively involved in civic-minded organizations in the community they serve. This social interaction can enhance becoming sensitive to the aspects of the desirable needs of the community which they cannot obtain elsewhere or receive in sufficient degrees.

The principal reasons for utilizing the humanistic and race relations center are:

1. A greater amount of general counseling could be provided to the community at large to meet its needs.
2. Seminars could be made which would arouse the community's thirst for more information and/or knowledge, and perhaps the conceptual level could be elevated.

The fundamental goal of the center should be to provide learning opportunities as in-service training for teachers.

The center can be a valuable facility that has an excellent utility for keeping teachers, students, and professional persons current on community affairs. In simplified terms, this facility can be developed into an excellent agency to carry out predetermined educational and technical objectives in the community, formal and informal courses on current issues of the community offered at the elementary, secondary, and college level, and incorporated with research. This approach will surely have implications for use in the current, unprecedented concern of education for inner-city pupils.

Therefore, the center should be designed to serve the needs of faculty, programs, and departments that have strong orientation toward research, as well as the community served. For example, the humanistic and race relations center is envisioned as being active in a variety of intramural and extramural projects. The intramural projects of the center can provide a strong core of learning, research, and information. The extramural activities of the center can range from discussion to programs and referral and consultation on the development of cooperative experimental and research projects. This can include working with community groups with respect to community development. Also, the extramural activities may draw upon the core of the intramural projects for new insights and ideas. Importantly, too, the extramural activities can assist in setting priorities and providing information for the intramural projects.

As a human service and community relations program, the following objectives should be set forth:

1. Promote and develop human relations in the community by affording opportunities to employees, community members, professionals, non-professionals, and students to increase their competence, and by encouraging and assisting organizations and agencies concerned with community problems to develop relevant activities and to work together in the interest of the community.

2. To receive and disseminate information about community needs.

3. To arrive at consensus within the center regarding those gaps which need to be closed between expectations and what is the actual case.

4. Establish priorities regarding the areas in which the center should direct primary interest.

5. Recommend ways in which the center and other groups and individuals can take action to help close the gaps.

6. Make public the resulting statements as a way of

increasing the visibility of the center and the cooperation of other entities, as a way of encouraging concentrated action by the various related groups and individuals in the community.

The expectations of the humanistic and race relation center should be the same for the community and participating organizations and individuals. All entities should be encouraged to provide information rather than seek it, and all should review social problems, in addition to attempting to solve them.

To be effective in this center, the instructors should seek to create the circumstances where individuals are maximally open, optimally free to receive feedback information. The purpose is to create a supportive, non-judgmental, encouraging, and rewarding climate within which ego protection is less important and defenses may be lowered. Continuing groups that develop norms which are favorable to openness and change and which reward efforts in these directions should be a major objective of this type of center.

A Model Proposed for
Afro-American Cultural Centers

This section describes a model proposed for Afro-American culture centers. This model is built utilizing research assistants and a performing artist in residence. This approach to Afro-American culture does not presume to cover the full range of black studies, but it is intended to be a coherent unit available to the community public schools as well as the institutions of higher learning.

A serious defect of the Afro-American cultural centers has been the haphazard approach and inadequate attention to the development of the concept into a realistic program, which frustrates the whole purpose of black culture enlightenment.

Black people's culture has gone too long unanalyzed by black scholars. An obstacle is the shortage of black scholars to research and teach in this area. Black scholars are needed who can cultivate and recapture black culture with a sense of continuity.

Between 1966 and 1970, universities and colleges across the nation made disappointing progress in searching for the type and quality of personnel needed for the vigorous emphasis on development of black culture programs which black students, black communities, and institutions of higher learning have requested.

If Afro-American cultural centers are to become truly effective in their endeavor to contribute to the refinement of black life, we must organize them around fundamental human needs, in terms of both individuals and groups; we must directly relate the cultural center programs with black life processes and problems; and we must provide extensive culture studies and service opportunities for university students, community youth, and adults alike.

Furthermore, only through extensive firsthand and vicarious experiences, academic and non-academic, can university students, adults, and faculty be able to attain realistic understanding of the black heritage. It is through this viable alternative that the Afro-American cultural centers and the university can fully justify their true, continued existence, and mutual concerns for black students.

Verbal support of the Afro-American cultural center on this viewpoint, regardless of how sound, is not enough. Instead of verbal embracement, guiding principles should be reformed and translated into specific policies of concern and commitment, and these policies must be implemented in terms of particular programs if anything really significant is to happen toward reconstructing the cultural center into a meaningful entity. I propose that the public educational institutions commit their resources of the reconstruction for the cultural center into a full dimension such that black people are able to enhance a keen awareness of their cultural heritage. Nevertheless, although the cultural center was created for black students, it is envisioned that the expanded concept can prove useful to all students, faculty, curriculum developers, educational advisory councils, the local community, and others desiring guidance and assistance in down-to-earth techniques of building a better institution and community. Only through the efforts of many persons in many places can we make a center of this kind possible. The scores of educators, community leaders, and the cultural center, being sensitive to the crucial needs of black students, can collectively point the way out of current confusion toward a deeper sense of community. With this support, we can clearly discern the road that separates the university from the community. This type of reciprocal cultural exchange with the black community and the academic concerns within public education should be coordinated, for social and cultural consciousness is part of being an educated person; individuals should be sensitive to the real essence of other individuals, their culture, experiences, viewpoints, life-styles, and needs; for such is part of the process of education.

Throughout the country, vast numbers of people are learning about black people or think they are—from higher education to public education, from commercial film and television shows. A small proportion of these are excellent examples of blacks' finest achievements in the visual arts, drama, music, and documentaries. Many others are certainly not "bad"—they are entertaining and reflect something of black humor, folklore, strengths and weaknesses, blacks' progress, and blacks' unsolved problems.

Taken as a whole, it seems fair to say that commercial films and television programs, while there is much good in them, present a lopsided and, in many ways, harmful picture of black people. What is most needed is to balance the diet of lighter entertainment with a large infusion of black cultural and documentary programs that display the more serious, creative, and cultivated side of black life.

Guidelines for Researchers

With the tide running strongly toward putting the bulk of the program development and refinement on researchers, their laudable goal for a respectable and relevant cultural program of action as conceived here calls for:

1. Research and labor in the vineyard of the Afro-American scene to make available and to give full account of black culture and the circumstances of their own people.

2. Research, study, and analysis of black culture for the light it sheds on black people.

229

3. Through teaching and writing, a description, definition, or explanation of their findings.

4. Their determination of what black intellectuals have offered in the way of descriptions, definitions, and explanations.

5. Documentation of their findings to enable all scholars and students to enrich their own perceptions. A series of works can emerge and have an impact on the world of scholarship.

6. Skillful analysis of the relationship of art, music, dance, drama, poetry, etc., to black culture, pointing out the interaction using examples of material and non-material culture; for example, the modification of cultural norms of art, music, drama, poetry, dance, and their effects on spiritual forms.

7. Taking students through the black experience with workshops, setting the scene elaborately, they would be required to conclude with an analytical summary ranging from the past to the future of black culture. These results should be a detailed study which can provide much valuable information about black people—their vocations, skills, ethos, modes of life, thinking, and religion, both indigenous and acquired. In short, black culture would be an indispensable compendium for anyone who seeks to understand black people, beginning from their past history and going on to their adaptations to modern conditions not only in the fields of art, music, dance, drama, etc., but in other aspects of blacks' cultural heritage.

8. The researchers to illustrate and supplement their work with critical analysis in conjunction with their research and teaching.

9. Research, teaching, and related suggestions for the participants to proceed with the lectures with their natural flow unhampered.

10. Describing the theory of culture diffusion and assimilation.

11. New evidence to lead to new conditions and conclusions. Thus, the research and teaching of black culture should be a historical, not a geographical, analysis, where

all those who wish can begin their understanding of Afro-Americans by studying in depth the culture of black people. The community, public schools, university students, and teachers should find this offering a treasure of knowledge, a mine of new information and a rational inquiry—all marshaled for the elucidation of the life and thought of black people.

The approach is proposed primarily because it can illustrate through teaching and research ways in which black culture experiences are organized and explained; major forces that bear and shape black culture and the typical approaches of black student scholars. The categories, therefore, include the mythic and imaginative capacities of the culture and the importance of ideas, of technology, and of communication.

Guidelines for Performing Artists

The performing artists should interpret the research and teaching of the research assistants. The tasks of the performing artist should be:

1. To interpret and transform the research and teaching of the researchers.
2. To provide an opportunity for all concerned to see the artist as a representative of blacks' most conscious values.
3. To plan black cultural programs with the university and community, assist when requested with pageants and plays.
4. To devote time to the development of black literature, and through their talent, show the longings and aspirations of black people and their intellectual contributions. Past and present black authors and their "slants" can be studied to interpret the varied viewpoints of the group.
5. To express the poetry and orations of outstanding black people.
6. To organize drama workshop-seminars, debating

seminars, and literary appreciative organizations. In the drama workshop-seminars, original plays can be written, directed, and staged by students and teachers on some phase of black achievements or problems. Members of the local community can take active roles in these plays.

7. In the literary appreciation organization, the original poems or phases of blacks' work and attainment can be read and presented.

8. To interpret and perform the works of famous black artists and their world-wide achievements, they should teach how to make posters, tapestries, and paintings depicting black reactions.

9. Dances of blacks and their historical meaning should be studied and learned and later performed in community and university programs.

10. In Music they can devote time to spirituals, blues, jazz, etc., to learn their true spirit and rhythm. Many of these can be presented in public performances of a glee club, chorus, and bands.

No one artist should be expected to teach and perform in all of these areas. The entire phase of this program offering should be divided up into categories, and each artist should be assigned to his area of competency.

For a program of this kind there is great need to increase the number of staff members. It is conceived that some non-degree person can qualify for several positions. Some people have lived as deep or deeper than most scholars have studied. Several staff members are needed because the ultimate effectiveness of our efforts depends heavily upon being able to implement several ongoing integral programs or projects. With adequate personnel and staff, for example, several staff members could spend specific time assigned by the program director teaching while others are researching or studying in the field, or attending workshops at other universities. The approach would enrich the cultural program staff's knowledge and magnify its teaching. This dimension is needed for a continuous, fresh, broader, and more realistic concept of what is required for successful program planning, research, and teaching.

Moreover, much greater use can be made of the younger

researchers and artistic talent from the culture program; they can establish rapport with youthful audiences at other universities and elsewhere. Or, they could be sent abroad to Africa to research and acquire new insights and broaden their experience. Also, we can bring in distinguished artists for guest appearances to participate and conduct workshops.

The offerings of the culture center hopefully will produce new insights about reality, race relations, and a major device for dissemination of that knowledge, and to place in perspective the legitimacy and worth of the experience of the black people.

Finally, the cultural center should be academically sound and respectable, with all the students and communities encouraged to participate in the program regularly. In this respect, the culture center should be a center for all students and communities. It should have a program which is relevant and responsive to the reality of black students' needs; respect all students' values in the broadest cultural terms; promote the self-determined growth of the students and community; and liberate the mind and mobilize resources within the university to develop and refine the existing program. The specific purpose is to liberate through research and rational discussion students' potential ways of fulfilling a number of kinds of potentials—political and/or social, through training for social change; intellectual and cultural protocol, through development of the critical facilities and creative abilities of all students; and the establishment of the relevance of the reconstruction of the existing curriculum and disciplines.

In summary, the Afro-American culture center activity is to build a firm base in the university for the understanding of black culture through the community, university, and mass media. The culture center activities should not be confused with, or subordinated to, information and propaganda programs. Nor should they be expected to serve short-term, political ends, but conducted rather with the expectation of long-term results.

There should be coordinated efforts to overcome the educational problems that bind the black community. There should be genuine interest to establish a contact with those within the ghetto. It should take the form of the establishment of various organizations within the inner-city ghetto and organizations, and social service bureaus which are operating in the black community, in the rapidly increasing groups and individuals who are attending civic and social affairs, there for varied reasons attempting to establish understanding and friendship with those within.

In many cases, this is no conscious attempt to break the inner-city bonds; indeed, it may be a deliberate attempt to go in and satisfy the needs of the inhabitants to prevent their leaving the ghetto.

Sometimes the ruse is successful, but more often, in the long run, it defeats its own end, for it sets an example of broadness that the ghetto-bound spirit eagerly seizes upon. Having secured a taste of the world outside the ghetto, youth is eager to get more of it and the determination to grow strong and break through increases.

There is another side of the picture; it is a tale of long dark years of dismal failure, of brave struggles to rise above mediocrity, of bitter fights for existence, a tale twisted with heartaches and heartbreaks, a tale drenched in sweat and blood, but still shot through with flashes of sunlight upon pure gold. It takes rare courage to fight a fight that more often than not ends in death, poverty, or prostitution of genius. But it is to those who make this fight despite tremendous odds, despite the deterring pessimism of those who see in the tangle of racism that surrounds the ghetto a hopeless barrier, that we must look for the breaking of the bonds now linked together by ignorance and misunderstanding.

NOTES

CHAPTER 1

[1]Thomas Woody, *Educational Views of Benjamin Franklin* (New York: McGraw-Hill, 1931).

[2]Roy J. Honeywell, *The Educational Work of Thomas Jefferson* (Cambridge, Ma.: Harvard University Press, 1931). See also Julian P. Boyd, ed., *The Papers of Thomas Jefferson*, Vol. II (Princeton: Princeton University Press, 1950), pp. 535-543.

[3]W. E. B. DuBois, *The Souls of Black Folk* (New York: The Fawcett Publishers, Inc., 1968), pp. 23-54.

[4]C. G. Woodson, *Education of the Negro, Prior to 1861* (New York: G. P. Putnam's, 1915), p. 2.

[5]William J. Edwards, *Twenty-Five Years in the Black Belt* (Boston: The Cornhill Company, 1918), p. 101.

[6]Booker T. Washington, "The Education of the Southern Negro," *National Educational Association Proceedings* (1904), p. 134. (The *National Educational Association Proceedings* became the *National Education Association Proceedings* beginning with the 1907 volume.)

[7]Charles T. Walker, "The Educational Needs of the Southern Negro," *National Educational Association Proceedings* (1903), pp. 123-129.

[8]Gustavus J. Orr, *The Best System for a Southern State* (Atlanta: J. P. Harrison, 1886).

[9]Louis R. Harlan, *Separate and Unequal* (Chapel Hill: The University of North Carolina Press, 1958), p. 138.

[10]*Ibid.*, p. 140.

[11]Horace Mann Bond, *The Education of the Negro in the American Social Order* (New York: Prentice-Hall, 1934), pp. 352-353.

[12]Bulletin, State of Arkansas, *Annual Report of Education Activities in Negro Schools*, June 30, 1922.

[13]Gunnar Myrdal, *An American Dilemma* (New York: McGraw-Hill, 1944), Vol. 2 p. 897.

[14]Dista H. Caldwell, *The Education of the Negro Child* (New York: Carlton Press, 1961), p. 3.

[15]Harlan, *op. cit.*, p. 139.

[16]*Ibid.*, p. 138.

[17]J. W. Holley, *Education and the Segregation Issue* (New York: William-Frederick Press, 1955), p. 26.

[18]*Ibid.*, pp. 35-36.

[19]Myrdal, *op. cit.*, Vol. 2, p. 900.

[20]H. V. Brown, *E-Qual-ity Education Among Negroes in North Carolina* (Raleigh, N. C.: Irving Swain Press, 1964), p. 31.

[21]A. A. Gunby, *Negro Education in the South* (New Orleans: H. C. Thomason, 1890) p. 51.

[22]Paul B. Barringer, *Negro Education in the South*, Report of the Commissioner of Education for the Year 1900-1901, Vol. 1, pp. 517-523.

[23]Gunby, *op. cit.*, p. 51.

[24]*Ibid.*, p. 54.

[25]Kenneth B. Johnson, *Teaching Culturally Disadvantaged Pupils* (Pleasantville, N. Y.: Science Research Associates, Inc.), pp. 7-12.

[26]Harry Miller and Marjorie Smiley, *Education In the Metropolis: A Book of Readings* (New York: Hunter College of the City of New York, 1964), p. 2.

[27]Virgil A. Clift, "Factors Relating to the Education of Culturally Deprived Negro Youth," *Educational Theory*, XIV (April, 1964), 76-82; and Edmund W. Gordon, "Characteristics of Socially Disadvantaged Children," *Review of Educational Research*, XXXV (December, 1965), pp. 377-388.

[28]Virgil A. Clift, "What Can Education Do?" *The Education Forum*, XXX (January, 1966), pp. 147-151.

[29]*Ibid.*, p. 150.

[30]John Niemeyer, "Some Guidelines to Desirable Elementary School Reorganization," *Programs for the Educationally Disadvantaged*. OE-35044, Bulletin, 1963, No. 17 (Washington: Government Printing Office, 1963), pp. 80-85.

[31]Bernard A. Kaplan, "Issues in Educating the Culturally Disadvantaged," *Phi Delta Kappan*, XLV (November, 1963) pp. 70-76.

[32]Samuel Tenenbaum, "The Teacher, The Middle Class, The Lower Class," *Phi Delta Kappan*, XLV (November, 1963), pp. 82-86.

[33]Harry S. Broudy, "Schooling for the Culturally Deprived," *The Teachers College Journal*, Vol. XXXVII (October, 1965), 4, pp. 14-18.

[34]*Ibid.*, p. 18.

[35]*Ibid.*

[36]Betty Levy, "Classrooms in the Slums: An Urban Teacher Speaks Out," *Harvard Graduate School of Education Association Bulletin*, X (Summer, 1965), p. 18-21.

[37]Bernard Bailyn, *Education in the Forming of American Society* (Chapel Hill: The University of North Carolina Press, 1960), p. 14.

[38]Lawrence A. Cremin, *The Wonderful World of Ellwood Patterson Cubberly* (New York: Bureau of Publications, Teachers College, Columbia University, 1965), pp. 46-47.

[39]Jonathan Kozol, *Death at an Early Age* (Boston: Houghton Mifflin Company, 1967).

[40]Nat Hentoff, *Our Children Are Dying* (New York: Viking Press, 1966).

[41]U.S. Commission on Civil Rights, *Racial Isolation In The Schools*, Vol. 1 (Washington: Government Printing Office, 1967).

[42]Peter Schrag, *Village School Downtown* (Boston: Beacon Press, 1967).

[1]Harold L. Hodgkinson, *Education in Social and Cultural Perspectives* (Englewood Cliffs, N. J.: Prentice-Hall, 1962), p. 3.

[2]Harry L. Miller and Roger R. Woock, *Social Foundations of Urban Education* (Hinsdale, Il.: Dryden Press, 1970).

[3]Arthur M. Schlesinger, "The Rise of The City," *A History of American Life,* Volume X (New York: The MacMillan Company, 1933), pp. 448-450.

[4]*Report of the National Advisory Commission on Civil Disorder* (New York: Bantam, 1968), p. 248.

[5]Arthur Vidich and Joseph Bensman, *Small Town in Mass Society* (Garden City, N. Y.: Doubleday, 1960).

[6]For specific reasons and basis of recommendations, see The Mayor's Advisory Panel on Decentralization of the New York City Schools, *Reconnection for Learning, A Community School System for New York City* (New York: Praeger, 1969).

[7]*Ibid.*

[8]*Ibid.*

[9]The Council of Supervisory Associations of the Public Schools of New York City, *Response to the Lindsay-Bundy Proposal,* "Interim Report No. 2" (New York City, January, 1968).

[10]C. Eric Lincoln, *Black Muslims in America* (Boston: Beacon Press, 1961), p. 45.

[11]James S. Coleman et al., *Equality of Educational Opportunity,* U.S. Office of Education (Washington, D.C.: U.S. Government Printing Office, 1966).

[12]*The Report of the National Advisory Commission on Civil Disorders, op. cit.*

[13]Jean-Jacques Rousseau, *Emile,* trans. Elenor Worthington (Boston: D. C. Heath and Company, 1906), pp. 42-43.

[14]Henry S. Reuss, *Revenue Sharing* (New York: Praeger Publishers, 1970), p. 72.

[15]Alvin H. Hansen and Harvey S. Perloff, *State and Local Finance in the National Economy* (New York: W. W. Norton and Company, 1944), p. 16.

[16]Reuss, *op. cit.,* p. 146.

[17]Ryland W. Crary and Louis A. Petrone, *Foundations of Modern Education* (New York: Random House, 1971), p. 129.

[18]Harvey S. Perloff and Richard P. Nathan, *Revenue Sharing and the City* (Baltimore: The Johns Hopkins Press, 1968), p. 64.

[19]William Anderson, "The Perils of Sharing," in Joseph F. Zimmerman, ed., *Subnational Politics*, 2nd ed., State University of New York at Albany (New York: Holt, Rinehart and Winston, 1970), p. 33. This letter can also be found in the *National Civic Review* (June, 1967), pp. 329-334.

[20]Ernest W. Burgess, "The New Community and Its Future," *Annals of the American Academy of Political and Social Science*, CIL (1930), pp. 161-162. Also see E. W. Burgess, "The Growth of the City," in R. E. Park, E. W. Burgess and Roderick D. McKenzie, *The City* (Chicago: University of Chicago Press, 1925), p. 51.

[21]Colin Clark, "Urban Population Densities," *Journal of the Royal Statistical Society*, Series A, CXIV (1951), pp. 490-496.

CHAPTER 3

[1]James Betchkal, "Rural Education: Caught in a Crossroads," *The Nation's Schools* (November, 1961), p. 84.

[2]James B. Conant, *Slums and Suburbs* (New York: McGraw-Hill, 1961), pp. 1-147.

[3]*1950 Census of Population*, U.S. Bureau of the Census, Vol. 1 (Washington: Government Printing Office, 1953).

[4]E. W. Burgess, "The Growth of the City," in R. E. Park, Roderick D. McKenzie and E. W. Burgess, (eds.), *The City* (Chicago: University of Chicago Press, 1925), p. 51.

[5]Homer Hoyt, *The Structure and Growth of Residential Neighborhoods in American Cities* (Washington, D.C.: Federal Housing Authority, 1939), pp. 112-122. See also his article, "The Structure of American Cities in the Post-War Era," *American Journal of Sociology*, XLVIII (January, 1943), pp. 475-492.

[6]Conant, *op. cit.*, p. 72.

[7]*Ibid.*, p. 73.

[8]R. I. Derbyshire, *The Sociology of Exclusion: Implications for Teaching Adult Illiterates*. Presented at Workshop on Adult Basic Education, College Park, Maryland, July 26, 1965. For an elaborate discussion of these and other American values, see Robin Williams, *American Society* (New York: Knopf, 1960), pp. 445-470.

[9]Stokely Carmichael and Charles V. Hamilton, *Black Power* (New York: Vintage Books, 1967), p. 164.

[10]Harold Benjamin, *The Cultivation of Idiosyncrasy* (Cambridge, Mass.: Harvard University Press, 1956), pp. 36-37.

[11]Martin Mayer, *The Schools* (New York: Harper Bros., 1961), p. xii.

[12]Charles F. Silberman, *Crisis In the Classroom* (New York: Random House, 1970).

[13]See section on "Compensatory Education," p. 162.

[14]Kenneth Clark, *Dark Ghetto* (New York: Harper and Row, Publisher, 1965), p. 128.

[15]Jean François Revel, *Without Marx or Jesus* (Garden City, N. Y.: Doubleday, 1971).

[16]William O. Stanley, *Education and Social Integration* (New York: Teachers College, Columbia University, 1953), p. 36.

[17]Hansom Prentice Baptiste, Jr., "A Black Educator's View," *Notre Dame Journal of Education*, Vol. I, No. 2 (Summer, 1970), p. 126.

[18]Seymour W. Itzkoff, "The Cultural Community," *Notre Dame Journal of Education*, Vol. I, No. 3 (Fall, 1970), p. 233.

[19]Barbara A. Sizemore and Kymara S. Chase, "White Values in Black Education," *Notre Dame Journal Education*, Vol. I, No. 3 (Fall, 1970), p. 244.

[20]Itzkoff, *op. cit.*, p. 233.

[21]Baptiste, *op. cit.*, p. 126.

[22]Bill Turner, "The Revolution and the Black Intellectual," *Notre Dame Journal of Education*, Vol. I, No. 2 (Summer, 1970), p. 138.

[23]John R. Dill, "Reflection of the Enigmas of Educating the Church," *Notre Dame Journal of Education*, Vol. I, No. 2 (Summer, 1970), p. 158.

[24]Charles Pleasant, Sr., "The Educative Functions of the Black Church," *Notre Dame Journal of Education*, Vol. I, No. 2 (Summer, 1970), p. 158.

[25]LaMar P. Miller, "The Discipline of Black Studies and Curriculum Theory," *Notre Dame Journal of Education*, Vol. I, No. 2 (Summer, 1970), p. 147.

[26]John Walsh, book review of Seymour W. Itzkoff's *Cultural Pluralism and American Education*. In *Notre Dame Journal of Education*, Vol. II, No. 2 (Summer, 1970), p. 186.

CHAPTER 4

[1]Alfred L. Hilliard, *The Form of Value* (New York: Columbia University Press, 1950), p. 1.

[2]Byron G. Massialas and C. Benjamin Cox, *Inquiry in Social Studies* (New York: McGraw-Hill, 1966), pp. 153-154.

[3]Frederick M. Raubinger and Harold G. Rowe, eds., *The Individual and Education* (New York: The Macmillan Company, 1968), p. 5.

[4]Myrdal, *op. cit.*

[5]Ralph Linton, *The Cultural Background of Personalities* (New York: Appleton-Century-Crofts, 1945), pp. 55, 75-82.

[6]Barton M. Schwartz and Robert H. Ewald, *Culture and Society* (New York: Roland Press, 1968), p. 183.

[7]Robert Lynd, *Knowledge for What?* (Princeton, N. J.: Princeton University Press, 1939), pp. 60-62.

[8]Robert J. Havighurst and Bernice L. Neugarten, *Society and Education* (Boston: Allyn and Bacon; Barton, Third Edition, 1968), p. 361.

[9]Miller and Woock, *op. cit.,* pp. 24-39, 220-234.

[10]Norman R. Yetman and Hoy Steele, eds., *Majority and Minority, The Dynamic of Racial and Ethnic Relations* (Boston: Allyn and Bacon, 1971), p. 183.

[11]Mathew W. Miles and W. W. Charter, Jr., eds., *Learning in Social Setting* (Boston: Allyn and Bacon, 1970), p. 407.

[12]*Education News,* Vol. III, No. 2, (August 5, 1968).

[13]Harold R. Isaacs, "Color in World Affairs," *Current,* No. 105 (March, 1969), p. 64.

[14]Quoted in Charles H. King, Jr., "A New Challenge to Human Rights Agencies," *Nation's Cities,* Vol. VII, No. 8 (August, 1969), pp. 23, 25.

[15]Burton R. Clark, *Educating the Expert Society* (San Francisco: Chandler Publishing Company, 1962), pp. 11-12.

[16]*Ibid.,* Ch. 4.

[17]*Ibid.,* pp. 122-130.

[18]*Ibid.*

[19]The New York Commission Report on the Quality, Cost and Financing of Elementary and Secondary Education, 1972, Vol. I, Ch. 5, p. 4.

[20]*Rochester Democrat and Chronicle,* Saturday, May 13, 1972, p. 3B.

[21]Helen Icken Safa, "The Case for Negro Separatism: The Crisis of Identity in the Negro Community," *Urban Affairs Quarterly,* Vol. IV, No. 1 (1968), p. 58.

[22]Bayard Rustin, "The Myths of the Black Revolt," *Ebony,* Vol. XXIV, No. 10 (August, 1969), pp. 102-104. Cf. Arnold Schuster's description of the position of Dr. Martin Luther King: "Dr. King . . . said that these pragmatic judgments may be shrewd and sound in the long run, but self-defeating in the short run. To make a man accept the ghetto as a fact of life is to tell him that he does not exist, even if in the same breath you tell him black is beautiful or superior. The ghetto, like the "nigger," is a white invention; acceptance of either undermines self-respect. Racism in America is a sign of moral bankruptcy, but so is acceptance of the consequence of racism." Arnold Schuster, *White Power Black Freedom* (Boston: Beacon Press, 1968), pp. 572-573.

[23]For example, see Stokely Carmichael and Charles V. Hamilton, *Black Power: The Politics of Liberation in America* (New York: Random House, 1967); Harold Cruso, *The Crisis of the Negro Intellectual* (New York: Morrow, 1967); issues of the Black Panthers' newspapers; Elliot Liebow, *Tally's Corner* (Boston: Little Brown, 1967); Anthony Downs, "Ways Out of the Ghetto," *Daedalus* (Fall, 1968), pp. 1331-1378; Ralph W. Conant, "Black Power: Rhetoric and Reality," *Urban Affairs Quarterly,* Vol. IV, No. 1, pp. 15-25; Nathan Wright, Jr., *Black Power and*

Urban Unrest (New York: Hawthorn, 1967); Albert and Roberta Wohlstetter, "Third Worlds at Home and Abroad," *The Public Interest,* No. 14 (Winter, 1969), pp. 88-107.

²⁴Dorothy A. Jones, *Community Control Decentralization: The Black Community* (New York: National Urban League, 1969), pp. 20-21.

CHAPTER 5

¹Black studies is the concept used to identify the union of African Studies and Afro-American studies. However, the author sees Afro-American studies as being synonymous to the section of black studies that focuses on the experience of black people in America.

²Clyde Kluckhohn, "The Student of Values," In Donald N. Barrett, ed., *Values in American Education* (Notre Dame, In.: University of Notre Dame Press, 1961), pp. 17-45.

³*Ibid.,* p. 20.

⁴*Ibid.*

⁵Daniel A. Prescott, *Factors That Influence Learning,* Horace Mann Lecture, 1958 (Pittsburgh: University of Pittsburgh Press, 1958).

⁶*Ibid.*

⁷*Ibid.,* p. 18.

⁸Felix M. Keesing, *Cultural Anthropology: The Science of Custom* (New York: Holt, Rinehart and Winston, 1962), pp. 420-421.

⁹W. E. B. DuBois, *The Autobiography of W. E. B. DuBois* (New York: International Publishers, 1969), p. 213.

¹⁰*Ibid.,* p. 313.

¹¹The National Council for the Social Studies: Forty-ninth Annual Meeting; Theme: Priorities for the Social Studies; Houston, Texas: November 24-29, 1969.

¹²Carmichael and Hamilton, *op. cit.,* p. 41.

¹³The report of faculty committee on African and Afro-American Studies, Harvard University, January 20, 1969, p. 3.

¹⁴DuBois, *op. cit.,* pp. 308-325.

¹⁵*The Journal of Negro Education,* quoted in DuBois, *op. cit.,* p. 318.

¹⁶*Ibid.,* p. 313.

¹⁷Maurice P. Hunt and Lawrence E. Metcalf, *Teaching High School Social Studies* (New York: Harper & Row, Second Edition, 1968).

¹⁸Massialas and Cox, *op. cit.*

¹⁹DeVere E. Pentony, "The Case of Black Studies," *The Atlantic* (April, 1969), p. 87.

[1]Benjamin S. Bloom, Allison Davis, and Robert Hess, *Compensatory Education for Cultural Deprivation* (New York: Holt, Rinehart and Winston, 1965).

[2]Earnest H. Austin, Jr., "Cultural Deprivation—A Few Questions," *Phi Delta Kappan*, Vol. XLVII, No. 2 (October, 1965), pp. 67-70, 75-76. And S. M. Miller, "Dropouts—A Political Problem." In Daniel Schieber, ed., *The School Dropout Project: School Dropouts* (Washington: National Education Association, 1964), pp. 11-24.

[3]J. Wayne et al., Evaluation of the Higher Horizons Program for Underprivileged Children, Cooperative Research Project No. 1124, New York: Board of Education of the City of New York, Bureau of Educational Research (1964), pp. 243-244; and D. A. Wilkerson, "Programs and Practices in Compensatory Education for Disadvantaged Children." *Review of Educational Research*, Vol. XXXV, No. 5 (December, 1965), pp. 426-440.

[4]W. W. Charters, Jr., "The Social Background of Teaching." In N. L. Gage, ed., *Handbook of Research on Teaching* (Chicago: Rand-McNally, 1963), pp. 739-740.

[5]Austin, *op. cit.*, pp. 67-70, 75-76.

[6]Dwight W. Allen and Robert A. Mackin, "Toward a Redefinition of Teacher Education," *Educational Technology* (February, 1970), pp. 65-70.

[7]Henry Ehlers and Gordon C. Lee, *Crucial Issues in Education* (New York: Holt, Rinehart and Winston, 1962), pp. 296-297.

[8]Sir Richard Livingstone, "On Residential Adult Education," *Continuing Education Report*, University of Chicago, No. 12 (1967).

[9]Helen J. Kenney, Polly Bartholomew, and William C. Kvaraceus, *Teacher Education: The Young Teacher's View*, Project Report No. 2, NDEA National Institute for Advanced Study in Teaching Disadvantaged Youth (July, 1968), pp. 9-10.

[10]Silberman, *op. cit.*, p. 377.

[11]Charles H. Monson, "On Teaching Teaching Assistants," *Phi Delta Kappan*, Vol. LII, No. 2 (October, 1970) pp. 93-94.

[12]Henry David Thoreau, "Walden." In *The American Tradition in Literature*, Bradley, Beatty, and Long (New York: Norton, 1962), Vol. I, p. 1167.

[13]Karen Duncan, *Community Action Curriculum Project*, U.S. National Student Association, Washington, D.C., November 15, 1968.

[14]Kenneth B. Clark, *op. cit.*, pp. 111-112.

[15]Louise Kennedy, *The Negro Peasant Turns Cityward*, (New York: Columbia University Press, 1930), pp. 193-195.

INDEX

244

245